D1756015

Endgame

The Hidden Agenda 21

Vernon Coleman

Vernon Coleman: What the papers say

'Vernon Coleman writes brilliant books.' – The Good Book Guide
'No thinking person can ignore him.' – The Ecologist
'The calmest voice of reason.' – The Observer
'A godsend.' – Daily Telegraph
'Superstar.' – Independent on Sunday
'Brilliant!' – The People
'Compulsive reading.' – The Guardian
'His message is important.' – The Economist
'He's the Lone Ranger, Robin Hood and the Equalizer rolled into one.' – Glasgow Evening Times
'The man is a national treasure.' – What Doctors Don't Tell You
'His advice is optimistic and enthusiastic.' – British Medical Journal
'Revered guru of medicine.' – Nursing Times
'Gentle, kind and caring' – Western Daily Press
'His trademark is that he doesn't mince words. Far funnier than the usual tone of soupy piety you get from his colleagues.' – The Guardian
'Dr Coleman is one of our most enlightened, trenchant and sensitive dispensers of medical advice.' – The Observer
'I would much rather spend an evening in his company than be trapped for five minutes in a radio commentary box with Mr Geoffrey Boycott.' – Peter Tinniswood, Punch
'Hard hitting...inimitably forthright.' – Hull Daily Mail
'Refreshingly forthright.' – Liverpool Daily Post
'Outspoken and alert.' – Sunday Express
'Dr Coleman made me think again.' – BBC World Service
'Marvellously succinct, refreshingly sensible.' – The Spectator
'Probably one of the most brilliant men alive today.' – Irish Times
'King of the media docs.' – The Independent
'Britain's leading medical author.' – The Star
'Britain's leading health care campaigner.' – The Sun
'Perhaps the best known health writer for the general public in the world today.' – The Therapist

'The patient's champion.' – Birmingham Post
'A persuasive writer whose arguments, based on research and experience, are sound.' – Nursing Standard
'The doctor who dares to speak his mind.' – Oxford Mail
'He writes lucidly and wittily.' – Good Housekeeping

Books by Vernon Coleman include:

Medical
The Medicine Men
Paper Doctors
Everything You Want To Know About Ageing
The Home Pharmacy
Aspirin or Ambulance
Face Values
Stress and Your Stomach
A Guide to Child Health
Guilt
The Good Medicine Guide
An A to Z of Women's Problems
Bodypower
Bodysense
Taking Care of Your Skin
Life without Tranquillisers
High Blood Pressure
Diabetes
Arthritis
Eczema and Dermatitis
The Story of Medicine
Natural Pain Control
Mindpower
Addicts and Addictions
Dr Vernon Coleman's Guide to Alternative Medicine
Stress Management Techniques
Overcoming Stress
The Health Scandal
The 20 Minute Health Check
Sex for Everyone
Mind over Body
Eat Green Lose Weight
Why Doctors Do More Harm Than Good

The Drugs Myth
Complete Guide to Sex
How to Conquer Backache
How to Conquer Pain
Betrayal of Trust
Know Your Drugs
Food for Thought
The Traditional Home Doctor
Relief from IBS
The Parent's Handbook
Men in Bras, Panties and Dresses
Power over Cancer
How to Conquer Arthritis
How to Stop Your Doctor Killing You
Superbody
Stomach Problems – Relief at Last
How to Overcome Guilt
How to Live Longer
Coleman's Laws
Millions of Alzheimer Patients Have Been Misdiagnosed
Climbing Trees at 112
Is Your Health Written in the Stars?
The Kick-Ass A–Z for over 60s
Briefs Encounter
The Benzos Story
Dementia Myth

Psychology/Sociology
Stress Control
How to Overcome Toxic Stress
Know Yourself (1988)
Stress and Relaxation
People Watching
Spiritpower
Toxic Stress
I Hope Your Penis Shrivels Up
Oral Sex: Bad Taste and Hard To Swallow
Other People's Problems

The 100 Sexiest, Craziest, Most Outrageous Agony Column
Questions (and Answers) Of All Time
How to Relax and Overcome Stress
Too Sexy To Print
Psychiatry
Are You Living With a Psychopath?

Politics and General
England Our England
Rogue Nation
Confronting the Global Bully
Saving England
Why Everything Is Going To Get Worse Before It Gets Better
The Truth They Won't Tell You...About The EU
Living In a Fascist Country
How to Protect & Preserve Your Freedom, Identity & Privacy
Oil Apocalypse
Gordon is a Moron
The OFPIS File
What Happens Next?
Bloodless Revolution
2020
Stuffed
The Shocking History of the EU
Coming Apocalypse
Old Man in a Chair
Endgame

Diaries
Diary of a Disgruntled Man
Just another Bloody Year
Bugger off and Leave Me Alone
Return of the Disgruntled Man
Life on the Edge
The Game's Afoot
Tickety Tonk

Animals
Why Animal Experiments Must Stop

Fighting For Animals
Alice and Other Friends
Animal Rights – Human Wrongs
Animal Experiments – Simple Truths

General Non Fiction
How to Publish Your Own Book
How to Make Money While Watching TV
Strange but True
Daily Inspirations
Why Is Public Hair Curly
People Push Bottles Up Peaceniks
Secrets of Paris
Moneypower
101 Things I Have Learned
100 Greatest Englishmen and Englishwomen
Cheese Rolling, Shin Kicking and Ugly Tattoos
One Thing after Another

Novels (General)
Mrs Caldicot's Cabbage War
Mrs Caldicot's Knickerbocker Glory
Mrs Caldicot's Oyster Parade
Mrs Caldicot's Turkish Delight
Deadline
Second Chance
Tunnel
Mr Henry Mulligan
The Truth Kills
Revolt
My Secret Years with Elvis
Balancing the Books
Doctor in Paris
Stories with a Twist in the Tale (short stories)
Dr Bullock's Annals

The Young Country Doctor Series
Bilbury Chronicles
Bilbury Grange

Bilbury Revels
Bilbury Country
Bilbury Village
Bilbury Pie (short stories)
Bilbury Pudding (short stories)
Bilbury Tonic
Bilbury Relish
Bilbury Mixture
Bilbury Delights
Bilbury Joys
Bilbury Tales
Bilbury Days
Bilbury Memories

Novels (Sport)
Thomas Winsden's Cricketing Almanack
Diary of a Cricket Lover
The Village Cricket Tour
The Man Who Inherited a Golf Course
Around the Wicket
Too Many Clubs and Not Enough Balls

Cat books
Alice's Diary
Alice's Adventures
We Love Cats
Cats Own Annual
The Secret Lives of Cats
Cat Basket
The Cataholics' Handbook
Cat Fables
Cat Tales
Catoons from Catland

As Edward Vernon
Practice Makes Perfect
Practise What You Preach
Getting Into Practice
Aphrodisiacs – An Owner's Manual

The Complete Guide to Life

Written with Donna Antoinette Coleman
How to Conquer Health Problems between Ages 50 & 120
Health Secrets Doctors Share With Their Families
Animal Miscellany
England's Glory
Wisdom of Animals

Copyright Vernon Coleman March 2021.
The right of Vernon Coleman to be identified as the author of this work has been asserted in accordance with the Copyright, Designs and Patents Act 1988.

Dedicated, as ever, to Antoinette
You are my treasure,
And my inspiration
My true love,
And my purpose
Always and all ways

Contents List

The Author

Dr Vernon Coleman MB ChB DSc FRSA was the first qualified medical practitioner to question the significance of the 'crisis' with which you may be familiar, telling readers of his website www.vernoncoleman.com at the end of February that he felt that the team advising the Government had been unduly pessimistic and had exaggerated the danger of the 'bug'. At the beginning of March, he explained how and why the mortality figures had been distorted. And on March 14th, he warned that the Government's policies would result in far more deaths than the disease itself. In a YouTube video recorded on 18th March, he explained his fear that the Government would use the 'crisis' to oppress the elderly and to introduce compulsory inoculation. And he revealed that the infection had been downgraded on March 19th when the public health bodies in the UK and the Advisory Committee on Dangerous Pathogens decided that the 'crisis' infection should no longer be classified as a 'high consequence infectious disease'. Just days after the significance of the infection had been officially downgraded, the Government published an Emergency Bill which gave the police extraordinary new powers and put millions of people under house arrest. Dr Coleman, a former GP principal, is a *Sunday Times* bestselling author. His books have sold over two million copies in the UK, been translated into 25 languages and sold all around the world. He has given evidence to the House of Commons and the House of Lords and his campaigning has changed Government policy. There is a short biography at the back of this book.

Preface

I wrote this book with one hand tied behind my back. Well, not literally, you understand, but figuratively.

In April 2020, I wrote a book which dealt with the decision in the early spring of 2020 to put large populations under house arrest, and to close factories, shops and all businesses not regarded as essential. It also dealt with the aftermath of those decisions. The part dealing with the early part of 2020 was based entirely on fact. The part dealing with what was then the future was, inevitably, largely conjecture. In order to publish this book I was informed that I had to remove all references to the name of the problem which triggered the close downs. And so you would not find therein any reference to a word describing a disease which begins with the third letter of the alphabet. Nor would you find any reference to a disease name which ends with a number which is slightly greater than 18 and slightly smaller than 20. In addition, in view of proposed new legislation which will make it illegal for anyone (including doctors) to share facts and opinions about a specific medical procedure, I avoided using a word beginning with 'v' and used the word inoculation instead. I also had to avoid using words which describe bits of material placed over the mouth and nose. And I cannot mention an organisation whose acronym has the same name as a rock band. There were several other things too.

In this book I have followed the same restrictions.

Readers may be puzzled by this censorship since other authors are allowed to discuss these things in their books. I am banned from writing about things which are open to other authors. And lest there be any doubt I would point out that someone stole the transcripts of my videos from my website, turned them into a book and put them for sale on the internet. I put the book for sale but did not charge a royalty on the paperback and charged only the minimum royalty allowed on the eBook. Sadly, however, within days my book was banned but the thief's book, consisting entirely of my copyright material, was offered for sale and allowed to remain on sale.

The mysteries of the world seem unending.

I sometimes think I must have wandered down a rabbit hole.

In the post civilisation technocratic society which is being planned (according to the great or global reset) nothing is ever going to be the same as it was.

My last two books were completely banned by just about every publishing and printing operation I could find.

Let's hope this one does better...

Introduction

This is a book about the future; the future which has been designed for us by the United Nations, the followers of Agenda 21, the Global Economic Forum and those eager to further the aims of the Great Reset and take us into what they call the 'new normal'.

This is not a history book; it is a future book; it is a book of predictions and conclusions. My forecasts since February 2020 have been proven absolutely accurate and are documented in my books, articles and videos. I decided it was time to look ahead and, based on what we know has been planned for decades, I have described the future we can expect and how their plans will impact on our lives in the years to come.

It has been clear almost since the beginning that the rules and restrictions which have been introduced will remain indefinitely. The arrival of the injections was never going to make any difference to those rules. The excuses were always predictable: the injections do not provide complete protection, that not enough people have had been jabbed to protect the whole community, that the target mutates, that the effects of the jab wears off and it has to be repeated at regular intervals and that it is not possible to produce enough of the injections to protect everyone. Testing programmes will be increased and the results will be used to justify a whole raft of new restrictions.

It is also necessary to accept that nothing is now impossible and that our new rulers are operating beyond satire. I think the wise probably realised that things may have changed permanently when in October 2020, the Welsh authorities introduced a ban on non-essential goods which at first included clothing, kettles, toasters and women's sanitary products. Defending the ban, one politician explained that he wasn't planning on buying any new clothes; the implication being 'why should anyone else?'

The immediate plan, of course, is to overwhelm us, bewilder us, terrify us and force us to concentrate our energies on the leaves so that we don't get to see the trees let alone the woods. They've been planning this for a long, long time, while we've been getting on with our lives, dealing with daily problems and ignoring the slowly developing take-over of our lives; the greatest threat there has ever been to humanity, our freedom, our democracy and our future.

They have deliberately exhausted us. They have created an unprecedented level of fear and then used restrictions and quasi laws to take control of us and to prepare us for the world they have planned.

The plan is to remove every aspect of our history and all structural obstacles. They will eliminate credit cards, cash, jobs, privacy, schools, medicine (as we know it) and democracy.

This is a carefully planned crime against humanity.

I make no apologies for the fact that the story I'm about to tell seems unbelievable. None of the predictions in this book is a result of my imagination. As difficult as it may be to believe, the events that have turned our world upside down since the start of the year 2020 have been carefully composed, orchestrated and conducted.

Everything that has happened was meant to happen.

Throughout 2020, we have been behind the battle; running to catch up but never getting anywhere close. It's time to get ahead and look into the future.

Foreword

Powerful egomaniacs and psychopaths have, for centuries wanted a world government.

Naturally, they want to run the world government themselves and not surprisingly, they have invariably been untroubled by such annoying niceties as democracy, controlling the globe as a private fiefdom – with themselves as some sort of combined Lord High Executioner and Grand Pooh-Bah.

It has, of course, all been about power and money. They've dressed up their primeval yearnings with all sorts of pretty nonsenses (I will show how the threat of climate change was introduced as a weapon with which to force society to accept their plans) and the sanity of the main protagonists is questionable, but it's been about power and money.

They have never admitted their ambitions, of course. In public, their dreams and conspiracies have always been covered in a confection of selfless yearning to make the world a better place for all those living in it, all those less fortunate, less gifted, less powerful and less wealthy than themselves. In private, their dreams and conspiracies are completely selfish and quite dangerous. The opportunists may have appeared to have the interests of the people at heart but they were acting in accordance with a sinister hidden agenda.

It is possible to trace the yearning of power hungry elites for total control back through most of human history and I am well aware that there are some who believe that this whole process has been in motion for centuries, millennia even, and that the origins of everything happening today can be traced back through the years. I sometimes suspect that Adam and Eve had long boring conversations about the need for some sort of world government.

But to keep this book manageable, readable, accessible and affordable, and to avoid the book stretching into 12 vast volumes, I have begun the story at the end of World War II, when the modern yearning for global control began in earnest when nations everywhere were weary of fighting and killing and susceptible to high-sounding, well-meaning promises made by political opportunists. The story outlined in this Introduction is given a little more flesh in Part One – How Did We Get Here?

For centuries there have been evil people (many of them bankers) who, for personal, largely financial reasons, wanted to create a world government, and who have worked tirelessly to win power over ordinary citizens. I think the evil plan for a global reset, a new normal, can really be traced back to 1909 when it was first suggested that it is far easier to control people if you have a good, long war going on. This was long before Orwell, of course.

We can then jump to 1932 when people at Columbia University had the idea of introducing energy as a new currency. They came up with the word 'technocracy' and the idea that the world would be a much better place if it were run by scientists. The technocrats wanted to abolish private property and change education so that it merely prepared students for the work that had been selected for them by people who knew better. It was this nonsense that gave Aldous Huxley the idea for his novel *Brave New World*.

After the end of World War II, the United Nations was founded. And that was the beginning of almost everything that is now happening. That is when the story really starts.

Then, after the formation of the United Nations, we jump to 1961 when a bunch of Kennedy Administration insiders, most of them Bilderbergers, unearthed the old idea of using war to keep the people under control. After much thought, however, they created a twist on that idea. They thought it would be a damned good wheeze to create massive, worldwide pollution and then blame the citizens of the world for the mess and, having blamed them for making the mess, to force them to clear it up.

If you're beginning to get the idea you know where this is going you're right – you do.

The next big step forward was the formation of the Club of Rome in 1968. Today, the Club of Rome consists, among others, of a variety of UN administrators, top politicians, rich businessmen and government officials. I'll come back to the Club of Rome in a moment.

And then in 1971, the World Economic Forum was founded – though it was originally called the European Management Forum and only became the WEF in 1987. This is the curious organisation which has a shindig at Davos every year where celebrities and billionaires swap cheek kisses and telephone numbers.

In 1976, there was another move towards what we now know as Agenda 21.

The United Nations decided to take control of the world's land and to control the world's population. This was all to be done for the good of the planet and mankind, of course. The plan, created by a bunch of unelected, interfering greedy, power-hungry individuals, was to put the rights of the community over the rights of the individual. This sort of nonsense used to be called communism but the would-be new world rulers dreamt up the name communitarianism which is as much fun to spell as it is to say.

Things moved quickly after that.

In 1980, they invented the idea of sustainable development – two words that ought now to strike terror into the hearts of anyone who cares about people, the world, integrity, respect and the environment.

And in 1983, they set up a commission to prepare us all for a new world order.

In 1987, the World Commission on Environment and Development (also known as the Brundtland Commission) reported to the United Nations and defined sustainable development as: 'Development that meets the needs of the present without compromising the ability of future generations to meet their own needs.'

Who could possibly object to that?

For the best part of a decade, they were all still fumbling around like teenage boys at a dance and then in 1991 the Club of Rome, which you will remember if you've been paying attention, decided that they needed to find a way to motivate and distract the masses. They dug around and with a total lack of imagination came up with global warming.

It was in 1991 that the Club of Rome published a book called, *The First Global Revolution*. In one important way this really was the beginning for it was this publication which gave the United Nations a way to take real control.

The book noted that history shows that individual countries have always been motivated, and given strength, by having an enemy. It isn't at all unknown for political leaders to start wars (usually small ones) in order to divert attention from problems at home and to unite the electorate. Bill Clinton did it when he was having trouble with allegations of sexual impropriety. Margaret Thatcher made what some felt was a rather exaggerated response when Argentina invaded the Falkland Islands at a low point in her electoral popularity.

The authors of the book from the Club of Rome concluded that leaders always like a scapegoat, an enemy of some kind, as a distraction when things are going badly. And if one isn't available they will usually invent one. It is, after all, the existence of enemies which gives leaders power and authority and which, as a by no means insignificant side effect, provides arms manufacturers, and many other industries, with their raison d'etre and their profits.

'In searching for a common enemy against whom we can unite,' they decided 'we came up with the idea that pollution, the threat of global warming, water shortages, famine and the like, would fit the bill.'

Global warming had been regarded as a problem since the 19th century but only a few environmentalists had ever taken it seriously. It was always a theoretical problem, rather than a practical danger. It was a cranky sort of thing to worry about and, in its way, as typical of the 19th century as electrically heated underpants and those frilly little mini-bloomers with which the Victorians hid the saucy, well-turned legs of the family piano.

The Club of Rome noted they needed to change people's attitudes and behaviour if they were to meet their aims. Pompously they concluded that: 'the real enemy is humanity itself'. Most people who noticed this hubristic nonsense dismissed it as hubristic nonsense. But it was, in retrospect, a truly ominous warning of evil things to come.

So the Club of Rome devised the agenda: global warming together with pollution, with food and water shortages as a side order. We (members of the human race) were designated as the cause of all these problems. We therefore became our own enemy. And this new policy gave the main movers, the promoters of the fake scares, an opportunity to move towards a world government. Since we were now to be our only enemy, a world government would be necessary to take control of us and to manage every aspect of our lives – for our own good, of course.

Now, as I have already said, global warming had been toyed with as a threat since the 19th century but every time anyone had suggested that the planet was getting hotter, it quickly became apparent that the idea was a load of rubbish because it wasn't.

The Club of Rome put a twist on this old bit of nonsense. They said it was all our fault; we had caused the global warming. In reality, global warming was no more of a problem than it had been in Queen Victoria's Day but because it was now our fault we were clearly responsible for accepting the changes that were necessary, and so the fact that there was no global warming was brushed aside as irrelevant.

And then in 1992, the United Nations held a conference in Brazil and Agenda 21 was born. This was the real start of communitarianism and the beginning of the end of individualism. Before you could say Tony Blair or Bill Clinton, or even Al Gore and a DVD which would get three out of ten for accuracy, the world was set to change.

The Agenda 21 policy was adopted at the 1992 United Nations Conference on Environment and Development in Rio de Janeiro where United Nations Agenda 21 Sustainable Development was born. (The 21 obviously refers to the 21st century.) The United Nations had found the way to take power, to control us and to move towards a world government which would, of course, be controlled by the United Nations itself. Who better?

Almost inevitably, 178 leaders immediately signed up to the Agenda 21 plan. The aims seemed laudable and no one dared say 'No'. It was decided that the world's nations would join together to fight these imaginary threats to our existence. The 'people', who had consumed too much oil and gas and coal were the new foe. The phrase 'sustainable development' was used to describe how the world's nations would move forward and the word 'communitarianism' became the new watchword for the new world.

Since we were now our own enemy, all fighting our own greed and wastefulness, we had to move towards a world government.

And thus began the nightmare.

With astonishing speed, and a good deal of behind-the-scenes political chicanery, the plan was put into action.

The United Nations went from being an organisation with some high flown good intentions best known perhaps for its peace keeping force of borrowed soldiers in smart uniforms, to an organisation with a steadily growing grip on every aspect of our lives.

The 178 governments which had signed up to the principle of sustainability (and the idea of 'making the world a better place') all set up their own groups to ensure that the principles of sustainable development were followed.

And global warming was the stick with which we were all to be beaten into submission. Everything could be blamed on global warming, of course, and it was decided (with no scientific evidence to support the decision) that the planet was being endangered by our use of fossil fuels and our reckless use of the world's resources. Celebrities and well-known politicians were recruited to give the new 'threat' credibility, and some pretty fancy graphs and fake statistics were glued together to give the whole thing a pseudo-scientific look.

Loads of big hitters came in at this point. Prince Charles, son of Queen Elizabeth and famous mostly for having a valet to put toothpaste on his toothbrush and for talking to the plants his gardeners grew, was one of those who saw this as a quick way to become terribly important and a world class hypocrite. Charles spent most of the following decades flying around the world in private aeroplanes telling people that they mustn't fly around the world in aeroplanes of any description.

And it wasn't just about power. There was money too: loads of it. It was clear that there was a ton of money to be made out of carbon trading – a completely nonsensical piece of chicanery which changed absolutely nothing except the size of the bank balances of the people running the carbon trading scam.

The Agenda 21 plan was to dumb down education, close all small companies, empty rural areas, force people to live in tower blocks in smart cities and shut down farms. Food would be grown in laboratories which would make tons of money for the right people (in due course, factory farms would end up being owned by people like Bill Gates).

It was also agreed that it was necessary to force the simple-minded citizens to learn how to take orders and to become compliant slaves. And so recycling was invented. It didn't matter that all the freshly washed yoghurt cartons ended up being transported to countries thousands of miles away to be burnt or buried. The recycling wasn't the point. This was all about compliance. Even when it became widely known that our recycling rubbish was being burnt or buried abroad, people still carried on washing their yoghurt cartons without making a fuss.

In America, the events of 9/11 enabled the US to create some wonderfully oppressive new laws, and bits and pieces of terrorism around the world enabled other countries to put the fear of God into their citizens. The threat of weapons of mass destruction enabled politicians to take away whatever privacy and freedom we had left. And diseases were used as threats too. AIDS and all those funny influenzas were such a threat that we were told we all had to change our lives and accept orders from those who had decided they were our betters.

Regionalisation was brought in as a first step towards globalisation and lovely, well-built old 19th century houses were knocked down because they didn't fit into 21st century building regulations. Many big, well-built old houses were replaced with crappy, apartment buildings and tacky little houses seemingly made out of cardboard which did satisfy the building regulations.

Cars were targeted as being bad for the environment, and we were all told that we had to stop using fossil fuels and start living on sunshine and wind. Since neither of these provides enough electricity to give everyone a lit light bulb (and weren't ever likely to do so) governments started chopping down trees, chopping them up, calling the result biomass, burning it and labelling it 'sustainable'.

Anyone objecting to what was clearly the beginning of a huge scam was dismissed as a conspiracy theorist and publicly shamed and demonised.

Rural living was made damned near impossible by letting roads go to ruin, by ruining water supplies and by introducing wild animals into country areas.

Everywhere we looked (or didn't look) the Agenda 21 followers were busy planning for a future to suit their purposes. The banks decided that they would get rid of cash and replace it with a digital system. Billionaires worked out ways to change the temperature, control the weather and force us to eat laboratory made food. Psychologists were hired to brainwash us all. The police were pushed into demonising themselves as well as us. ID cards and microchips were promoted as 'a really good thing' and there was much talk of the need to depopulate the world.

And that took us up to the start of 2020.

But they still needed something else with which to control us all.

They needed something they could use to terrify us and force us to do as we were told. They'd tried AIDS and various types of flu and none of them had worked.

So, what happened during 2020 was merely the culmination of years of common purpose, quangos, civil servants, corporate insensitivity and local planning.

It's enough to say that nothing happened by accident.

Much of the rest of this book simply explains the full consequences of these plans, what the new normal will look like (unless we call a halt to it) – and how the United Nations plan will affect every aspect of our lives.

Our future is based on Agenda 21, and it is the future we can expect if people continue to comply, mindlessly and uncritically accepting mainstream media, the BBC, the lies of the sponsored fact checkers, and the various but widely spread nonsenses. It is a lie to claim that the policies being created by governments have 'followed the science'. Governments and the WHO have steadfastly ignored the science, and their policies have been as far removed from evidence and research as it is possible to get.

The journey into the hinterland where we now all live has taken many decades but today political leaders around the world, aided and abetted by common purpose apparatchiks, a compliant media (bought and paid for with taxpayers' money) and professional trolls have turned millions of petty bureaucrats into witless traitors, cold-bloodedly and mindlessly working against the citizens of their own countries.

Already, Governments everywhere are taking increasingly greater control of every aspect of public and private life.

Part One: How Did We Get Here?

There can be no doubt about it: our world has been taken over. It was, in old fashioned terms, a coup – though few people recognised it as such. Our world, our lives, our present and our future have been taken over by a bunch of self-serving criminals who have cleverly slid into positions of power (mostly without ever standing for public office, let alone being elected) and who now control governments, banks, global organisations and, of course, the United Nations. Dishonesty and immorality are now so commonplace among those holding public office that even the most egregious examples of both are ignored or dismissed as simply inevitable.

It would be a mistake not to understand that everything that has happened so far has been deliberate. Some commentators have criticised politicians and scientific advisers around the world for the errors they appeared to have made in 2020. But I don't think the apparent mistakes have been errors. Everything that has happened has been deliberate. No politician or scientific advisor could be as incompetent as these have been.

And it is certainly inconceivable to think that politicians, administrators and advisors around the world could all be making exactly the same mistakes.

So, what has been going on?

Powerful egomaniacs and psychopaths have, for centuries wanted a world government.

Naturally, they've wanted to run the world government themselves and, not surprisingly, they have invariably been untroubled by such annoying niceties as democracy. They have always planned to run the world government themselves, controlling all those upon the earth as servants within a private fiefdom – each considering themselves to be some sort of combined Lord High Executioner and Grand Pooh-Bah.

It has, of course, all been about power and money. They've dressed up their primeval yearnings with all sorts of pretty nonsenses and the sanity of the main protagonists is questionable, but it's been about power and money.

They have never admitted their ambitions, of course.

In public, their dreams and conspiracies have always been covered in a confection of selfless yearning to make the world a better place for all those living in it, all those less fortunate, less gifted, less powerful and less wealthy than themselves.

Back in 1932, Columbia University in the US backed a new economic system designed by engineers and scientists that was intended to replace free enterprise and, indeed, capitalism. It was claimed that the system could 'rescue' the whole world (though from what was not made clear). It was called technocracy and it was, in practice, intended to be the science of social engineering: controlling every aspect of human life. In a way this early manifestation of technocracy was a blueprint for much of what was to come. The basic idea was that energy would be the new currency and that citizens would be issued with energy certificates which they could use to buy whatever goods or services they could afford. Goods and services would be priced according to the amount of energy that had been used in their creation. There were other aspects to technocracy: private property would be abolished (on the grounds that it was wasteful and inefficient) and education would be designed to do no more than prepare students for a lifetime of work – and their work would be chosen for them by the authorities.

When he read about the technocracy plans, Aldous Huxley realised that if these aims were followed we would be heading towards a scientific dictatorship. He was inspired to write his most famous novel, called, *Brave New World*.

But, in order to keep this book manageable, readable, accessible and affordable, I have begun with things that happened at the end of the Second World War when nations everywhere were weary of fighting and killing and susceptible to high-sounding, well-meaning promises made by political opportunists.

Those opportunists appeared to have the interests of the people at heart but they were acting in accordance with a sinister hidden agenda.

For centuries there have been evil people (many of them bankers) who, for personal, largely financial reasons, wanted to create a world government, and who have worked tirelessly to win power over ordinary citizens.

What's happening today can largely be traced back to the days after the end of World War II when the United Nations was founded. That was the real beginning of almost everything bad that is now happening.

Another important early milestone was the meeting of a number of Kennedy Administration officials, including Dean Rusk, Robert McNamara and McGeorge Bundy (who also happened to be Bilderberger members) at a place called Iron Mountain, near New York – a huge underground corporate nuclear shelter.

The authors of the subsequent report stated that war was both desirable and necessary as an economic stabilizer and an organising force. They argued that war could not be allowed to disappear until there was something to put in its place.

'The possibility of war,' they wrote, 'provides the sense of external necessity without which no government can long remain in power…the basic authority of a modern state over its people resides in its war powers. War has served as the last great safeguard against the elimination of necessary classes.'

The theory was that international rivalry (with regular wars) was necessary to create a community of interest between rich and poor. And the Kennedy administration think tank also concluded that: 'A possible surrogate for the control of potential enemies of society is the reintroduction, in some form consistent with modern technology and political process, of slavery…The development of a sophisticated form of slavery may be an absolute prerequisite for social control in a world at peace.'

It was at the Iron Mountain meeting in 1961 that other forms of control were discussed. These included a space program aimed at unreachable targets, a permanent arms inspection force, a global peacekeeping force, a comprehensive eugenics program and massive global environmental pollution which would need cleaning up.

None of this was particularly new, of course. The same theory had been espoused by other groups. In their book, *Illuminati Agenda 21* Dean and Jill Henderson report that in 1909, the trustees of the Andrew Carnegie Foundation for International Peace concluded: 'There are no known means more efficient than war, assuming the objective is altering the life of an entire people…How do we involve the United States in a war?'

The World Economic Forum was for many years often regarded as a rather pointless and potty organisation, and the ludicrous annual Davos beanos which it organises were widely dismissed as nothing more than expensive networking for the rich and self-important who can display their wealth to one another and plan our future. It all seemed rather James Bond baddie type of stuff. As it turned out, the World Economic Forum and its Davos parties were much, much more than that. The founder of the World Economic Forum is a man called Klaus Schwab. Schwab is to me the most frightening human being of the post-Hitler era. I don't know why but whenever I see him or hear him I am reminded of the maniacal Dr Strangelove as played by Peter Sellers. The subheading of the WEF is 'The International Organisation for Public-Private Cooperation'. Schwab is author of a book called, *Shaping the Future of the fourth Industrial Revolution* – one of the most frightening (and virtually unreadable) tomes I have ever read.

In 1976, the United Nations decided that it would control the use of land around the world. And that it would also take upon itself the job of managing populations everywhere. All this was to be done for the good of the planet and mankind, of course. This was, I suppose, the beginning of communitarianism: the idea that the community's needs must be put first and individuals cannot have rights.

Rosa Koire, writing in *Behind the Green Mask* points out that the slogan of the UN Agenda 21 is: 'to protect the rights of future generations and all species against the potential crimes of the present'. She points out that the philosophy is that by living we are a danger to the earth and that those who campaign for the rights of the individual are selfish and/or immoral. Arguing that it is 'saving the planet' the UN's plans are, she says, restricting and suffocating our civil liberties and drowning liberty. The UN's supporters claim that they are working to protect the planet and the environment and to protect the rights of those who are alive in the future. But, of course, the price is that we have to abandon our rights in order to preserve our rights.

To the followers of Agenda 21 the only thing that matters is an amorphous, ill-defined entity known as 'the community'. In order to protect the community we must all obey the regulations devised as part of Agenda 21 and, of course, we must all become accustomed to having our regular health jabs – however dangerous they might be to us as individuals. To protect the community, the UN has already criminalised almost every activity; it has demonised free speech; suppressed debate and given massive rights to specific, individual groups who claim that they are communities in need of protection. Anyone who questions the myth of global warming or the onerous demands of Agenda 21 is deemed to be a conspiracy theorist or worse.

In 1980, the United Nations' International Union for Conservation of Nature and Natural Resources produced a document entitled 'World Conservation Strategy' which stated that its aim was 'to help advance the achievement of sustainable development through the conservation of living resources'.

That was, I think, the first time that the now widely dreaded phrase 'sustainable development' had been used.

In 1983, the United Nations set up a World Commission on Environment and Development and appointed as chairman a former Prime minister of Norway called Gro Harlem Brundtland who was enthusiastic about environmental issues and a member of the Trilateral Commission (the organisation dedicated to creating a new international economic order). In 1987, the World Commission on Environment and Development (also known as the Brundtland Commission for short) produced a book called, *Our Common Future* and reported to the United Nations. Sustainable development was defined as: 'Development that meets the needs of the present without compromising the ability of future generations to meet their own needs.'

Who could possibly object to that?

But there was still a need to find a way to turn all this theory into action.

In 1991, the Club of Rome published a book called, *The First Global Revolution*. It was this publication which gave the United Nations a way to take real control.

This is what they said: 'In searching for a common enemy against whom we can unite, we came up with the idea that pollution, the threat of global warming, water shortages, famine and the like, would fit the bill.'

Global warming had been regarded as a problem since the 19th century but only a few environmentalists had taken it seriously. It was always a theoretical problem, rather than a practical danger. In the decades that followed, data was falsified and misrepresented time and time again to support an argument that had absolutely no scientific merit.

The Club of Rome noted that it is only through changed attitudes and behaviour that the problems they had identified (the ones they had created) could be overcome, and concluded that: 'The real enemy is humanity itself'.

This policy was then adopted at the 1992 United Nations Conference on Environment and Development in Rio de Janeiro where United Nations Agenda 21 Sustainable Development was born. The 21 in the title obviously refers to the 21st century and the key word, the word that would eventually define every aspect of our lives, was 'sustainable'. Never before has such an innocent, honest looking, well-meaning sounding word be used to promote and sustain such a genuinely evil, Luciferian plan. The Agenda 21 programme for 'sustainable development' bears an uncanny resemblance to the plans for technocracy.

The United Nations had, in reviving the technocracy plan created in the 1930s, found the way to take power, to control us and to move towards a world government which would, of course, be controlled by the United Nations itself. Who better? The plan was to punish the people of the world because they had, through their consumerism, destroyed the world. Later the world's consumers would be vilified for upsetting a small Swedish girl and filling her with rage – to add to her other mental health issues. She was chosen as the poster child for global warming and used to recruit children to the cause in the knowledge that there is no easier way to control adults than to control children. The Nazis, masters of manipulation, had used this trick to great effect.)

Eventually, the punishment was enhanced with laws, restrictions and, just as in Biblical times, a suitable plague. This was 'sold' as a way of saving the environment from the consequences of the manufactured hazard of global warming but it was always a plan to take control of the world and the bodies, minds and souls of every living being. It was, in essence, a plan to take control of humanity.

Maurice Strong, a Canadian oil and mining billionaire, played a huge part in promoting the new paradigm.

Almost inevitably, 178 leaders immediately signed up to the Agenda 21 plan. The aims, carefully crafted to create both fear and a solution for the fear, seemed laudable and so no one dared say 'No'. It was decided that the world's nations would join together to fight these threats to our existence: environmental damage and global warming. The 'people' who had consumed too much oil and gas and coal, and who had therefore put the entire planet in peril, were easily defined as the new enemy. It was not global industries which had caused environmental damage but the people who had used their products. The solution was said to be centralised control over all resources and a 'new international economic order' (soon to be shortened to 'new world order'). There would be a global smart grid with everything controlled by the UN and its supporters. There was to be no place for democracy.

The phrase 'sustainable development' was constantly used to describe how the world's nations would move forward. And the word 'communitarianism' became the new watchword for the new world. Bill Clinton, shortly to become President of the USA, and Tony Blair, shortly to become leader of the Labour Party and then Prime Minister of the United Kingdom, were, and would continue to be, keen supporters of a new world order which would take power from the people and give it to the bankers and the billionaires working in the computer industry. How ironic that the betrayal of the people should be in the hands of two men who were allegedly leaders of democratic and socialist parties. Al Gore, Clinton's vice president, later became a spokesman for the new fear-makers and promoted a hugely profitable DVD which was ruled by a judge in the UK to contain nine errors. Gore also became a multi-millionaire.

There was much talk of the need for less spending and for more austerity. Carbon footprints, carbon trading and smaller houses became the order of the day. Biofuels were promoted as an alternative to fossil fuels, despite (or because of) the fact that biofuels were being made out of food and leading to mass starvation. The banks were deregulated, inoculation programmes were increased massively (with the dangers being actively suppressed and the critics being silenced), genetically modified foods were approved (without any proper testing) and the very real hazards of cell phones and Wi-Fi were also suppressed.

Not everyone was convinced. Two participants in the UN meeting held in Rio in 1992 were Pratap Chatterjee and Matthias Finger. In 1994 they published a book called, *The Earth Brokers*. They argued that the UN had 'boosted precisely the type of industrial development that is destructive for the environment, the planet and its inhabitants'. Moreover, they concluded that as a result 'the rich will get richer, the poor poorer while more and more of the planet is destroyed in the process'. And that, of course, is exactly what is happening.

Since we had now been proven to be our own enemy, we were encouraged to fight our own greed and wastefulness and in order to train us to be compliant we were introduced to the joys of recycling (though we were not told, of course, that much of the carefully sorted material would be burnt, buried or dumped).

Our unelected leaders could, at last, start to move us towards a world government which would remove traditional democracy (which had clearly failed because it gave the people too much power).

And thus began the nightmare.

With astonishing speed, and a good deal of behind-the-scenes political chicanery, the plan was put into action.

The world has always been chaotic.

But it was largely our sort of chaos. It was human chaos. We often voted for the wrong people. In some countries there were corrupt governments. In other countries totalitarian governments or military juntas took power.

But what started to happen as a result of Agenda 21 was quite different: it was an end to democracy, freedom and humanity.

The United Nations went from being an organisation with some high flown good intentions best known perhaps for its peace keeping force of soldiers in their smart UN uniforms and blue hats, to an organisation with a steadily growing grip on every aspect of our lives.

The 178 governments which had signed up to the principle of sustainability (and the idea of making the world a better place) all set up their own groups to ensure that the principles of sustainable development were followed. Prominent environmentalists were given money and power and anyone who voiced criticism was silenced. Debate was suppressed and those who questioned the science of global warming were demonised. Prince Charles of the British royal family, either through malignant intentions or through ignorance and stupidity, was among the most prominent voices promoting the need for a new world order.

The Agenda 21 plan included an end to national sovereignty, a restriction in the ease of movement around the world, an increased role for the State in the rearing of children, an end to private property and the breaking down of the family unit.

Although most people didn't realise it at the time, the plan included an increase in the rules for those wanting to take on certain jobs (through licensing arrangements), the emptying of rural areas and the building of new, densely populated 'smart' cities whose inhabitants would never have to leave, and a dumbing down of education so that children were indoctrinated and tested rather than being taught in the traditional sense.

Local politicians were dragged into this plan, too. The word 'sustainability' became a keyword in all new planning programmes. Organisations such as 'Local Governments for Sustainability' and 'Common Purpose' were set up to ensure that the Agenda 21 protocols were followed as widely as possible. The environmental movement was given huge amounts of money to create shame and guilt and to help promote the United Nations plan.

And, most terrifying of all, there was a plan to reduce the world's population – not by a few million here and a few million there, but by billions. The plan was to reduce the global population by 75% or more. The mysterious Georgia Guide Stones appeared and called for the world's population to be taken down to under 500 million – meaning that around 7 billion people would have to be removed. A United Nations Global Biodiversity Assessment called for the world's population to be kept under 1 billion – though it was never clear how this was to be attained.

And global warming was the stick with which we were all to be beaten into submission. Everything could be blamed on global warming. It was decided (with no scientific evidence to support the decision) that the planet was being endangered by our use of fossil fuels and our reckless use of the world's resources. Celebrities and well-known politicians were recruited to give the new 'threat' credibility and some pretty fancy graphs and fake statistics were glued together to give the whole thing a pseudo-scientific look.

In America, the events of the 9/11 were used as an excuse to bring in stringent and oppressive new rules taking away the rights of all citizens. Similar laws were gradually introduced around the world and the rights of the individual were slowly banished. Protests held up some of the plans (such as Tony Blair's ambition to introduce ID cards in the UK) but the promoters of these plans merely kept re-introducing them.

There was no doubt at all that the promoters of Agenda 21 wanted our bodies, our minds, and our souls. And they wanted a good many of us dead.

Today, there are still many millions who still don't realise precisely what is happening. Everything that is happening was planned decades ago – and is only now coming to fruition. Every strange planning decision was deliberate. The rows about gay marriage, trans-sexuality and black lives matter campaigns were all designed to erase our culture and make us ashamed of our history, to cause chaos and confusion, to spread dissent and to divide populations. Even the introduction of bicycle lanes, bizarre street furniture and smart motorways were all part of a United Nations plan which was created decades ago. The promoters of Agenda 21 want to get rid of the motor car because they want us all living in smart cities. Regionalisation, as promoted by the European Union, is a step towards globalisation. The European Union itself became part of Agenda 21 some years ago and the phrase 'new normal' was also created a good while ago.

The plan all along has been to get rid of all nationalities. Those patriots who wave their Scottish, Irish, English, American flags can say goodbye to those flags. There will soon be no nations.

The leaders of Agenda 21 want us all living in small apartments. Have you ever wondered why local planning officers want to get rid of well-made old houses and replace them with poorly built, cramped apartments in tower blocks? It's all part of the Agenda 21 plan. Have you ever wondered why the EU pays big landowners to do nothing with their land – to grow nothing, to grow no food? Well, it's all part of the plan to force us to eat factory made food. Bill Gates hasn't just invested in inoculations. He doesn't just control world health. He has for a long time been dictating global food policy and has money invested in a company which makes fake meat. The internet is pretty much under the control of a handful of billionaires. The main search engine controls 80% of search requests. The biggest internet seller controls a similar number of sales. Data mining will soon by the most profitable (and arguably the only profitable) industry on earth. The internet of things is intrusive. Governments and bureaucrats care nothing about the people who pay their salaries and fat pensions. It is worth remembering that every totalitarian state has relied on collecting data about its citizens. Stalin was pretty good at it. And so were the Nazis.

The deaths caused by the closure of hospital departments in 2020 were all part of the plan. The world's billionaires decided some decades ago that the world was overpopulated. They want to kill a few billion of us. The closure of farms is part of the plan too. They need many of us to starve to death. Most of those who die of starvation will be in Africa. (Ironically, black lives matter campaigners have completely missed this and have been persuaded to put their energy into removing statues and eradicating history.)

It was no accident that many elections have been cancelled. It is no accident that some politicians are being demonised while others are lauded by the media. And it is no accident that the media has betrayed citizens en masse globally.

The crime has been built upon the false threat of global warming. That was always part of the plan. Those questioning the honesty of the global warming mythology, or the virtues of Agenda 21, are dismissed as 'conspiracy theorists' but the only conspiracy is the one leading towards a World Government and a World Church.

This is the most evil, most carefully planned, most deadly conspiracy in human history. A senior official at the United Nations has talked of a Luciferian initiation. The plan is wicked beyond belief.

Our governments have been bought. They have no respect for us. Common purpose drones do the dirty work and the billionaires build their wealth.

In her brilliant and astonishing book, *Behind the Green Mask*, published in 2011, Rosa Koire, described how many of the things which have been damaging our way of life in Europe were already beginning to destroy American life.

Energy saving programmes and the abandonment of fossil fuels were introduced to force us into smart cities. Remaking roads to suit bicycles was a plan to stop us using motor cars – and thereby force us into living in their smart cities. Do you ever wonder about smart motorways – which create traffic jams and accidents? All that crazy road furniture? Ever reducing speed limits? Higher and higher taxes on motor cars? All these seemingly absurd developments were designed to stop us using cars, move into high rise tower blocks in cities where we would be forced into tiny flats and ticky tacky box houses. And, of course, everything is conveniently blamed on climate change.

It's all part of the plan.

We are being told we have to cut carbon emissions to levels measured decades ago. But carbon emissions weren't measured in those distant days.

The plans to replace local police forces with sneaks and snitches were put in place many years ago. The aim was to create mistrust.

Property inspections for houses and energy assessments were all devised to force us out of old-fashioned, well-built houses into badly built, but profitable, new tenement buildings.

All those licences and certificates we need for our jobs? They were planned years ago to disrupt and force us into living in fear. They were designed to be expensive and disruptive. If you don't have the right licence then you can't work. And then when you have one licence they want another. And another.

Immigration policies were devised as a deliberate well thought out plot designed to disrupt society, break down nations, increase fear and create racism.

Nothing is accidental.

Do you remember reading that they were releasing wild animals such as wolves into the countryside? That was all planned years ago. It's another part of forcing us to live in cities and away from the countryside.

Forcing people out of the countryside isn't difficult. Public transport links are cut. Electricity supply problems are ignored. Landline, broadband and cell phone coverage is poor. Water supplies are blocked. Rural roads are not repaired or are closed for long periods. Town and village dwellers are allowed to have a garden or an allotment to make them feel they are reaching independence. But for most people it's impossible to grow enough food to live on. The proponents of Agenda 21 want us all to be dependent. And they talk regularly of terrorism to create fear and obedience. People living in rural communities (including those owning and working on farms) will be moved into 'islands of human habitation' or 'smart cities' so that the countryside can be left wild.

Do you enjoy playing sports such as football or golf? Forget it. The land used for such activities will be allowed to go back to wild land. Agenda 21 calls for governments (and, eventually, the world government) to take control of all land and to remove all decision making from individuals. The assumption is that bureaucrats will make wiser decisions (on behalf of communities) than individuals. Civil and legal rights will disappear. Standards of living must all be reduced to a lowest common denominator. Planning departments all over the world have been given identical blueprints for legislation so that the Agenda 21 requirements can be met. New supermarkets and shops are built with residential flats built above. Sadly, a lot of the flats remain empty and a good many of the shops are struggling, too. If you wonder why street lights are turned off, why verges are scruffy, why even the potholes have potholes, why there are few bus services, why services for the elderly and the disabled are either non-existent or priced out of reach for most people and why local hospitals are closing, you need look no further than Agenda 21 and the United Nations.

Much of the money your local council collects has to be spent on projects, such as redevelopment, which are mandated by Agenda 21. If you've wondered why there is so much absurd road furniture decorating roads and pavements and why so many chicanes are being built then look no further than Agenda 21. All those cycle lanes which cause traffic jams on narrow roads are there because of Agenda 21. Restricted car parking (and ever narrower spaces) is a result of regulations from the United Nations. Even the pretty coloured paving stones used are mandated by the United Nations. Every aspect of your daily life is managed not by local councillors or officials but by bureaucrats who were never elected and who have probably never been within a thousand miles of your home.

And if you're worried about who will grow our food when the farms have gone you can stop worrying. (Or start worrying.) Our food will be grown in factories.

The UN's Agenda 21 is a huge document but the big giveaway is, perhaps, this statement: 'The precautionary principle states that if an action or policy has a suspected risk of causing harm to the public or to the environment, in the absence of scientific consensus that the action or policy is harmful, the burden of proof that it is not harmful falls on those taking the action.'

The whole of the European Union's law making process works along these lines. And it is used effectively to defend the claim that global warming is dangerous. Those promoting the danger don't have to prove their claim. It is up to those who disagree to prove that global warming isn't a threat. And proving that something isn't happening, or isn't a threat is, of course, impossible.

Do you think it's an accident that veganism has suddenly become popular? It isn't. They don't want us eating animals. It takes up too much time. It's a slow, messy process. They want us eating the food they are making in laboratories. Some of it will, of course look and taste like meat. And the billionaire food factory owners will be the ones making the money.

Towns are growing to look the same, like hotel chains. Many strong, old buildings, good to look at and full of character, are demolished to save the environment from their presence and us from the memories they harbour. They are replaced with buildings as ugly and as durable as cardboard boxes.

Privacy is going, shortly to be gone. 'Why does anyone need or want privacy? What terrible secrets have you got to hide?' Webcams, CCTV and social media have banished privacy. We are tracked, traced and tested. We zoom in and out of each other's homes because we are told it is better that way. The NSA in America can monitor tens of millions of phone calls every second. If they can do it they will.

Better for whom?

Better for the spies, perhaps.

When we chat through the internet they can spy on us all the time. Another piece of our privacy gone. Only those with evil secrets need privacy, they say. And now they know everything about you, and your life is not yours any more.

Traditions are reviled because our history must be forgotten. Everything we may have thought of as great is apparently an embarrassment. Our ancestors, they say, were all racists or worse.

And so we bury ourselves in shame and obediently forget the people who came before. Our history will begin tomorrow and they will tell us what to believe and what to think.

It has all been planned for decades.

Look back at the United Nations plans – published decades ago – and in your shock you will recognise life as we have grown to know it, predicted in those now almost ancient documents.

Everything was planned.

Today, most people have absolutely no idea what is going on. They dutifully pick out their pretty face coverings, and they feel quietly confident that their selfless actions and their thoughtful government will save them from the plague threatening their lives.

These people are blind.

They are sleeping walking to their deaths. They have been brainwashed by carefully organised psychological operations. Governments have admitted they want us terrified, and they use professional psychological operations to achieve their aims.

The endgame has started. We must work fast. We are in the fight of our lives for they want to kill many of us and enslave the rest.

Life will never be normal again unless we smash the 'new normal', deny the new world order and reject the global reset.

There isn't a single world leader we can trust.

If we are to save humanity we all have to fight as we have never fought before.

We have to spread the word. We have to show people what has happened. We have to help them understand the horror of what is being done to our world. We have to show them that nothing – nothing – that has happened is an accident. It has all been deliberate. The sleepwalkers must be encouraged to watch, listen and read the truth. Our lives are the stake in this war.

The whole Agenda 21 fraud has been built on two lies.

The first lie is global warming. The earth sometimes gets hotter and it sometimes gets cooler. There is no evidence of any dramatic change in the global temperature – just fraudulent figures and lies. Inevitably, therefore, there is no evidence that man is responsible for any dramatic change.

The second lie is that the world is overpopulated. It isn't. There is plenty of land and food for everyone. People starve only because the food that is available is in the wrong place.

This isn't George Orwell's 1984.
This is real.
Orwell got most of it right. All he really got wrong was the date.
Everything that has happened was meant to happen.
I've glimpsed the future. And I don't like the look of it.

Part Two: What the World Will Look Like

Important Note (A reminder)

As you read on, please remember, I wrote this book with one hand tied behind my back. Well, not literally, you understand, but figuratively.

In order to publish this book I had to remove all references to the name of the problem which triggered the 'house arrests'. And so you will not find therein any reference to a word describing a disease which begins with the third letter of the alphabet. Nor will you find any reference to a disease the name of which ends with a number which is slightly greater than 18 and slightly smaller than 20.

In addition, in view of proposed new legislation which will make it illegal for anyone (including doctors) to share facts and opinions about a specific medical procedure, I had to avoid using a word beginning with 'v' and use the word inoculation instead. I have also had to avoid using words which describe bits of material placed over the mouth and nose. And I am not allowed to mention an organisation which has a name which could be mistaken for a rock band. There were several other restrictions.

Readers may be puzzled by this censorship since other authors are allowed to discuss these things in their books. The reality, however, is that I am banned from writing about some things which are open to other authors.

So, please bear with me if some material seems slightly obtuse. I sometimes think I must have wandered down the rabbit hole.

The world is never going to go back to normal – unless we take control. Those who say things will be normal in a few months or a year or two are either lying or they are ignorant.

In this part of the book I am going to describe what we can expect in a simple, alphabetical analysis of our future.

Adenauer (Konrad)

'The good Lord set definite limits on man's wisdom, but set no limits on his stupidity – that's just not fair.'

Affirmative action

Affirmative action is most accurately described as politically acceptable racism.

Africa

There is a disaster in Africa which is going almost unnoticed. It is a disaster of unimaginable proportions. I forecast what would happen many months ago in one of these videos. This man-made disaster was always going to be worse than any natural disaster; worse than any tsunami, any plague or any volcanic eruption.

'Expert' mathematical modellers advised the United Nations, and as a result of their advice the official forecast from the UN was that there would be up to 1.2 billion cases and 3.3 million deaths from a new virus. African countries told everyone to stay indoors and did all the things they were told to do.

Inevitably, things went terribly wrong.

Cases of malaria and tuberculosis went undiagnosed and untreated and both are now spreading and killing millions. Maternal mortality is soaring and so is infant mortality. Around 10% of Africa's population will descend into extreme poverty. The number of deaths from starvation will soar. Was that really by accident? Or could it have been part of the depopulation plan?

Proof that the chaos was avoidable comes from Malawi. The wise government there did not impose strict house arrest rules, even though it was predicted that without house arrest there would be 50,000 deaths. The result was that out of a population of 19 million there were, at the time of writing, just 176 deaths.

Agenda 21

Under the auspices of the World Economic Forum, the United Nations and a bunch of unelected billionaires and officials, politicians and policymakers around the world are determined on creating a global technocracy and introducing what they call the Great Reset or the Global Reset – a crude form of social engineering designed to manipulate and 'own' every citizen on earth. The world we know now, in 2021, is just a taste of what we can expect in the future.

The aim of those following Agenda 21 is to create their own version of a Utopia, a global technocracy with a guaranteed income for every citizen and a system of reward, punishment and control modelled on China's social credit system. Global warming is the excuse. Once the Global Reset has been completed citizens will be monitored. Those who behave well will be rewarded. Those who fail to comply with the orders they are given will be punished and excluded from much of society. Agenda 21 is organised, legalised corruption.

The plan is to remove all signs of human dignity; with every piece of dignity disappearing too slowly for most people to notice. The people who have planned this coup rely on the mass of people being too busy, too distracted, too complacent, too lazy and too fearful to realise what is happening. And they know that they can ensure that those who speak up can be smeared, demonised and dismissed as right wing conspiracy theorists.

The result will be that individuals will be forced to submit to the tyranny of a technocratic state with so-called, self-appointed experts managing every aspect of human life. Our behaviour will be controlled in minute detail and we will be forced to be dependent on the State.

This is tyranny on a scale never known before, and the events of 2020 were planned to give governments an opportunity to force us to obey and become accustomed to a 'new normal' in which all individuality is suppressed and the power of the State (and its self-appointed functionaries) is everything.

The fact is that everything strange, bad, restricting and destructive that has happened in the last three decades is a result of Agenda 21. All of those things which happened, but which seemed wrong, inexplicable, damaging, unnatural and unreal, were a result of

Agenda 21. Most of them occurred without even the slightest nod towards democracy since the crucial decisions were made by individuals working for the UN, the EU or the World Economic Forum, by huge, powerful Non-Governmental Organisations (NGOs) with staff on million dollar salaries, by quangos and by regional parliaments and so on – none of whom was staffed by individuals who had been elected.

Our lives have steadily deteriorated in every notable way. Health care, education, increased taxation (local and national), rapidly deteriorating services, reduced standard of living and increased corruption.

Campaigns demanding more rights for homosexuals and transgender individuals have created conflict, broken up the traditional family unit, done a great deal of permanent harm to religions and will have the acceptable by-product of helping to reduce the population. Doubters and those who object can easily be demonised as homophobic or transphobic.

Fear and confusion have been caused by deadly warnings and by constantly changing advice and impenetrable laws. None of this has been accidental. All trust and sense of fair play and decency have been eradicated. (Ironically, it is inevitable that the destruction of fair play and trust will lead many young people to become rebellious and to stand up against authoritarianism. But that is some way ahead and the rebellions will be quashed ruthlessly.)

Kindness and dignity are the main currencies of value in private life, and honesty, trust and honour are the only currencies of value in public life. Tragically, these qualities have, for years, been steadily devalued and in the last few months they have been shot, knifed, stamped on, kicked, spat on, shredded and attacked with brutal disregard for sense or sensibility. There is no grace, no serenity and no soul among our new leaders who have, without ever being elected to anything, clawed their way through life with their progress based on deceits built on avarice and jealousy. As a result, millions now consider themselves to be refugees in their own countries. Tony Blair (who is, in my view, quite possibly the most evil man in modern history), Gordon Brown and Boris Johnson are reported to have called for the creation of a global bureaucracy with more power than the World Health Organisation – all part of the end of sovereignty and nation states.

What happened in 2020 was merely the culmination of years of common purpose, quangos, civil servants, corporate insensitivity and local planning.

Nothing happened by accident.

Much of the rest of this book simply explains the full consequences of these plans, what the new normal will look like (unless we call a halt to it) – and how the United Nations plan will affect every aspect of our lives.

AIDS

Looking back I can see when I became a target and when commissions and media invitations suddenly dried up.

In 1988, I wrote a book called, *The Health Scandal* for a London publisher called Sidgwick and Jackson. They were incredibly excited about it. There was much talk of heavy promotion. At a special reception, the chairman of the company, Lord Rees Mogg told me how excited he was by the book.

But the book contained a small section questioning the Government's line on AIDS. I produced evidence proving that the disease was not, as we had been told, going to affect every family in Britain by the year 2000. And suddenly, without explanation, *The Health Scandal* was abandoned. The planned publicity and advertising disappeared. And Sidgwick and Jackson refused to sell the paperback rights. The book had become too hot to handle. It seemed to me clear that my questioning of the AIDS myth was clearly embarrassing to the company. (I had previously written much along the same lines for the national newspaper to which I was contributing a weekly column.)

When my agent asked what had happened about arranging a paperback edition of the book, she was told that we could have the rights back since the company didn't want to offer the book. Within less than a week we'd sold the book to a paperback house and since Sidgwick and Jackson didn't want anything further to do with the book, I kept the entire paperback payment. Neither my agent nor I had ever come across anything like it. Publishers don't usually turn up their noses at a chance to collect thousands of pounds in rights money.

I had exposed the AIDS fear as a lie. I produced figures which blew away the claim that we would all be affected by it. And suddenly, virtually overnight, I became a non-person. Regular appearances on television programmes were cancelled. Invitations to appear on BBC television and radio programmes ceased. I still wrote contracted newspaper columns but I had clearly been marked as dangerous. My books were only rarely reviewed in the UK. Requests to make keynote speeches stopped suddenly. As far as the establishment was concerned I had become a nuisance and clearly had to be silenced.

After I exposed the way the AIDS 'crisis' had been exaggerated, I found that publishers around the world suddenly let my books go out of print or remaindered them – and refused to consider new titles. My German publishers had been selling fairly large amounts of my books (for example, one year I received a royalty cheque of around £30,000 for sales of *How to Stop Your Doctor Killing You* and *Bodypower*) but the books then disappeared, and the following year I received nothing in royalties. The publishers did not respond when I asked what had happened or when I sent them other titles. And I was banned in China (where my books had been bestsellers) after I wrote a column on a forbidden topic for a leading Chinese newspaper. Much the same sort of thing happened around the world.

Only now does it seem obvious that the AIDS virus was being promoted as the plague that would prepare us for Agenda 21. They massively increased the global mortality figures by, for example, including just about everyone who died of tuberculosis (among other common disorders).

I am not alone in thinking that AIDS was a rehearsal. I received a note from a reader who said: 'I worked in several Genito-Urinary Medicine clinics between 1989-92 and then again between 1997-2002. One of my duties in the latter post was reporting the monthly numbers to CDC Colindale. The Government used to manipulate those figures, the BBC and other mainstream media were happy to unquestioningly report them.'

There have, of course, been a number of other attempts to find a scary story with which to terrify the world: avian flu and swine flu, to name but two.

And what did these threats have in common?

They were all subject to dramatically exaggerated forecasts from Professor Neil Ferguson at Imperial College, London – the one with links to the Bill and Melinda Gates Foundation and a man who seems to me to be so incompetent that if he designed a cup he'd put the handle on the inside.

Alcoholism

The incidence of alcoholism has been rising fast since April 2020. Shutting pubs and restaurants, but continuing to allow supermarkets to sell cheap booze, has meant that increasing numbers of people are drinking heavily at home. The number of alcoholics (or nearly alcoholics) in the UK had within months doubled from around four million to over eight million. The number of deaths from alcoholism has soared. (It is no accident that the closure of pubs has also led to the closure of a number of small brewers – leaving the market open for large, international companies.)

I suspect that the next move will be to restrict the sale of alcohol in supermarkets (or to increase the tax on alcohol) ostensibly because of the increase in alcoholism caused by the closure of pubs. This will cause much pain and distress. The real reason will, of course, be to reduce overall alcohol sales. This will be done to reduce the damage done to society by alcohol consumption and also help lead us to the world religion of Chrislam.

It is interesting to note that wildfires have become an existential threat to the entire American wine industry. There have been seven big fires affecting the wine industry between 2015 and 2020. The fires have destroyed vines and damaged every aspect of the wine industry. It is difficult not to conclude that this is deliberate.

As an associated aside, it is worth noting that during the same period, the amount of tobacco being smoked has also risen while gambling is much more of a problem than it was before the events of 2020.

Naturally, as always, everything that is happening is part of a plan. Nothing that happens today happens by accident. Everything is a consequence of deliberate actions.

Alienation

It isn't difficult to see why some are calling this 'the age of alienation'.

Those of us who attempt to share the truth are lied about, demonised, harassed and often arrested. The very idea that anyone might offer an alternative point of view terrifies the heavy booted brigade who have put themselves in charge. Telling the truth has always been a crime in fascist and totalitarian regimes.

And since the rules change from one area to another, we never quite know what punishments to expect. In one part of America, you can be sent to prison for a year if you fail to cover your mouth and nose. In another part of America you have to pay a 2,000 dollar fine but there is no prison sentence. In Texas, some people have been told that they should wear face coverings in their own homes. In one shop, a guard pulled a gun on a man who was not wearing a face covering. In California, people have been telephoning the police if they've heard a neighbour coughing or sneezing.

The snitches and sneaks, eager to please the system, are part of the mass surveillance system.

Alternative energy

Huge amounts of fossil fuel are being used to build solar farms, wind farms, electric car batteries and a variety of other forms of renewable energy (some of which, such as barrages and tidal wave energy recovery, have never been proven to work). There is little doubt that many of these new forms of energy are of negative value (building and running a wind farm, for example, requires more energy than the wind farm will produce) and some are absurd. Solar is useless when the sun isn't out (which, in Northern Europe for example, is most of the time) and wind power is useless when there isn't any wind (which is surprisingly often). Biofuels are promoted as a clean way to keep engines running but it has been recognised for years that turning corn and other crops into biofuel merely increases the number of people starving to death. Biomass is quite possibly the most hypocritical invention of all time.

Global warming extremists want to stop funding so that oil companies will not find more oil. They want us to stop using oil. However, the International Energy Agency has stated that by the year 2040 our planet will still obtain only around 5% of its energy needs from renewable sources (including burning trees or 'biomass'). Without fossil fuels, billions will die of starvation and the cold.

We need to take a hard, scientific look at the various alternative sources of energy which are recommended as alternatives to the fossil fuels.

First, there is wind, is a clean, long established and renewable technology and the energy it produces doesn't require sending men underground to do dangerous jobs in difficult circumstances. There is no pollution (unless you count the alarmingly annoying noise pollution made by windmills and the destruction of wildlife caused by the turning blades). The energy produced by wind is relatively cheap and competitive with other sources of energy.

Unfortunately, you do need rather a lot of windmills to provide even a relatively small amount of electricity.

In his book, *The Coming Economic Collapse* Stephen Leeb reports that in order to replace 10% of America's coal consumption (at the time around 5% of America's electricity supply) with wind, would require between 36,000 and 40,000 windmills. To meet all America's electricity needs would require twenty times that number and take a decade to construct.

Inevitably, there are snags with obtaining energy from wind.

First, we would need vast numbers of windmills. There is no sign of anyone wanting to build them in sufficient quantities.

Second, building windmills uses up large amounts of fossil fuel. And yet the greens who want the windmills don't want oil companies to continue looking for oil. Will the world's motorists, airline travellers and military agree to vast quantities of the planet's remaining oil being used to make windmills? Somehow, I doubt it.

Third, to build enough wind turbines to fill our fuel needs would cost billions. One estimate suggests that building enough windmills in America would cost £2,500 per man, woman and child in America. Will citizens be prepared to spend £2,500 each today to provide themselves with fuel tomorrow? And will they put up with the environmental cost? Who will want the windmills in their backyard?

Fourth, most countries are not windy enough for windmills to work effectively. For example, even the UK is not as windy as some people think, and the idea that wind turbines could generate even a fifth of the UK's energy needs by 2020 is nonsense. There are, quite simply, too many calm days when the windmills would stand idle. When the wind doesn't blow you don't get any electricity. Indeed, electricity has to be used from other sources to keep the windmills moving and to stop them seizing up. The problems with wind reliability are vast. Germany has a lot of wind farms but these can only produce a sixth of their potential capacity. There is no way to store wind generated electricity when the wind blows very hard and there is no way that any developed country could obtain its power from wind farms unless the demand for power was dramatically reduced (to about a tenth of current levels.)

Fifth, wind turbines affect the environment too. They don't just look horrid and make an awful noise. (Try building one near to a country cottage owned by a politician to find out how unpopular wind farms really are.) If you erect enough windmills to produce useful amounts of electricity they will change the climate and change the surface drag of the earth.

It is clear that even politicians don't have much faith in wind energy. In some parts of Europe, home owners who spend money on eco-friendly wind turbines (or, indeed, on solar panels or other energy saving measures) are forced to pay higher taxes.

Ironically, the most practical use of wind and windmills may be to grind corn in small communities.

Solar power has been around a long time. The ancient Chinese are believed to have used glass and mirrors to harness the sun's rays and make fire.

Solar energy sounds wonderful. It's clean and quiet and sunshine is abundant in some parts of the world. But solar cells aren't very efficient (converting only about a tenth of the light they receive into electricity) and they are expensive. Solar power is, at best, a niche energy source. It cannot be used to provide chemicals for farmers and it cannot easily be used to power the world's fleet of cars, lorries and aeroplanes.

What else is there?

Well, there are biofuels, of course.

And biofuels, remember, are the fuel of choice for global warming cultists. However, it is worth pointing out that the stuff known as biofuel, crops such as corn, is known to much of the world as food. By encouraging the use of biofuels, the global warming enthusiasts are condemning much of the world to death by starvation.

And there is always biomass, said to be the biggest source of renewable energy. Biomass is the 'green' word for wood, and we have to remember that although wind farms and solar panels get a great deal of publicity, they produce a marginal amount of electricity. The greater part of the energy which is said to come from renewables comes from burning wood pellets – biomass – and in the UK most of the biomass is imported from America. So the trees which the planet needs are chopped down, chopped up and shipped to the UK in big ships driven by diesel. And once the trees get to the UK, they are renamed biomass and burned to produce clean electricity. Curiously, a politician called Chris Huhne who was arrested, convicted and jailed for perverting the course of justice, and who was the Liberal Democrats' environmental spokesman, and an energy and global warming consultant was, soon after his sentence, appointed European manager of a biomass firm which makes wood chip pellets in the US and which sells them around the world as green energy. While he was energy and global warming secretary, Huhne championed the use of green subsidies for wood pellets and subsequently several hundred million pounds of British taxpayers' money was been spent on buying the pellets. It has been estimated that cutting the trees, turning them into pellets, bringing them across the Atlantic and burning them does more damage than burning coal – and costs a good deal more.

It is, of course, perfectly possible to obtain electricity from moving water. Mill owners have been using rivers to power their water mills for centuries. Today, almost 10% of American electricity is obtained through hydroelectric projects.

And rivers and reservoirs aren't the only source of water power. The sea is another relatively untapped source and some people claim that we can harness wave power. The first problem is that waves vary constantly. Sometimes they are high. Sometimes they are almost invisible. The result is that the electricity obtained from the sea tends to be intermittent. And you can't run cars or jets on wave power. Nor can you make fertiliser from the sea. The second problem is that the energy required to obtain energy from the sea is enormous. Building and maintaining the infrastructure would require a tremendous amount of oil. So obtaining electricity from wave power is pretty much out.

Hydrogen is a favourite among those who claim we will be able to replace oil with something else. And, superficially, it looks good. Hydrogen fuel cells provide a renewable, clean energy source. They combine hydrogen and oxygen chemically to produce electricity, water and heat. But the main problem is that there isn't enough hydrogen to go around. In addition, hydrogen is neither cheap nor environmentally friendly. And hydrogen fuel isn't terribly efficient for although it's true that the by-product of using hydrogen as a source of energy is clean water (so the process is environmentally friendly), the other big problem is that collecting the hydrogen requires vast amounts of oil, natural gas or coal. There are no wonderful underground reservoirs of hydrogen waiting to be exploited. Hydrogen has to be manufactured from hydrocarbon sources such as coal or natural gas or extracted from water. So we're back where we started – needing a fossil fuel supply.

It is possible to generate small amounts of hydrogen using electricity generated by windmills. And hydrogen fuel cells can be used to power cars so it might be possible to provide fuel for a few cars in this way. We would, however, need to build an entirely new infrastructure to support and fuel those hydrogen powered cars. It isn't really much of an answer to any problem. Finally, the big, insurmountable problem is that producing hydrogen always uses more energy than is obtained. Hydrogen, like windmills and biofuels, is a negative source of energy. And it just doesn't make sense to turn oil, or anything else, into hydrogen.

So, there we are.

We give thanks for the oil, the gas and the uranium which God supplied us with, and we carry on using them.

Or…

Well, there isn't really an or…

Animals

There is no place for animals (either farm animals or pets) in the Global Reset. Animals are considered to be a threat and must be eradicated.

The United Nations wants to keep animals away from people and to reduce the number of animals on earth. Their policy of keeping space between animals and people is, bizarrely, called biodiversity. The short, medium and long-term aim is to install people in smart cities and to feed them with laboratory produced meat. There will be no need or place for farm animals or pets when the Great Reset has taken place.

Animals, wild and domesticated, are being demonised and are now being blamed for epidemics past and present. We are warned that animals could create new plagues. In the last year or two, millions of hens, ducks, geese, pigs, cows and even mink have been slaughtered because of alleged threats of disease.

A few years ago, a team at Imperial College in London, involving Neil Ferguson, the mathematician, warned that a foot and mouth problem needed to be dealt with by a massive slaughter of animals. Their modelling of foot and mouth disease led to a cull of six million sheep, pigs and cattle. The cost to the UK was around £10 billion. But the Imperial's work has been described as 'severely flawed'. (Ferguson, of course, has an appalling track record. In 2002, he predicted that up to 50,000 people would die from mad cow disease. He said that could rise to 150,000 if sheep were involved. In the UK, the death total was 177. In 2005, he said that up to 200 million people could be killed by bird flu. The total number of deaths was 282 worldwide. In 2009, he advised the Government which, relying on that advice, said that swine flu would kill 65,000 people in the UK. In the end, swine flu killed 457 people in the UK.)

The UN Convention on Biological Diversity has said that things have to change in order to stop an on-going 'decline in nature'. It is not entirely clear what is meant by this but the UN has stated that 'the vast majority of outbreaks of new disease are a result of animal disease affecting people'.

There is, of course, no evidence for this absurd claim.

You might as well argue that 'the vast majority of outbreaks of new disease are a result of people watching rubbishy programmes on television' or 'the vast majority of outbreaks of new disease are a result of the United Nations spending its money on producing pseudo-scientific reports which are of absolutely no value'.

A BBC programme fronted by David Attenborough is reported to have claimed that modern diseases such as swine flu, SARS and Ebola were caused by our having more contact with animals.

In my view, there is as much evidence for this as there is that these diseases were caused by our watching stupid programmes on the BBC.

It's all just part of Agenda 21.

Arts

As 2020 progressed, so various aspects of the Arts began to demand government financial support. By the end of the year, a wide variety of the Arts had become subsidised and government controlled. They had, in practice, been nationalised – effectively owned and controlled by State bureaucrats.

And magazines (like newspapers) were also being controlled by governments through the medium of advertising – bought by the Government and paid for by unwitting and largely unwilling taxpayers.

Bacterial pneumonia

It has been shown that many of those who appear to die of viral infections (such as flu and the one ending in a number that I can't mention) actually die of bacterial pneumonia which could be treated with antibiotics. The evidence proving this was published in 2008, and one of the co-authors of the paper involved was Dr Fauci, who in 2020 became one of the American President's chief advisors.

This evidence means that the doctors who refused to treat elderly residents in care homes should be charged with murder rather than manslaughter.

They should have known that by withholding simple antibiotic treatment they were deliberately sentencing those people to death.

Bankruptcy

The Great Reset, as advertised by Prince Charles, doesn't include any provision for private property – unless you're already a billionaire or a member of the British royal family.

If you don't believe me check out the Agenda 21 promotional guff, as published by the United Nations. And take a look at Pope Francis's words on private property.

So, I hear you asking, how are the sturmbannfuhrers and obersturmbannfuhrers planning to take away our private property?

Silly question, I'm afraid, because they've already started their five point plan to bankrupt us all. The only people able to own private property will be the billionaires and the royals. (You didn't think they'd give up their wealth, did you?)

They don't want us to own anything because people who own a home or a pension or who have a few quid in the bank have an unacceptable tendency to assume that they are free citizens. The aficionados of the Great Reset want to remove every last vestige of our independence, and they'll be ruthless.

First, of course, crashing the global economy has buggered up any investments you may have. And don't think you are OK if you don't have any investments because unless you work for the State and have a State pension your retirement fund will have been savagely damaged by the destruction of the economy. Wrecking the global economy was deliberate not accidental; it was part of the Agenda 21 plan. Billionaires such as Gates and Musk did amazingly well during 2020 – their wealth grew massively. But I bet yours didn't. But then Bezos controls much of the internet, the Gates Foundation has shares in a variety of drug companies making specific products and Musk has the electric car industry tied up. The rest probably just shorted the markets to get rich. Remember the Rothschilds at the end of the Battle of Waterloo? They tricked all the other traders into thinking that Napoleon had won and then cleaned up and made a huge fortune.

Second, they have reduced interest rates to a level never seen before. If you have a million pounds sitting in your Government savings account, the annual interest will just about buy you a tankful of petrol. And just to add to the excitement, the central banks are all talking about negative interest rates. Put a few quid into a deposit account and you'll have to pay interest to the bank.

Third, the crashing economy will destroy millions of jobs. The United Nations said in 2020 that 50% of all jobs are going to disappear and we can trust them because it's their game, their ball and their packet of sandwiches. Those without jobs will have to rely on government hand-outs – renamed the universal basic income.

Fourth, if you own your own home, or think you do, or own part of it, then you're in trouble. Interest rates are going to remain the lowest in history for a while – to make sure that those with savings see their savings slowly disappear. And then interest rates will go up. Not a bit. But a lot. I'll explain why in a moment. And when interest rates are up to 8, 9 or 10 per cent – or even higher – imagine what mortgage payments will reach. They'll be even higher. And most people won't be able to afford to keep their homes. That will be the end of private home ownership and another step towards a successful Agenda 21.

Fifth, why are interest rates going to soar? Well, because when interest rates rocket so too will inflation. And massive inflation is the best way for governments to get rid of their massive, otherwise unpayable debts. And massive rates of inflation also destroy any savings that people have hung onto.

Oh, and there is a special, sixth trick up their sleeve: taxes.

Governments everywhere have been throwing money around with great joy. Ten billion here, a hundred billion there. They'll need to replenish the coffers and pay off the debts. And so taxes are going to rise. They'll invent new taxes you've never dreamt of – and the main aim will not be to raise money but to impoverish everyone.

They don't want us to own anything. It's the plan. Check it out – I'm not making this up.

And when we're all impoverished they will generously pay us all a universal basic income, and we will all be entirely dependent on Bill Gates, Klaus Schwab and company for our daily bread. If we misbehave or criticise our masters then our payment won't come through and our digital bank account will remain empty.

If we were to lose this war, which we won't because we can't, the dissidents would all be living in mud huts and eating grass and slug pie while the billionaires would get forever richer.

The people controlling the system are not inept or incompetent. They are deceitful, devious and far more wicked than anything most of us have ever come across.

When I was a GP, I worked as a police surgeon for some years. I have met, examined and interviewed a number of murderers. I never met any as evil as the deceitful and devious politicians, scientists and doctors now determined to destroy everything we value – for power and money. Make no mistake about it the end of civilisation is coming towards us at the speed of light.

There are still people who think things will get better. They won't. Next year is going to be far, far worse than this year and it is going to be ever harder to break the hold the evil people have on our lives. If you are awake and you care about life, your family, your friends and your community then you have to do everything you can to stop these people and halt the Agenda 21 plan.

Banned

I have banned and censored and suppressed a good deal in my life but during the last twelve months the banning, censoring and suppressing has gathered pace.

I have lost track of the number of internet platforms which have banned me and my work. My videos and books have been deleted although videos and books on the same subjects have been left alone.

Bats

Most bats are among the commonest animals in the UK but they are treated as a protected species.

Why?

I believe that making bats protected means that rural country, the lofts and eaves of which often provide homes for bats, are impossible to repair or restore. The presence of bats means that essential building work simply cannot be done or the cost of working around the bats is so great as to make the repair or restoration work impractical.

The bats are being used by the followers of the Agenda 21 guidelines.

A number of species of animal are protected by law. In some cases this is understandable because some animals are, without doubt, endangered and close to extinction. Sometimes this is a result of man's activities and sometimes it is not.

But there are some puzzles.

Absurd regulations are used to protect species which are not endangered (and which could often be moved somewhere else) in order to stop essential road or building works which are not considered essential for the progress of Agenda 21.

There are many paradoxes sewn into the lining of Agenda 21.

Beehive mentality

The Agenda 21 is a plan to turn the world into a giant beehive in which the vast majority of us will be drones, beavering away as slaves. The Queen bees, living lives of glorious luxury, will be people like Blair, Schwab, Gates, Prince Charles, the Rockefellers, the Rothschilds and so on – plus their families.

Benzodiazepines in drinking water

It has been suggested that tranquillisers (such as benzodiazepines) should be put into the drinking water to calm citizens who are upset by fears about the present and the future. This is not a new idea. The suggestion was dismissed when it was first made around half a century ago. I fear it might not be dismissed so easily today.

Big Lebowski

'A man is someone who is prepared to do the right thing whatever the cost.'

Bikeable

Why they needed to create this word I cannot imagine. It means a route upon which you can travel with the aid of a bicycle. In the old, pre-Agenda 21 days, we used to use words such as 'road' and 'path' but the Agenda 21 fascists want to destroy everything –including our language.

Bilderbergers

Bilderberg meetings began at the Hotel de Bilderberg in Oosterbeek in the Netherlands in May 1954. They began with a conference organised by Prince Bernhard of the Netherlands. Today, Bilderberg meetings take place in many different locations.

A great deal of secrecy surrounds these regular meetings which receive substantial financial support from a number of institutions, including the American Government and the CIA. The meetings all follow a simple pattern: politicians, company directors, bankers, university professors, strategists, journalists and lobbyists all meet in luxury and great secrecy. There are usually around 130 people in attendance with two thirds coming from Western Europe and a third from North America. Governments usually provide the heavy security (at taxpayers' expense) but nothing that is discussed is published for public consumption. None of those who attend is allowed to talk about the meetings – indeed they are sworn to secrecy before being allowed to attend. Since many powerful press barons attend, there is little risk of there being any publicity.

So, what do the Bilderbergers do at their meetings?

Well, they certainly don't all simply drink whisky, smoke fat cigars and ogle waitresses in French maid costumes. These are heavy duty elitist meetings at which important decisions are made. It is said that the euro was introduced as a result of a Bilderberg conference, and that the Trilateral Commission (a lobbying organisation) was founded on the recommendation of a Rockefeller. The Bilderbergers are also credited with drafting the Treaties of Rome, and there is little doubt that some aspects of Agenda 21 originated among conspirators attending these elitist, annual, three day long meetings. The Bilderbergers are a lobbying pressure group, consisting entirely of rich and powerful individuals.

Occasionally, there are leaks.

So, at the Bilderberger conference in 1991, Henry Kissinger said that when faced with any sort of threat (be it terrorism, famine or plague) people would accept tyranny as the excuse for safety.

Today, some unexpected individuals are Bilderbergers. So for example Michael O'Leary, the boss of Ryanair is on the Bilderberger committee. At the end of 2020, O'Leary's airline took a strong position by using the promotional phrase 'Jab and Go' to encourage people to accept the recommended answer to the advertised crisis.

Billionaires

This is the best time to be a billionaire. Between January 2020 and August 2020 most people in the world became increasingly impoverished. The world's billionaires, however, increased their wealth massively. Even the so-called philanthropists ended up with far more money than they started with. Jeff Bezos made $80 billion during those months. Bill Gates made $8.4 billion. Mark Zuckerberg made $21 billion. Elon Musk ended up richer by $62.8 billion. Larry Page was richer by $9.6 billion. MacKenzie Scott gained $25.6 billion and Eric Yuan improved his wealth by $10.4 billion. How nice it must be to be a billionaire in these difficult times.

The billionaires are still doing extremely well out of a crisis which has been used as an excuse to destroy economies everywhere – damaging savings and taking jobs by the million. The wealth of billionaires in the US alone had increased by nearly $800 billion by the end of 2020. The world's richest 500 people, according to the Bloomberg index, collectively gained 23% or $1.3 trillion in 2020.

The billionaires will continue to become ever richer because the New World Order is designed, in part, to fit their businesses. Their investments are in technology, they have well-stocked balance sheets, their outgoings are minute and yet their income has risen because their internet businesses are well suited to a world in which people are locked in their homes and have little to do but spend their time online – often shopping.

Electric cars are the fashionable flavour of the month with the intensely hypocritical and ignorant global warming cultists because no one bothers to ask where the electricity is coming from and no one worries about the 14-year-olds digging in the mines for the essential ingredients for the car batteries the cars require.

It is also worth noting that by providing loans and grants to businesses, governments are quietly taking control of much of the economy. In the UK, the State is getting bigger and more powerful every day. Curiously, a conservative government is nationalising everything it can lay its hands on.

Biofuels

I never really understood why governments were so keen on converting food into fuel – and promoting 'biofuels' as an alternative to fossil fuels. But once you realise that it is Agenda 21 policy to reduce the global population, this policy becomes understandable. Biofuels are promoted to ensure that more people die of starvation.

Biomass

Most renewable energy is derived from biomass – which is the fashionable and acceptable name for wood – the stuff that really does grow on trees. The electricity which is obtained from biomass is obtained by burning the wood in power stations – in exactly the same way that coal used to be burnt.

In the UK, the biomass which is burnt in the power stations mostly comes from America. Trees are chopped down by the thousand and then turned into little pellets of wood. The pellets of wood are then put into diesel-powered lorries and taken vast distances to ports. The pellets of wood are then transferred from the diesel-powered lorries to large gas or diesel-powered ships. The large ships then sail across the Atlantic (if sail is what large, modern, diesel-powered ships are still said to do) and then the pellets of wood are unloaded from the diesel-powered ships and put into diesel-powered lorries. The diesel-powered lorries then take the pellets of wood to the power stations where the pellets of wood are burnt.

Not surprisingly, the carbon footprint produced by burning biomass is massive – possibly higher than it would have been if oil, gas or coal had been burnt. (Much coal, remember, was dug out of the ground in the country where it was burnt.)

But since biomass is counted as renewable energy, the global warming cultists do not mind.

Incidentally, the odd thing is that in the UK there are moves to ban the burning of wood in fireplaces in the home. Instead, home owners will be encouraged to use electricity obtained by burning wood in power stations.

Birds and bees

The earth constantly emits low frequency waves which birds use as a sort of compass to help them migrate. The massive increase in the amount of electromagnetic activity on the earth (as a result of all the cell phones and cell phone towers) is having a damaging effect on bird migration. And the same thing is causing a collapse in the number of colonies of honey bees.

Without birds and bees the balance of nature will be irreversibly damaged. Bees in particular are essential for the pollination of trees, bushes and plants and without them many crops will fail.

It's not surprising that birds have been seen attacking new cell phone towers.

Bitcoin

Promoted as the alternative to central banks and national currencies, bitcoin is actually a prologue for the cashless society. It is against freedom not for it.

Blair (Tony)

Tony Blair, the infamous war criminal and former Prime Minister of the UK, has his fingerprints all over the Agenda 21 wickedness. What a surprise.

Blair is now positioning himself to be the first One World President. Don't bet against it happening.

Incidentally, Blair is probably the wealthiest ex-Prime Minister in the UK. He and his family have built up a £35 million portfolio of 39 houses and flats. Tony and Cherie Blair own a £10 million mansion in Buckinghamshire and a London mews house worth £1.7 million. Cherie and Euan Blair co –own a portfolio of 31 flats.

In my book, *Rogue Nation*, when discussing Blair's support for the illegal and immoral invasion of Iraq, I did predict that he might well find some personal financial benefit awaiting him upon his retirement.

In the UK, Blair has been the most enthusiastic advocate for health passports. When he was Prime Minister, Blair tried to force through legislation forcing UK citizens to carry ID cards. The electorate was more feisty in those days and rejected the idea.

Health passports, now widely accepted by many Britons, are merely a more intrusive and dangerous version of the ID cards which were rejected.

The irony is that Blair, widely recognised as a serial traitor and liar as well as a war criminal, is so loathed that his words tend to have the opposite effect to the effect he intends. So, Blair was an obsessively enthusiastic Remainer (inspired by his support for Agenda 21), and his support for the EU helped ensure victory for the Brexiteers. His support for health passports may well be the best endorsement those opposed to health passports could possibly hope for.

Incidentally, the BBC is desperately pro-Blair. If he has a view on anything the BBC will give him unlimited time to share his opinions.

Finally, although Blair appears to be a fervent supporter of the global warming cult, he opposed the building of a wind farm near to one of his homes.

Body ownership

You might think that whatever else they take away from you, your body will remain your property. If you thought that you would be wrong.

In the UK, for example, your organs can be taken by the State after you have died. That is the default position. If you want to stop this happening then you must sign a form insisting that your organs are not to be 'harvested'. I think it is doubtful whether anyone will take any notice of such a form – which is unlikely to be available when you are being wheeled into the operating theatre so that surgeons can help themselves to your vital bits and pieces (and hoping that you no longer need them).

And what are you going to do about it if they have ignored your wishes? Sue them for return of your heart, liver, kidneys and whatever else they have snatched?

John Locke included property when he wrote about our having rights. But property doesn't just mean houses, land, cars and socks. It also means your body. Indeed, a body is the only property we all have when we are born and which we all relinquish when we die.

Book burning

In the 7th century BC the Neo-Assyrian king Ashurbanipal's library at Nineveh was burnt.

Book burning took off in England during the Reformation when hundreds of thousands of books were destroyed (invariably by burning) as the monasteries where they were housed were dissolved and broken up (often literally).

And in Europe, before and during WWII (from 1933 to 1945), the Nazis destroyed an estimated 100 million books.

Of course, you don't have to burn books to stop people reading them. In 2009-10 there were 4,356 public libraries in the UK. By 2018-19, that number had fallen to 3.583. There were never as many public libraries and reading rooms and educational institutes in the UK as there were during the much maligned Victorian era.

And today, you don't have to burn books or close libraries. You just persuade the large social media companies to refuse to allow books which do not fit the approved demands to be sold on their platforms. I have personal and painful experience of this new version of book burning.

I wonder how many of those directly involved in suppressing truths and replacing them with propaganda and pseudoscience realise just how dramatic the consequences will be.

Journalists and broadcasters and members of the 77th brigade of the British Army (paid to protect British citizens but currently involved in a propaganda and brain washing campaign designed to hide the truth and to spread disinformation and to promote deceit) have all positioned themselves alongside Hitler and the other book burning giants of history. By suppressing truths, supporting lies and deleting facts they are betraying everything that is decent and allying themselves alongside some of the worst tyrants in history. I wonder how many of those involved realise what is happening, why they are being used and what the long-term consequences will be for them and their families.

I wonder how many realise that one of Agenda 21's plans is to break up families and couples. People who are alone, isolated and frightened are much easier to bully and to control than people who have friends and family around them.

Brainwashing

Governments around the world have, since the start of 2020, been attempting to brainwash their citizens. And they have been doing very well at it.

Actually, the brainwashing and manipulations started some years ago. Students at school and university have for some time now been trained to question and disapprove of dissenters and critics of the establishment. Political correctness and virtue signalling have fathered a bizarre new race of obedient, compliant non-thinkers.

Governments have been using a range of Orwellian mind control tricks during the 'crisis'. The slogans, the clapping and the symbols have all been carefully used to enable the authorities to take control of our thinking.

I am grateful to Dr Colin Barron, a former NHS doctor and eminent hypnotherapist who is the author of the book, *Practical Hypnotherapy*, for pointing out to me just how our minds were taken over in 2020 and how we have been very successfully and skilfully manipulated into believing the lies we have been fed.

Elected governments, aided by specialist behavioural scientists, have been brainwashing millions into accepting their propaganda.

The mind is a wonderful thing. It responds in sometimes unpredictable ways. So, for example, if you see a headline which says: 'Boris Johnson is an alien' then most people will probably dismiss it quite readily. But if the headline says 'Is Boris Johnson an alien?' readers will be more likely to suspect that the British Prime Minister might indeed be from another planet. And research shows that if people see a headline which says 'Boris Johnson is NOT an alien' then their suspicions will be raised still higher.

Manipulating and tricking the mind is a professional business.

You've been brainwashed and the brainwashing has been very subtle. We've all been quietly hypnotised and indoctrinated to accept the new mass hysteria generated by governments everywhere. Many people now enjoy staying at home, being paid by the Government to do nothing, and don't want it to end. It enables them to avoid responsibility for their own lives.

Do you remember who said: 'Through clever and constant application of propaganda, people can be made to see paradise as hell and also the other way round, to consider the most wretched life as paradise.'?

It was Adolf Hitler, who was a master at mass manipulation and the use of subliminal techniques. And it was Hitler who also commented that it was good fortune for governments that the mass of people did not think.

The Nazis were very good at controlling people's minds.

Goebbels, who was Hitler's propaganda chief, once said that if you repeat a lie often enough then people will believe it. He also pointed out that if you want to control a population and you have to deal with opposition then you should accuse the other side of the sin or the trickery which you yourself are using.

So, governments everywhere have been accusing those who are telling the truth of spreading fake news. Anyone who doesn't toe the party line is dismissed as a dangerous conspiracy theorist – though the big conspiracies have all been coming from governments.

Countries around the world have been promoting slogans to persuade their citizens to behave as required. In China there was a slogan which said, 'If you love your parents, lock them up'. In Taiwan people were told: 'To visit each other is to kill each other'.

At first glance the slogans which have been heavily advertised in the UK seem harmless enough. We all recognise them.

Some such as 'We're all in this together' seem fairly innocuous, though we might all be forgiven for adding the rider that we are all in this together unless we work as advisors to the Prime Minister.

The first trio of phrases which were promoted everywhere were:

Stay alert, Control the virus, Save lives
Keep your distance, Wash your hands, Think of others
More recently new phrases have been added to the repertoire:
Wash hands, Cover face, Make space
Stay home, Protect the NHS, Save lives

The rhythm and pattern used in these phrases is not a coincidence. There are usually three words in each phrase and the phrases run in threes. This isn't a coincidence; it isn't happenchance.

Using phrases of three words, presented in groups of three, is a technique known as the rule of three in psychological conditioning.

And that's the reason for the three phrases with which we are all being bombarded. We've being trained and taught at the same time. It's behavioural psychology.

Other hypnotherapists have pointed out that if we repeat phrases often enough then the words and thoughts become implanted in our subconscious minds and then become a belief which motivates our behaviour. And so governments repeat slogans which become beliefs. It's called auto suggestion – along the lines of 'every day in every way I am getting better and better'.

Hitler was also a believer that if a lie was repeated often enough it would eventually be confused with the truth by the greater part of the population.

'People more readily fall victim to the big lie than the small lie,' said Hitler, 'since it would never come into their heads to fabricate colossal untruths, and they would not believe that others could have the impudence to distort the truth so infamously.'

Hitler used these techniques to control and manipulate the German people and to persuade them to accept the evil things he wanted them to do.

George Orwell who invented Newspeak also understood the importance of the triple three word phrase. In 1984, his futuristic novel which was written in 1948, Orwell invented the slogan: 'War is peace, freedom is slavery, ignorance is strength'.

If you want a picture of the future, wrote Orwell, imagine a boot stamping on a human face – for ever. Power, he reminded us, is not a means, it is an end.

Everything else that has been happening since February 2020 has been part of the brainwashing process.

It has been noticeable that the instructions we have been given have been more like orders. The signs that have popped up like dandelions say 'Stand here', not 'Please stand here'. And why not? Because you don't say 'Please' to prisoners do you?

And then there are the weeks of clapping for carers and medical staff.

Clapping, which probably started innocently, and with good intentions, covers up the paradox – the quiet insistent terror that comes from knowing that for all practical purposes there is no health care and we have all been betrayed by politicians and bureaucrats who decided to devote entire health care programmes to caring for a relatively small number of patients who have, or might be thought to have or be susceptible to a flu like virus.

Dr Milton Erickson, an eminent hypnotist, used to give his patients simple tasks to do. He would send them home to clean the attic or count the books they owned. All this was done as part of the process of mind control. The clapping was quickly and enthusiastically adopted and promoted by the people influencing our lives. Telling people to stand on their doorsteps at 8 p.m. on Thursdays and to clap is a simple, repetitive task which is part of the mass hypnosis. Persuading people to do what you want them to do is part of the hypnotherapy process. Getting people to clap was also important in that it made people believe in the danger of the virus and the bravery of those working in health care. It helped people accept the fact that there were no beds available for patients with cancer or any other disorder.

The rainbow which appeared everywhere is another part of the brainwashing process. Thousands have been so successfully brainwashed that they willingly take part in promoting the symbols and the slogans. The psy-op specialists also understand that a question mark at the end of a headline strengthens the message and that putting quotation marks around a statement means that more people will believe it. Many of these tricks were perfected by marketing gurus and mail order specialists.

Even the confusing rules about who we can and cannot see were part of the programme. A minister recently told Britons that two people could meet one person but that one person could not meet two people.

If you confuse and bewilder at the same time that you are frightening people then you unsettle them and create an anxious and obedient population.

Bearing all this in mind, I prepared my own triple phrased slogan. Three words and three phrases:
Distrust the government
Avoid mass media
Fight the lies
My slogans fit the brainwashing requirement perfectly.

Brainwaves

Many workers in China now wear caps which monitor their brainwaves. The data acquired is used to monitor production and to redesign the way work is done. The management even claim that they can increase efficiency by manipulating the length and frequency of breaks. The system is used in the military and on public transport.

Brain surveillance, measuring emotions as well as other mental activities, is already used in China and it won't be long before it is coming to an office, store or factory near you. Lightweight, wireless sensors monitor the wearer's brainwaves and send the data to computers which can measure brainwaves and assess anxiety, depression or anger.

Brandt (Willy)

'If I were asked to say what, apart from peace, was most important to me, then my answer would be: freedom.'

Brexit

British people voted to leave the EU but Agenda 21 will take us much further along the same route – to a dangerous mixture of fascism and communism. Leaving the EU won't make any difference to the way Britain is run – unless the British people vote in a new parliament which stands firm against the United Nations' plans for the world.

Brexit was always doomed to be a disaster because no one in the establishment (on either side of whatever fence might divide political parties) wanted to damage the EU or the Agenda 21 aims and objectives.

Meanwhile, I have a strong suspicion that Britons are being punished for voting Brexit. The laws have all been tougher in Britain than almost anywhere.

Incidentally, the BBC, which fought against Brexit with all its might (and even admitted that its coverage was biased) continued to draw attention to all the drawbacks of Brexit after the UK had left the European Union.

Building regulations

The Grenfell Tower fire appears to have involved cladding which was used as part of the attempt to reduce carbon emissions. Seventy two people died in that fire. Nearly two million people are living in potentially lethal and now un-saleable flats which have the same cladding. That appears to be yet another hollow victory for the global warming cultists. The flats, which were built to satisfy existing building regulations from the EU, are so badly designed and put together that they are failing newer regulations on walls, balconies, insulation and cladding. Would-be buyers cannot obtain a mortgage on the flats which will cost a fortune to rebuild.

Bunkers

The establishment has for years been building deep bunkers which are designed to be used not just by the Government but by the military, the billionaires and the Bilderbergers. These bunkers (built and maintained with great secrecy) are designed to enable those living in them to survive for over 50 years. I'm not sure I'd want to live in a bunker for 50 years – especially if I had to share it with Mr and Mrs Gates and the British royal family.

Campaigners

It has always been up to us to shout 'stop' when we have had enough of the wickedness around us. We all have a voice we can use and we all have a duty to make sure that our voice is heard. If we remain silent then we are just a part of the evil which is corrupting and destroying our world.

We have to ignore the sad individuals who scoff or mock – either because they have been bought with a purse of silver or because they are too unintelligent to understand the nature of the war we are fighting. We must not allow ourselves to be put off by scorn, derision, undisguised contempt or a lack of support or encouragement from others.

Look through history and we can all see that imaginative, thoughtful and creative individuals have always had a hard time.

Look back and you will find countless examples of citizens who were harassed or persecuted simply because they dared to think for themselves – and tried to share their thoughts with others.

The sad fact is that our world has never welcomed the original, the challenging, the inspirational or the passionate and has always preferred the characterless to the thought-provoking.

Those who dare to speak out against the establishment have always been regarded as dangerous heretics. The iconoclast has never been a welcome figure in any age.

Confucius, the Chinese philosopher, was dismissed by his political masters and his books were burned. Those who didn't burn his books within 30 days were branded and condemned to forced labour. Two and a half thousand years later, Confucius's influence was still considered so dangerous that Chairman Mao banned his works.

Described by the Delphic Oracle as the wisest man in the world, Greek teacher Socrates was accused of corrupting the youth of Athens, arrested for being an evildoer and 'a person showing curiosity, searching into things under the earth and above the heaven and teaching all this to others'. Socrates was condemned to death.

Dante, the Italian poet, was banished from Florence and condemned to be burnt at the stake if ever captured.

After they had failed to silence him with threats and bribes, the Jewish authorities excommunicated Spinoza in Amsterdam because he refused to toe the party line, refused to think what other people told him he must think and insisted on maintaining his intellectual independence. He and his work were denounced as 'forged in Hell by a renegade Jew and the devil'.

Galileo, the seventeenth century Italian mathematician, astrologer and scientist got into terrible trouble with the all-powerful Church for daring to support Copernicus, who had the temerity to claim that the planets revolved around the sun.

Aureolus Philippus Theophrastus Bombastus von Hohenheim (known to his chums as Paracelsus) made himself enemies all over Europe because he tried to revolutionise medicine in the sixteenth century. Paracelsus was the greatest influence on medical thinking since Hippocrates but the establishment regarded him as a trouble-maker.

Ignaz Semmelweiss, the Austrian obstetrician who recognised that puerperal fever was caused by doctors' dirty habits was ostracised by the medical profession for daring to criticise practical procedures.

Dr John Snow fought two huge battles. He introduced anaesthesia for women in confinement, and by removing the handle from the Broad Street pump in Soho he helped prevent the spread of cholera in London. Both battles brought him enemies.

Henry David Thoreau, surely the kindest, wisest philosopher who has ever lived, was imprisoned for sticking to his ideals.

These are all my personal heroes. They show that original thinkers and people who do not fit neatly into the scheme of things have never gone down well.

Camps

There has been much talk that dissenters, those who dare oppose the official lies, will be placed in quarantine camps or internment camps. It is difficult to see why these should not be named concentration camps.

Camus (Albert)

'The welfare and safety of the people is always the alibi of the tyrant.'

Cancel culture

The supporters of Agenda 21 do not approve of free speech. Citizens everywhere must obey the rules and the regulations and whatever laws the bureaucrats decide to impose.

From the early years of the 21st century, much new legislation has been introduced to control what people say, as well as do. Much of it has been wrapped up in legislation ostensibly designed to stop religious hatred, but that was just an excuse to impose stricter and stricter rules controlling free speech. Almost anything which can be described as 'insulting' or a 'hate crime' is now illegal and severely punished.

Moreover, the problem has spread to schools and universities where it has been encouraged by teachers and lecturers and taken up with great enthusiasm by students. Today, students refuse to be taught aspects of history which they find upsetting, uncomfortable or any way disagreeable.

And, of course, lecturers who attempt to talk about something which is deemed unpopular, unfashionable or unacceptable will be refused the right to speak. Those who disobey are 'called out' and censured. Institutions are forced to cancel lectures by those who have been targeted, publishers will refuse to produce their books, broadcasters will refuse to allow them on air and periodicals will refuse to print articles by them.

The cancel-culture (whereby lecturers and others are banned if they attempt to say or write something which is considered unacceptable by the far left) started in universities but has spread. In the beginning lecturers considered unacceptable were 'no platformed' (they were not allowed to speak) and the excuse was that if they did speak the students might be upset by what they had to say. This brutal attack on tolerance has now spread widely within society. In the UK the Government has talked about renaming the 'Churchill Room', because Sir Winston Churchill is considered unacceptable for a variety of bizarre reasons. And senior civil servants have discouraged the use of the word 'blacklist' because it is alleged to have racial overtones.

Capital letters for emphasis

Throughout its existence, the virus in the news (which I cannot name) has usually been dignified with unnecessary capital letters. This was done deliberately to suggest that the infection was more important than any other disease. No one in the media or government writes about Tuberculosis or TUBERCULOSIS or about Malaria or MALARIA – even though these infectious diseases kill more people than the virus in question.

It has also become popular in left leaning, politically extreme circles to use an initial capital when referring to Black people while retaining the lower case initial letter when referring to white people.

Carbon trading

When politicians choose to fly off on their latest freebie holiday, instead of spending a fortnight camping in Cornwall, they respond to critics (who want to know why they are polluting the environment and adding to global warming) by claiming that they have purchased 'carbon offsets' to balance their carbon 'footprints'. Carbon trading is one of the biggest confidence tricks in history.

In 2007, the British Government said that everyone should have their own carbon swipe cards forcing them to take more care of the environment. When former US Vice President Al Gore found himself under fire for using 20 times as much electricity in his Nashville mansion as the average American, he defended himself with the same argument. He claimed he offset all his carbon dioxide emissions by buying green credits. What most people probably don't realise is that Al Gore, and a bunch of investors, helped create the idea of carbon credits whereby companies buy a licence to pollute. The cost of the carbon credits (the licence to pollute) is simply passed onto the public. And brokers who sell the carbon credits are making a fortune. The disgraced Ken Lay, of the disgraced and now defunct Enron, helped Gore set up the structure for carbon credit trading. Gore is not the only one heavily invested in the global warming scam. Many other leading politicians and scientists stand to gain billions from this fraud.

And all the time we must remember that the global warming scam, together with whatever pandemic is the flavour of the month and recurring financial crises are all part of the pathway to Agenda 21 and a world government. The global warming scam was invented for a reason but the protagonists are not above making huge sums of money from the fraud.

Public figures all like to portray themselves as 'green' and 'environmentally aware'. When asked about the fact that he has three Hummer vehicles, the former Governor of California, Arnold

Schwarzenegger, announced that two of the vehicles had been converted to take ethanol. Managing to say this with a straight face must have required more acting skills than I realised he had.

Politicians and millionaire pop stars buy carbon emission offsets in order to 'balance' their flying around the world in private planes.

But this doesn't help the planet at all because carbon trading is practical hypocrisy.

The European Union, the world's largest and most corrupt fascist organisation, has set up its own carbon trading programme and, if nothing else, it is a good example of how carbon trading works.

The EU's programme is called the Emissions Trading Scheme and as you might expect the European Union's scheme is of no benefit to the environment, the planet or you and me. As you might equally expect, it is of enormous benefit to the large companies which are responsible for global warming.

Officially, the EU's carbon trading scheme was set up to encourage dirty power stations to switch to cleaner forms of energy. Governments made it an integral part of their drive to reduce greenhouse gas emissions.

In practice the scheme has allowed the dirtiest polluters, the companies really responsible for global warming, to push up their bills and increase their profits without lowering the level of their greenhouse gas emissions.

Even industry experts admit that the EU's carbon trading scheme has been a windfall which has allowed the big power companies to increase their profits massively.

Here's how the scheme was set up.

The EU gave permits to major electricity producers and manufacturers allowing them to produce a fixed amount of carbon dioxide every year.

Any company which reduced its allowed ration of pollution could sell its unused permit to pollute on the open market. A company which exceeds its allowed level of pollution had to buy extra credits in order to continue polluting.

But here's the best bit: the EU succumbed to pressure from the polluters and handed out the permits free of charge.

In case you thought that might be a misprint I'll repeat it: the EU gave the power giants their permits entirely free of charge.

The minute the big electricity producers had their permits, they simply cut their output of electricity in order to reduce their level of pollutants. They could then be able to sell their spare polluting capacity to other companies. Having cut the amount of electricity they were producing, the big electricity companies were also able to put up their prices.

It was a double whammy!

A bunch of the world's biggest polluters made extra money by charging more for their electricity. And they made extra money by selling off part of their permit to pollute. A permit which, remember, the EU had given them free of charge.

Carbon trading is all a bit like the system of 'indulgences' which was in vogue during medieval times. Sinners haggled with and then paid a corrupt priest a fee to absolve their sins.

Carlin (George)

'I have certain rules I live by. My first rule: I don't believe anything the Government tells me. Nothing. Zero.'

Cash

One of the aims of Agenda 21 is to get rid of cash and replace it with digital money. This will make life much easier for the banks and for governments who will, with a few keystrokes, be able to separate dissidents from their money.

Early in 2020, it was suggested that a taxi driver had died because he had come into contact with cash contaminated with a virus. There was, of course, no evidence for this.

Later, researchers showed that the virus in the news could survive for 28 days on surfaces such as bank notes. This discovery was given huge publicity and used as evidence that we shouldn't use cash but should rely on credit cards and credit card machines (which, of course, do not ever get contaminated).

What no journalists bothered to mention was that the experiment was conducted in the dark and that ultraviolet light kills the virus.

On the same day as I read about this piece of nonsense, a report by *Which?* magazine showed that consumers were having difficulty buying essential foodstuffs because shops were refusing to accept banknotes and coins.

By early 2021, the shortage of shops willing to accept cash had become a real problem for the millions of people who (for one reason or another) do not have a credit card and do not have access to the internet.

People had become accustomed to paying for things and services with their credit cards or mobile telephones, and the events of 2020 pushed cash further into the background. Cashpoints will soon be as uncommon as telephone boxes. This is the future.

Cash gives us freedom so you can see why they are so keen to get rid of it. Besides, the ubiquitous Bill Gates has a patent on a method of controlling digital currency and human body functions. The 'Better than Cash Alliance', lobbying for, among other things, an end to cash, was partly funded by the Bill and Melinda Gates Foundation.

Governments everywhere want to eradicate cash and replace it with digital money. Helped by the mass media, they are using the new excuse to force us all to stop using real money and, instead, to pay for everything with credit cards or phone Apps. In China, 85% of all transactions are already done by mobile phone.

Despite the fact that governments and banks persistently claim that cash carries disease, the risk is no greater than it has always been. All you need to do is wash your hands after handling cash.

And cash gives us freedom and privacy. Below are some facts explaining why cash is vital.

Cash gives us freedom of movement and behaviour. Without cash 'they' will be able to track our every move. They will always know where we are, what we are buying and what we are doing. Privacy will be gone.

Cash helps teach children the value of money. It gives a sense of reality and the importance of money.

Cash helps stop people going into debt.

Many people rely on cash and without it will be unable to buy food. Nearly one in five people in Britain relies on cash and would struggle to survive without it. The millions (including the elderly and the homeless) who do not have bank accounts, or access to the internet, would find life impossible.

Cash may be vulnerable to thieves but if you lose your wallet or purse, all you lose is the cash you were carrying. Using a phone or plastic card for every transaction means that your details are at greater risk of being stolen. If your phone or plastic cards are stolen you can lose everything – including your identity.

When cash has disappeared, banks may charge a transaction fee for every item bought – and, possibly, for every item sold.

If you rely entirely on credit cards the banks will be able to cut off your access to your money very easily. If you misbehave you will be denied access to your own money. If, for example, you are a diabetic, the authorities will be able to prevent you from buying sweet foods. It will be easy to prohibit the sale of certain items – such as alcohol. If you are considered a troublemaker you will be prevented from travelling.

The immediate aim is to get rid of plastic cards and replace them with a universal phone App – so that all financial transactions have to be managed by phone. The medium term plan is to replace phone Apps with implanted chips which will make us all slaves to an electronic system. Implanted chips are already being trialled. Eventually, the implanted chips will contain every bit of information about you. It will be possible to turn these chips 'off' in an instant from afar.

Without cash, and by forcing us to keep all our money in banks, the big banks will be able to extend negative interest rates.

Shops which ban cash are excluding many citizens and helping to remove our basic freedom and privacy rights. To keep cash alive, we should all insist on paying with cash whenever possible. And we should try to avoid stores which refuse to accept cash.

CCTV

New CCTV cameras have been made that will block people from entering a shop if they are not obeying the rules about face coverings. The cameras will 'help staff tackle difficult customers' and will prevent the disabled, the mentally ill and those with hidden infirmities such as asthma or heart disease from entering shops and buying scarce food supplies. The cameras are used to operate shop doors. If a shopper without a covering approaches, the door remains firmly and resolutely closed. Only when an obedient shopper approaches does the door open.

Celebrities

In the early days of 2020, a surprising number of celebrities, politicians and world leaders fell ill with the virus. In view of the remarkably small number of non-celebrities affected by the virus it seems clear that this was part of a plan to help promote the significance of the infection and to create fear.

Later, as the anger at the lies grew, governments around the world started hiring minor celebrities to endorse the fraud and to promote the roll-out of a medical procedure.

Did any of the celebrities actually know anything about the procedure they were promoting? I suspect not.

Cell phones

It is impossible to talk, write, hint or even dream that there might be something just the teeniest bit worrying about 5G without being dismissed as a traitor, a cheat, a liar, a conspiracy theorist and probably someone who parks in those supermarket bays reserved for mothers with small children.

But there are now thousands of scientific papers proving that electromagnetic field radiation can cause serious health problems – particularly for children, whose bodies are still growing and whose skulls are much thinner than adult skulls.

When I first wrote about these dangers in the late 1980s, I was regarded as a madman. But today the evidence is unequivocal. The problem is that wireless products such as cell phones were never safety tested properly – they were just assumed to be safe and although the industry has done some tests, no long-term assessments have been done. Insurance companies are so concerned that they won't give health cover to cell phone companies. Here are some facts:

Wi-Fi and cell phones can cause long-term infertility and psychological problems such as depression, suicide and paranoia and sleepiness. Other problems include DNA changes, endocrine changes, developmental changes, behavioural problems and cancer. Parkinson's disease and dementia may also be caused.

Many schools (particularly in the UK and USA) are boasting that they have boosted their Wi-Fi capability, but some countries have banned Wi-Fi and cell phones in schools where small children are taught.

In 2008, it was reported that Switzerland, France, Germany, Belgium and England had begun removing Wi-Fi from schools. Now Wi-Fi is back in English schools.

The Austrian Medical Association has stated that electromagnetic fields and radiation accumulate, and concluded that children should categorically not use mobile phones.

On July 20th 2020, the Russian Government recommended the banning of Wi-Fi and cell phones in all elementary schools. The Russians were experimenting with radio frequency weaponry in the 1940s and know a good deal about the dangers.

In June 2011, the Council of Europe called for a ban on Wi-Fi and cell phones in schools.

In 2012, UNICEF found that Wi-Fi in schools caused an increase in central nervous system disorders, epilepsy, psychological problems and blood and immune system disorders.

France banned Wi-Fi in nursery schools in 2018 and restricted its availability to children under the age of 11.

The WHO has confirmed that electron magnetic fields can be carcinogenic – doing more damage to children because of their thinner skulls and developing bodies. The bone marrow of a child's head absorbs ten times more radiation than that of an adult.

The Council of Europe has warned of the dangers of installing routers in schools.

There are thousands of relevant scientific papers. If you want a list of papers available I recommend the book, *Hidden Dangers* by Captain Jerry G. Flynn. A simpler overview (without references) is available in my book *Superbody*. Also look out for videos by Barrie

Trower, a British former naval officer. I recommend Captain Flynn's book for those who want references to show to head-teachers, etc.

Censorship

Politicians and scientists who promote the idea that we are all at risk, threatened by a dangerous plague, have persuaded the media to refuse to allow any discussion or debate about the significance or otherwise of the disease. Indeed, the media have been paid (with massive advertising expenditure) to suppress all those who raise questions about the validity of the claims made by scientists promoting the plague. Doctors and nurses who dared to speak up were told they would be sacked or lose their licences. Some, indeed, did have their licences taken from them. Never before in modern history has medical debate been silenced so ruthlessly and so dangerously – though there have been warning signs for some time.

Let me explain.

A few years ago, I was invited to speak at an important conference in London.

The conference was, I was told, intended to tackle the subject of medication errors and adverse reactions to prescribed drugs. The company organising the conference was called PasTest.

'For over thirty years, PasTest has been providing medical education to professionals within the NHS,' they told me. 'Building on our commitment to quality in medical and healthcare education, PasTest is creating a range of healthcare events which focus on the professional development of clinicians and managers who are working together to deliver healthcare services for the UK. Our aim is to provide a means for those who are in a position to improve services on both national and regional levels. The topics covered by our conferences are embraced within policy, best practice, case study, clinical management and evidence based practice. PasTest endeavours to source the best speakers who will engage audiences with balanced, relevant and thought-provoking programmes. PasTest has proven in the past that by using thorough investigative research and keeping up-to-date with advances in healthcare and medical practice, a premium educational event can be achieved.'

Iatrogenesis (doctor induced disease) is something of a speciality of mine. I have written numerous books and articles on the subject. My campaigns have resulted in more drugs being banned or controlled than anyone else's. A previous Government admitted that they had taken action on prescription drug control because of my articles.

The conference organisers offered to pay me for two hours of my time. In addition to speaking at the conference, they wanted me to help them decide on the final programme. I thought the conference was an important one and would give me a good opportunity to tell NHS staff the truth. I signed a contract, and PasTest duly wrote to confirm my appointment as a consultant and speaker for the PasTest Conference Division.

And then there was silence. I repeatedly asked for details of when and where the conference was being held. The result was silence. Eventually, a programme for the event appeared on the internet. Curiously, my name was not on the list of speakers.

Here is part of the blurb promoting the conference: 'Against a background of increasing media coverage into the number of UK patients who are either becoming ill or dying due to adverse reactions to medication, our conference aims to explain the current strategies to avoid Adverse Drug reactions and what can be done to educate patients.'

Putting the blame on patients for problems caused by prescription drugs is brilliant. Most drug related problems are caused by the stupidity of doctors not the ignorance of patients. If the aim is to educate patients on how best to avoid prescription drug problems, the advice would be simple: 'Don't trust doctors. Too many are incompetent buffoons who do what they are told to do by drug company representatives.'

The promotion for the conference claimed that errors in medication account for 4% of hospital bed capacity.' And that prescription drug problems 'reportedly kill up to 10,000 people a year in the UK'.

As I would have shown (had I not been banned from the conference) these figures were absurdly low. I had already published evidence showing that one in six hospital beds is occupied by patients who had been made ill by doctors. And there was, and is, plenty of evidence showing that doctors are now one of the top three causes of sickness and death (alongside cancer and circulatory disorders such as heart disease and stroke).

The list of speakers included a variety of people I had never heard of including one speaker representing The Association of the British Pharmaceutical Industry and another representing the Medicines and Healthcare Products Regulatory Agency.

Delegates representing the NHS were expected to pay £250 plus VAT (£293.75) to attend the event. Delegates whose Trust would be funding the cost were asked to apply for a Health Authority Approval form.

And so the bottom line was that the NHS paid to send delegates to a conference where someone representing the drug industry spoke to them on drug safety. But I was banned.

I was banned from the conference because 'certain parties felt that he (Vernon Coleman) was too controversial to speak.'

It seemed to me that the drug industry, or people acting on their behalf, were deciding who they would allow to speak to doctors and NHS staff on the problems caused by prescription drugs.

Why are the people who had me banned so frightened of what I would say? It can surely only be because they know that I would have caused embarrassment by telling the truth.

Details of the ban were sent to every national and major local newspaper in Britain. None reported it.

I am by no means the only doctor to have found him or herself silenced in some way by the medical establishment.

Consider what happened to J. Meirion Thomas, a former specialist cancer surgeon at The Royal Marsden Hospital in London.

Dr Thomas's troubles began when he wrote a newspaper article in which he commented that 'the GP service is hopelessly outmoded'. The article had been written in response to a report from the Care Quality Commission. He wrote the article because he wanted to help improve patient care. And at the age of 68, he rightly thought he had experience which made his views worthwhile.

Nothing too controversial in that, you might think.

But the authorities thought otherwise. The medical establishment does not approve of doctors trying to improve things. And it does not approve of criticism – however valuable or well-intended.

Here is what happened to Dr Thomas (a widely respected surgeon with many years of experience) immediately after the publication of his article:

1) He received a letter (which he describes as 'aggressive') from the Imperial College, where he was Professor of Surgical Oncology. The letter demanded that he immediately sever all relations with the college.

2) A petition was started to have him struck off the medical register by the General Medical Council.

3) He received a message from the Royal Marsden Hospital where he worked as a specialist cancer surgeon. He was summoned to a meeting where he was told he had brought the hospital into disrepute and would not be allowed to attend until further notice. He was forced to take 'authorised leave' from his work.

4) The chief executive of the Royal Marsden Hospital received a complaint from the Professor of General Practice at Imperial College. Dr Thomas reports that 'this included a financial threat, querying why GPs should be expected to refer patients to The Royal Marsden Hospital when there are many others in London with which they had very good working relationships with the staff.'

5) Dr Thomas was then told that his Lifetime Achievement Award for 31 years of service at the Royal Marsden Hospital (due to be presented at a ceremony the following evening) was to be withdrawn.

6) He was eventually told he could return to work if he signed a document agreeing not to write any more articles unless he showed them to the chief executive in advance so that she could make sure they wouldn't harm the hospital's reputation.

All that happened because Dr Thomas dared to write one sensible article about general practice.

The tragedy is that this sad story is not, I fear, in any way exceptional. It is, rather, the norm. Whistle-blowers, truth-tellers and critics are not welcomed by the medical establishment. The doctors who are seen on television and heard on the radio are, I fear, largely vetted or approved by the pharmaceutical industry and the medical establishment (the two are pretty well interchangeable) for their willingness to toe the official line. The same is true, to a slightly lesser extent, of doctors who write for or are quoted in newspapers and magazines. Doctors who speak up on behalf of patients, or who try to expose problems within medical practice, will be quickly silenced.

All this happened a few years ago.

After writing several thousand articles and scores of books about medical practice! I have been censored and banned and the subject of numerous complaints. Today, the combined efforts of the pharmaceutical industry and the medical establishment mean that no one will interview me, review my books or print my articles.

It is hardly surprising that very few doctors dare to write anything critical of established medical practices – however damaging or dangerous they might be.

During 2020 things got even worse and the UK started to introduce bans which matched those which have been current in China for some time.

It is important to note that China censors rumours on the internet because they 'could cause social harm' (it has never explained what this phrase means) and the UK is planning to make 'content which has been disputed by reputable fact-checking services less visible to users'.

There has never been any attempt to explain what the phrase 'reputable fact-checking services' really means. And there is no doubt that many fact-checking services are paid for and controlled by governments and billionaires with their own financial and political interests to pursue. The UK Government is planning to appoint a regulator who will decide what is the truth and what is accurate.

Finally, it is worth remembering that the world's governments now regard China as having the system to aim at.

Things are now so absurd that although I would like to write a book about censorship I know that no one would publish it.

Since the very beginning of 2020 I have been banned, suppressed, libelled, defamed, monstered and demonised. (Curiously other authors have been allowed to write about topics even though my books on those subjects have been banned. A thief stole one of my books and reprinted the whole thing under his name – taking the royalties from the sales. The publishing platform did not ban the book although exactly the same book had been banned and removed from sale when it had my name on the cover.

As I mentioned a little earlier in this book, I have experience of Chinese censorship myself. Nearly a decade ago I wrote a weekly column in one of China's biggest circulation newspapers. After a few weeks I sent in a column criticising some aspects of inoculation. The editor's response was immediate and dramatic. He insisted that I replace the column with something else. It seemed that no one was allowed to criticise this procedure. But the matter didn't end there. A very short while later I received an email from my Chinese book publishers telling me that they would stop selling my books (which were bestsellers in China at the time) and that they would not publish any more of my books. When I showed some surprise at this they told me, rather shamefacedly I thought, that they had been instructed that foreign authors writing on medical subjects were no longer to be published in China and that, indeed, only selected publishing houses would, in future, be allowed to publish books on medical matters.

It seems that for some time any criticism of inoculation has been frowned upon very severely. In 2011, I wrote a book on the subject. I sent out around 620 review copies (a very high number). As far as I am aware not one review was published anywhere. Several books were actually sent back by editors who were obviously unhappy even to have the book in their offices. The book has, for nearly a decade, been an international bestseller.

Chains

We all create chains for ourselves – burdens and responsibilities. But this natural phenomenon has changed. The chains are now being made by those in authority – and imposed upon us whether we want them or not.

Chemtrails

It has been known for years that chemtrails are used to change our weather. But there is now also evidence that chemtrails are being used to distribute nanoparticles into the air. Just what purpose these have is the subject of rumour and conjecture but the absence of any clear cut information from the authorities means that the rumours and conjecture will continue and will, in the end, probably be proved correct.

The solution?

Well, there is no certain way to avoid the chemtrails but it seems wise to stay indoors and to keep the doors and windows closed if you can see a chemtrail in the sky near to your home or workplace.

Children

From the beginning of this fraud, children have been used to control their parents and the whole agenda. Using Greta Thunberg, the ever-young Swedish truant girl (that seems more appropriate than calling her a school girl) as a figurehead was a clever ploy because Ms Thunberg attracted a huge following among children of all ages. Her end of the world scenario, and forecasts of doom and a lost future, created massive fear among children and many became psychologically disturbed by what they were told. The children duly started to control their parents – demanding that recycling be taken very seriously, that fossil fuels be eschewed and that the climate and environment be put at the top of their thinking.

This was a ploy used by the Nazis during the 1930s. If you control the minds and fears of the children then you can more easily control the minds and fears of the parents.

The same technique has been used since the start of 2020. Children were deliberately terrified. They were told that they would die and that if they took the virus home then they would be responsible for killing granny and grandpa. The constant bickering about whether to open schools, and the absurd rules which were introduced, were designed to heighten the anxiety in the knowledge that the uncertainty and the fear would be transmitted to parents.

One of the most significant Agenda 21 plans is to take children away from their parents and to allow the State to bring them up – so that they think the 'right' way and have the 'correct' attitudes.

It is worth remembering that Lenin believed that by 'brainwashing' children early enough he could train them to become genuine communists.

And, of course, Francis Xavier, co-founder of the Jesuit Order, is famous for his saying: 'Give me a child until he is seven and I will give you the man.'

China

China is the model for the new world order. Every government in the world now wants to be like China. And the world government which is being planned will be very similar to the China of today. That's the plan. So, that's something to look forward to. If you want to know the sort of world we'll be living in then take a close look at China.

Billionaires and ambitious world government types realised long ago that China had become the West's most serious competitor in business. This helped drive their interest in promoting Agenda 21. If you look closely at the aims of Agenda 21 and the way China is run, you will quickly find that there is virtually no difference between the two.

China is the blueprint for all our futures. China has proved itself very capable of growing economically. And so it is that their system is well loved by billionaires.

Meanwhile, Britons should be aware that much of their country is now owned and controlled by China – through firms which are, in practice, an extension of the Chinese communist party (a close relative of Agenda 21's communitarianism). The General Nuclear Power Group (which is owned by China) owns two British wind farms and a big chunk of Hinkley Point nuclear power station. It wants to be involved in the building of two more nuclear plants. The State owned Huaneng Group is building Europe's biggest battery storage facility in Wiltshire. And Cheung Kong Group bought a big chunk of the UK electricity networks in 2010. China could close Britain in a minute if it chose to do so.

And it's worth remembering that Chinese citizens living outside China are legally obliged to help their country's intelligence services if told to do so.

Chrislam

There is a plan afoot to merge all religions into one – creating a new global religion suitable for a world which has a global government. There are several names for this new religion but the one which seems most popular among the movers and shakers such as Tony Blair, the Pope and the UN Secretary General is 'Chrislam'. There was even a World Chrislam Day (held on May 14th in 2020, if you're interested).

Those who find this difficult to believe should just key 'Tony Blair' and 'Chrislam' into a favourite search engine. Or try 'Pope and World Chrislam Day'.

Christianity and other religions will, in due course, become illegal

Christmas

By late summer 2020, it was patently clear that one of the main plans of the restrictions being engineered would be to ensure that there were very little opportunities to celebrate Christmas. I have no doubt that this policy will be maintained in future years.

There are several reasons for this.

First, of course, Christmas is (despite the commercialism) a Christian festival. Our future world government needs a world religion and Christianity has to be contained within the new global religion (which has a number of names but which, for obvious reasons, is usually referred to as Chrislam).

Second, the aim is to remove a festival which (even for non-Christians) is very much an annual focus. People look forward to Christmas as a party season. It is an opportunity for celebrations and feasts and for people to get together with friends and relatives they may not see for the rest of the year. In order to push fear and anxiety deeply into a nation's psyche, it is necessary to remove all chances for pleasure, relaxation and joy – and to make people's lives as deeply miserable as possible. Cancelling Christmas also helps to isolate people (who may be lonely for much of the year) from their friends and relatives.

We must never forget that the people running our lives are truly evil who will do anything to further their luciferian aims.

The followers of Agenda 21 have weaponised Christmas and will doubtless weaponise other crucial holidays. There are several advantages to making Christmas nigh on impossible.

First, of course, they want to damage Christianity. The Christian church establishment seems to be keen on this because they are committed to Agenda 21 and the one world religion. Christmas is, of course, the most significant and well-known Christian festival.

Second, closing Christmas will mortally damage small businesses. Most small businesses make most of their annual profit in the month of December – selling gifts and treats to those who want to celebrate Christmas. The Agenda 21 plan is to destroy these small businesses, and cancelling Christmas is an excellent way to do this. There are still those who don't understand why they would want to do this but the answer is simple: the plan is to destroy all small businesses (something constantly favoured by the European Union for example) so that large international businesses (with their many lawyers and lobbyists) can grow into complete monopolies. If you doubt this then just look at the way billionaires' wealth was boosted during the first few months of 2020.

Third, closing Christmas (or even just threatening to stop it, to turn it into a digital Christmas or to prevent families meeting) is all part of the policy to break down families and communities and to isolate us all as much as possible.

Fourth, holding people under house arrest increases ill health, increases the number of deaths and increases fear. Even the World Health Organisation has confirmed that keeping people shut in their homes is of no value in preventing the spread of flu or flu-like viral infections.

Church

Places of worship are shut or open only for an hour or two at a time and for the first time since the general papal interdict placed on King John in 1208 our parish churches were shut at Easter in 2020.

Wars, invasion scares, the Black Death and so on have come and gone but still the churches didn't close. They were indeed places of refuge. But church leaders of all colours, committed to the Tony Blair backed global religion Chrislam, have locked the doors and hidden away. Where have all religious leaders been hiding?

The Church of England has been a political party for some time. After the electors of Britain voted to leave the European Union, the Church of England continued to campaign against Brexit. It seemed that the Archbishop of Canterbury and a congregation of his colleagues decided that they knew better than the electorate. This was, of course, a policy entirely in accordance with Agenda 21.

Churches, mosques, synagogues and other places of worship are likely to remain completely or partly closed. Religious leaders of many types have been convinced by the plan for a world religion and they are accepting official guidance to stop their congregations worshipping in traditional ways. Even when places of worship are open, strict guidelines will remain in place and singing and the sharing of prayers will be banned.

In recent years, the Church of England appears to have been doing everything it can to destroy its relationship with its congregation. In one short period recently, Norwich cathedral introduced a 55 foot tall helter-skelter. The result was described as poisoning the very medicine the cathedral offered to the human soul. Rochester cathedral put a crazy golf course down the central aisle. And Southwark cathedral had a frock show as part of London fashion week.

Ironically, in early 2021, churches which were closed for services were opened to be used as inoculation centres.

Class division

An entirely new class system is being designed as part of the Agenda 21 programme. There will be two classes: the controllers (the UN employees, global warming mythmakers) and, as a serving class, the drones (who will be everyone else and who will effectively be slaves).

Communities are going to be divided into two – those who work for the Government or local authority and those who don't. Individuals who have secure civil service appointments will have far more job security. They also enjoy regular pay rises and good secure pensions and they work far fewer hours. The problems of 2020 have exacerbated the size of the gulf between the two halves. During the shut downs, civil servants did little or no work but continued to receive their full pay – and were comforted by the thought that when the restrictions ended, their jobs would be waiting for them.

Clauswitz

It was Clauswitz, the legendary German military author who pointed out that it is never sensible to make your plans according to what your enemy might do, or intends to do, but only according to what he can do.

Cognitive dissonance

I suspect that cognitive dissonance is greater with age. The longer you've lived the more likely you are to find it hard to believe just how much people are now lying.

Hitler and Goebbels were, perhaps, the first to realise that if the lies you tell are big enough, and you tell them often enough, then people will believe you. Most people are fairly trusting, and although they realise that politicians are liars they do not believe that even politicians would introduce national house arrest, force members of the public to wear face coverings and destroy a nation's culture and economy without good reason.

But, of course, it has been clear since March 2020 that politicians have been doing all those things without good reason – and that they will continue doing all those things until they are stopped by the courts or removed from office.

Voters are faced with three problems.

First, the courts are now largely controlled by what we must regard as the enemy. The justice system no longer operates to protect the public but now exists to protect the politicians and their billionaire friends.

Second, in Britain at least the Government halted all elections. For how long will democracy be suspended? Permanently, perhaps?

Third, most people accept what is happening because they believe that the restrictions are necessary and have been introduced to protect them. The longer the fraud continues the more difficult it will be to persuade individuals that they have been misled, that the virus is no more of a threat than the ordinary flu (indeed, for people under 80 it is probably less of a threat than the ordinary flu). There are two reasons for this. First, people have invested a good deal of faith in the new rules. They will be reluctant to admit that they were hoodwinked. Second, the face coverings in particular are causing brain damage and as the weeks and months pass by, the brain damage done by hypoxia and hypercapnia will be considerable.

Collaboration

The Agenda 21 definition of collaboration appears to be: 'The people do what they are told to do.'

Common Purpose

'Common Purpose' is a UK charity which apparently claims to develop leaders, to remove prejudices and to create 'elite' leaders. It seems to critics and sceptics that the organisation has much in common with the aims of the European Union and, therefore, Agenda 21.

Communitarianism

The principle behind communitarianism is that individual rights are always a threat to the community – whether the community is local or global.

You may believe you have rights over your body, your mind and your spirit. You may believe you have a right to own a home, maybe with a garden, and have a family and to plan your future the way you would like it to be.

You may believe that you have a right to earn money to feed and clothe yourself and your family. You may believe you have a right to move about freely.

But under communitarianism (devised by Agenda 21) you have none of those rights.

Your rights are a danger and so you must be watched, regulated and controlled.

The United Nations has given itself all the rights you thought you had. And through Agenda 21 and communitarianism it will decide what you do, where you go, where you live and how you live.

The Big Society nonsense devised by former Prime Minister David Cameron was, of course, a version of communitarianism.

Company directors

New rules mean that companies must now have some female directors and some ethnic minority directors regardless of the availability of suitable candidates.

What this means, of course, is that a few people will be given lots of directorships regardless of their talent, knowledge, experience and suitability.

Computerised medicine

Back in the early 1980s, a friend and I wrote the first medical software for home computers. I wrote the algorithms and my friend, Russell Smith, wrote the computer code. The software sold around the world but not many people had computers so the project wasn't an enormous commercial success. Still, it was the first attempt to produce medical software for home use. The original idea was based on a book of mine, consisting of a series of flow-charts, which was called 'Aspirin or Ambulance', and the concept was quite simple:

readers would use the software to decide whether or not a particular problem required a doctor or hospital (the 'Ambulance' in the title) or could be dealt with at home (the 'Aspirin').

Today, of course, that simple concept has been taken a good deal further and computer programs now are so sophisticated that computers have been ranked as better diagnosticians than human doctors. They are also better at selecting the most appropriate treatment. And now that robots can perform surgery there is no real place left for the human doctor.

A few decades ago, human doctors had an edge over computers: the human placebo response gave 'real' doctors a considerable edge. A kindly, sympathetic physician who was trusted by the patient he was treating would have a much better 'cure' rate than a cold, unemotional doctor who merely asked questions, did a little prodding and poking and then scribbled out a prescription.

Sadly, that edge has long since been lost. Modern doctors now work the same sort of hours as council officials and librarians and the vast majority no longer provide a 24 hour service for 365 days a year. Worse still, GPs are extremely reluctant to do home visits and many are deeply reluctant to see 'live' patients at all – preferring to speak to patients via the telephone or a video link.

It is difficult to avoid the conclusion that human doctors have little or no future. Whatever happens to the Agenda 21 plan there is little doubt that the changes in the way medicine is practised will be permanent.

A young person who wants to work with people and help mankind, would be wise, if they are also good with their hands and prepared to make home visits, to consider a career in plumbing rather than a career in medicine.

Confiscation

The huge costs of the shutdowns in 2020 and 2021 cannot possibly be met out of new taxes. Inflation will be used to help eradicate government debts but even that will not be enough. Governments will introduce confiscation policies. The events of 2020 gave politicians and bureaucrats the chance to provide grants and other forms of financial support for a wide range of organisations. When interest rates rise those debts will be un-payable and governments will claim control of companies, large and small, and of many types of private property. Astonishingly, governments around the world have proposed increased funding for local authorities and organisations which face budget shortfalls. The plans for Agenda 21 mean that there is absolutely no incentive for public officials to balance their budgets. All this leads directly to central control.

Confucius

'If a state is governed by the principles of reason, poverty and misery are subjects of shame; if a state is not governed by the principles of reason, riches and honours are the subjects of shame.'

Conspiracy theory

Everything which is not officially accepted is now regarded as a conspiracy theory. And the phrase is always used as a term of abuse. Anyone who tells the truth about just about anything is now labelled a conspiracy theorist by the fascists at Wikipedia and the BBC.

In reality, a conspiracy theorist is someone who believes that politicians lie and the antonym of conspiracy theorist is 'moron'. (I mention this with some hesitation. When my book, *Gordon is a Moron* was published, describing the mis-adventures of Gordon Brown as Prime Minister, I received a number of complaints from readers who thought the title genuinely unfair to morons.)

The truth, of course, is that those who are planning to take over our world and our lives are conspirators and could accurately be described as conspiracy practitioners.

Control

We have to be aware of the tricks being practised by our governments – under the advice of their mind control experts and warfare specialists. They attack in many ways and on many fronts. Take a look at my video on brainwashing techniques to understand more of how they do it. The transcript is on my website www.vernoncoleman.com

There are a number of traditional military techniques.

First, they want to suppress the truth. To do that they must silence journalists who might share facts with the public. The mainstream media has been bought with massive advertising budgets – paid for by taxpayers and designed to promote official lies. Suppressing the truth also involves demonising individuals, by using Wikipedia and other websites to make truth-tellers look bad and untrustworthy. And, of course, platforms such as YouTube are helping by censoring, deleting and banning videos which contain the truth. But, oddly, no one fact checks Prince Charles. He now claims that we need four planets to sustain us. This is pseudoscientific nonsense, of course, There is plenty of food on the planet – it's just usually in the wrong place. And much of it is wasted.

Second, while suppressing the truth, they plan to deceive us. This simply means lying. They tell us lies all day long and these lies are disseminated by the mainstream media with remarkable enthusiasm. In the old days, journalists used to check press releases. These days they just put their name at the top of the press release and hand it to their editor – who prints it. Governments keep the lies coming at a rapid rate so that we can't keep up and don't have time to check their allegations. And compliant media organisations constantly run propaganda campaigns. A day or so before the UK Government announced its latest restrictive laws, the BBC website ran an article quoting apparently ordinary people who wanted more rules.

Third, they want to distract us by constantly changing the rules and by pointing us in the wrong direction when we try to work out what is going on. They hope that in the end we will be so committed to trying to work out whether or not we must recite nursery rhymes when we go shopping that we hardly know what day of the week it is. The constant rule changing is not a sign of confusion in government. It is a sign that they are simply trying to increase their control over us by making us more stressed and fearful. The media is essential in this ploy.

Fourth, they want to exhaust us. An exhausted enemy is one that is easy to conquer. They deliberately want to exhaust us, confuse us, humiliate us and depress us. Our own governments want to increase the amount of depression among the population. Governments all around the world are responsible for the massive increase in suicide – particularly among children and young people. What sort of evil is this? In the UK, the Royal College of Psychiatrists has estimated that 8.4 million people are now drinking hazardous levels of alcohol.

Fifth, they must abuse those who are not convinced by their lies. They want to separate us and isolate us. In the UK, the rule that only six people can meet together is a standard trick to prevent the resistance movement gaining strength. They know well that revolutions invariably start in cafés where people meet and talk. When folk are isolated in their own homes, and cannot meet up with friends, then the risk of revolt is reduced. The rule of six, as they call it, is partly designed to stop demonstrations and meetings.

Remember: everything that has happened was meant to happen.

Within a few years (or even less time) the one world government will (if the plans are not stopped) be controlling every aspect of our lives – including our access to our own money and our access to food.

Cromwell (Oliver)

'You have sat too long here for any good you have been doing. Depart, I say, and let us have done with you. In the name of God, go!'

Oliver Cromwell's speech to the rump parliament in 1653

Cycling, cyclists and cycle lanes

Cycle lanes are being created around the world. Huge sums of money are being spent on marking off parts of existing roadways or pavements for the exclusive use of cyclists. When roads lose a large portion of their area there are inevitable extra queues for cars and lorries. This causes extra pollution and lowers productivity.

Cyclists think they are 'green' and are saving the planet but they are actually selfish and intensely annoying individuals (usually equipped with cameras, Lycra and an attitude problem). They cycle along (usually a yard and a half from the nearside curb or in pairs) and a huge queue of traffic builds up behind them travelling at 10 mph. At this speed, cars and lorries are far less efficient and so they throw out far more toxic fumes than if they'd been able to travel at a more reasonable speed. Drivers who travel too slowly may be arrested for causing a long tailback. Cyclists, who are the darlings of Agenda 21, are never arrested. Nor do they pay any road tax for the use of the roads and special cycle lanes.

Death

Death is not what it used to be. Most of the people who die are now given entirely false death certificates.

GPs in the UK want to certify death by using an application called Zoom. This allows them to certify patients as dead without having to leave their armchair or the golf course. Just how doctors can certify a patient as being dead without using old-fashioned methods such as listening to the deceased's chest or looking for a pulse has not yet been explained and probably never will be.

Debt

The US Federal Government now owes $27 trillion that it cannot possibly ever repay. Individual Americans owe another $53 trillion. And the American Government has signed IOUs worth $210 trillion in pensions and social security benefits that it will never be able to pay.

And to make matters worse the American president, Joe Biden, has pledged to spend $2 trillion over four years to ensure that the US economy is completely powered by 'clean' energy by 2050.

Declaration of Independence (United States of America)

'We hold these truths to be self-evident, that all men are created equal, that they are endowed by their Creator with certain unalienable Rights, that among these are Life, Liberty and the pursuit of Happiness.'

Delphi Technique

This is a technique which is designed to persuade a group of people to accept a point of view that they probably would never agree with if they thought it through, while at the same time managing to convince those individuals that whatever it is that they've agreed to was their idea in the first place. The Delphi Technique has nothing to do with the Delphic Oracle but is a plain, old-fashioned mind control technique – brainwashing, if you like. The Delphic Technique is often used in public meetings where Agenda 21 is on the menu and trained Common Purpose enthusiasts may be present.

The basic principle is that anything which you say, and which is not part of the plan, will be ignored. It may be written down. But it will be ignored.

The professionals who are presenting the meeting (which may be 'real' or 'virtual') will have lots of charts and graphs and statistics. The room will contain shills who will be there to deflect concerns away from delicate areas, to sneer at critics and to steer the conversations in the intended way. Anyone who objects to an Agenda 21 plan will be demonised as 'not caring about others'. The constant theme is the 'community'. Communitarianism depends on using social pressure to force people to conform in order to avoid being shamed.

Agenda 21 isn't just a global process: the plan, which is working frighteningly well, has always been to create fake citizen involvement by developing regional agencies, non- governmental organisations, non-profit groups, charities, commissions and special programmes. Local media report on all these agencies and groups and make it sound as if local people are involved in planning their own future.

But local people have no power. And local councillors and officials have no power.

Everything is coming to us from the faceless people behind Agenda 21 – assisted by lobbyists, facilitators, shills and 'bought' editors and media owners.

And the citizens, trying to get on with their lives, tend to shrug their shoulders. Exhausted by the confusion around them they tend to say nothing.

Anyone who speaks or writes about all this is dismissed as a 'conspiracy theorist'.

Democracy

These days, democracy is not considered very important. Politicians have accustomed themselves to making decisions without bothering to assess public support. So, politicians in the UK approved same sex marriage when there were clear signs that the majority of the public were opposed to it.

When voters are allowed to vote on issues they are often forced to vote again and again until they produce the acceptable, 'correct' answer. This has been the case with many votes on EU issues and, of course, when British voters decided to leave the EU there were many calls for there to be another vote. Scottish citizens voted against independence but Scottish politicians have repeatedly demanded a second vote. (Breaking up the United Kingdom would suit the EU, the UN and Agenda 21 very well.)

Democrat

A democrat (particularly a social democrat) is someone who believes that power is too valuable to be entrusted to the people.

Dentists

The British Dental Association has reported that dentists provided around 19 million fewer treatments between March and November

2020. The new rules about the cleaning of dental surgeries between patients mean that many dentists are closing their doors permanently.

Unbelievable though it may seem, most people in England had no access to a dentist from March until November in 2020. There was no one to drill and fill bad teeth, no one to remove teeth that had passed their pull by date, no one to clean teeth or preserve gums. Patients had no choice but to treat themselves with whatever home-remedies they could find. Quite a number removed their own teeth – using the time honoured method of tying one end of a piece of string to the painful tooth and the other end of the string to a doorknob. (And then slamming the door.)

In 2020, only around half the usual number of child dental appointments were arranged. The long-term consequences are impossible to quantify. But they will be awesome.

In early November 2020, it was announced that partial NHS dental services would be restored.

A short time later it was announced that England would be put under house arrest again.

De-platforming

Refusing to allow a speaker to speak by banning them or cancelling a planned lecture or series of lectures is known as de-platforming. It is a way of silencing dissenters, and encouraging compliance

Depopulation

One of the basic principles of Agenda 21 is that the global population needs to be reduced dramatically. The argument is that there are too many people around and not enough food to feed them. It is also argued that it is overpopulation which is leading to global warming and also damaging the environment. All of this is tosh, of course. There is plenty of food to feed the world's population – the only problem is that the food is often in the wrong place. And, of course, while millions starve to death, millions more are gorging themselves to death. The global warming myth has been thoroughly discredited, and talk about the environment being irreversibly damaged is also politicised nonsense.

Making plans to reduce the world's population is nothing new, of course. It's something that has been going on for many years.

In the 1950s, American scientists suggested using perpetual warfare to decrease the world population. They also suggested releasing deadly viruses. The first suggestion fitted in well with the requirements of the military-industrial complex and the second suited the pharmaceutical industry which would, of course, make billions out of providing drugs to help protect some people from the viruses.

In 1969, it was revealed that the US Defence Department (DoD) planned to produce new viruses designed to target and destroy the immune system – therefore making individuals more susceptible to infection. There is still much discussion about precisely which viruses were developed by the DoD.

There have been numerous other depopulation policies and programmes, and pressure has been applied to Third World countries to try to force them to reduce the size of their populations. There have been reports that birth control drugs have been included in a number of inoculation programmes. And there are reports that many of the wars which started in Africa and Latin America were encouraged in order to reduce populations.

Many of the individuals who are involved in the Agenda 21 process are keen to reduce the size of the world's population. Bill Gates and Boris Johnson both believe there are too many of us and are both keen to bring the world's population down considerably. So does Prince Charles and so does Prince Philip who wanted to be reincarnated as a virus to kill most of us. And Boris Johnson's father has said the same thing.

Digital currencies

Digital currencies are now being discussed by central banks (which originally rather disapproved of them).

The central banks have become enthusiastic because digital currencies (cryptocurrencies) will enable them to avoid or replace traditional banking systems. Digital currencies will also enable the central banks to get rid of cash completely. The Great Reset plan is to give everyone a digital currency account with the central banks. Payments will be made into or out of personal bank accounts as the central banks see fit. So, when a universal basic income is paid it will all be purely digital and the recipient will spend their money using a phone or, more likely, an identifying chip implanted under their skin. No one will need cash at all. And, of course, the central bank will be able to deduct taxes or negative interest rate payments as and when it wants to. The individual account holder will have absolutely no real control over their money. All the power will be with the central banks – ultimately under the aegis of the Bank of International Settlements in Switzerland. This system will enable the authorities to take payments for fines directly from an individual's account and it will give behavioural scientists running social credit schemes the power to introduce incentives, rewards and punishments in whatever form they consider appropriate.

Digital ID

The plan is to bring in a digital ID for all humans by the year 2030. There is an ID2020 alliance. The health passport and mandatory jabs are regarded as a useful way to force through a digital ID for everyone.

Governments, together with banks, are planning a digital financial identity for every global citizen. Some countries are already well on the way to developing these.

Digital tax

Governments are forcing all individuals to deal with their taxes online. The British Government, for example, has announced that it will no longer issue tax forms in paper format. Those who do not have the necessary software, or access to the internet, will either have to hire an accountant or find a neighbour, relative or friend willing to manage their affairs for them. The aim is not just to cut paperwork and reduce costs but also to take more control over the finances of individual citizens and small companies. The additional costs and time consuming work that digital tax creates will mean an increase in the number of small companies and self-employed individuals going bankrupt. This is no accident but is part of a deliberate policy to destroy small businesses.

Disaster

Whatever calamity befalls us, whether it appears to be man-made or a natural disaster, an increasingly large proportion of the world population is now so justifiably suspicious that they will believe it to be deliberate.

Dissident

In the new world order a dissident is anyone who prefers the truth to the lies told by the authorities.

Do not resuscitate

The letters DNR (standing for Do Not Resuscitate) used to be put (very occasionally) on the medical charts of very old, very ill patients who had no chance of recovering. Together with the patient and with relatives, where available, a team of doctors would discuss this option and, if it was generally thought best, recommend that if the patient had a heart attack then they should not be resuscitated.

That was a fairly passive form of manslaughter and it was generally used to protect patients according to the old tenet: 'thou shall not strive officiously to keep alive'.

Things have changed.

Today, patients are labelled with DNR notices without any consultation and without discussion with the patient or with relatives. And instead of a team of doctors discussing the DNR notice, individual doctors and nurses now decide that patients should be allowed to die. The notification is often done according to age. In some parts of the UK, it is reported that patients as young as 45 are automatically labelled DNR if they fall ill. In other areas, DNA notices are automatically applied to patients who are over 60 or 65 years of age.

Moreover, whereas patients with a DNR notice attached to them or their medical notes used to be allowed to die naturally, without treatment, the concept has developed noticeably.

Today, when the DNR letters are scrawled on a patient's chart the patient may well be quite well and the dying process will be accelerated not by denying them any medical treatment but also by denying them food and water. Patients who have been given a DNR notice will literally starve or dehydrate to death.

Dreams and ambitions

In the new world, after the Great Reset, dreams and ambitions will be gone forever. The rules of the 'new abnormal' have destroyed the music business, the theatre, the opera and much sport.

This is no accident. The aim is to abolish dreams and ambitions so that young people are content to live their lives as slaves, living in high rise buildings and working in dull, routine, slave type jobs.

Indeed, for today's teenagers the dream job will be one working for the local Health and Safety and Global Warming Compliance Department. Young people can forget about careers as actors, singers, footballers, ballerinas or models.

Dresden (James)

'When a well packaged web of lies has been sold gradually to the masses over generations, the truth will seem utterly preposterous and its speaker a raving lunatic.'

Drinking water

Drinking water is going to be the world's most sought after commodity. Over half of the world's population live in areas where there is too little drinking water. China, India, Africa and the Middle East are already dangerously short of drinking water. The problem is exacerbated by waste and by pollution rather than simply by an increase in the number of people living in those countries. Washing out yoghurt cartons, and so on, so that they are clean when they are taken half way round the world to be dumped, wastes a good deal of water.

Driverless cars

The driverless car is possibly the most stupid idea since electrically heated trousers were promoted in the time of Queen Victoria. Companies are spending huge fortunes trying to design cars which can operate themselves – without too much intervention from humans. It will be possible to control the vehicle from afar – to stop it, redirect it or deliberately crash it.

These vehicles might work well on motorways but on smaller, narrow, country roads where there are many side roads, blind bends and blind junctions there is a good chance that when two driverless cars meet they will come to a permanent halt – isolating and possibly imprisoning their passengers. I see no future for driverless cars outside the US.

And in the end, of course, the UN's Agenda 21 programme will mean that no cars (driverless or not) will be acceptable.

Drivers

In Britain, the number of young people with driving licences is falling rapidly. In 1994 around half of all those aged 17 to 20 had a driving licence. Twenty years later, the percentage had fallen to well under a third. And since then the number has continued to fall rapidly. The main reasons are the rise in the cost of insurance and the increasing complexity of the driving test and the way that driving has been made unpleasant by a rise in the number of laws and restrictions. New cycle lanes, pointless chicanes, speed bumps, street furniture and an ever expanding range of fines for misconduct have made driving unpleasant and expensive.

None of this has happened by accident.

The Agenda 21 plan is to eradicate private motoring completely and to force people to walk, cycle or use public transport if they must travel. In the cities of the future, people will live in high rise blocks and work within walking distance of home. Their purchases will largely be done online.

Dystopian society

A dystopian society is one where everything is unpleasant, bad and seemingly without hope; it is the opposite of a utopian society. Dystopian societies are typically totalitarian.

Eastwood (Clint)

'In this world there are two kinds of people, those with loaded guns and those who dig.'
(from the film 'The Good, the Bad and the Ugly')

Economy

The world's economy is deliberately being trashed.

'But why would governments want to destroy their own economies?' is a standard question from those who find it difficult to believe that any group of politicians would willingly self-harm their own economies.

And the self-harm has been remarkable.

Governments have destroyed small companies with new laws and absurd and scientifically indefensible rules about free movement. Central banks have printed money by the metaphorical ton and government deficits have grown massively. Money has been given to consumers (in 'furlough' schemes), small businesses have been lent huge sums at nominal rates of interest and large companies (some of with solid balance sheets) have been given access to huge amounts of money. By providing loans and grants to businesses, governments are quietly taking control of much of the economy. In the UK, the State is getting bigger and more powerful every day. Curiously, our conservative government is nationalising everything it can lay its hands on.

Furlough schemes have disguised the extent of the damage which has been done but there is no doubt that the capitalist system has been destroyed – with small companies, entrepreneurs and the self-employed being damaged most severely. Since tomorrow's large companies always grow from today's small companies, it is clear there will be no strong new companies in the future. Zombie companies, those which are surviving because interest rates are so low, will continue to stay alive and to ensure the failure of small companies which might have been able to grow.

At the same time savers have been punished, as though they were guilty of some heinous crime. Interest rates have been slashed to nothing and there have been threats of negative interest rates.

And what is all this for?

It is part of the Great Reset.

It was planned and it is all quite deliberate.

The aim is to eradicate private wealth (except for that of our new 'leaders' – such as Bill Gates, Prince Charles et al) and to force individuals to live on a modest 'Basic Universal Income'. The furlough schemes sound generous and kind but they exist to accustom yet more people to obtaining their income from the Government – and being totally reliant on the State.

It is worth remembering that during 2020 most of the world's billionaires did extraordinarily well. Between them their wealth rose by more than a quarter between April and July. Most of us got much poorer. The billionaires just got much richer. The bosses of Google and YouTube saw their wealth rise by a third.

Throughout 2020, professional financial advisors were convinced that the economy would quickly rebound. In their terms they predicted that the inevitable recession would be V shaped – in other words there would be a quick recovery, back to the old normal.

But the financial 'experts' were always going to be wrong either because they were lying or because they didn't understand that the economic chaos was not an accidental consequence of a global infection but a well-planned part of a huge fraud.

If the Agenda 21 plan goes ahead then the world's economies will never recover. Companies (particularly small, growing ones) will collapse. New companies will fail at, or shortly after, birth. Small investors and pensioners will be ruined. And billionaires will get ever richer.

Education

Followers of Agenda 21 (and environmentalists) believe that educated individuals consume more resources than the uneducated. They also believe that the educated are more difficult to control. And so, in order to reduce consumption and to achieve the UN's goals it is planned to change the education system. Education will be dumbed down, with exams being ever easier so that students think they are being well educated when they aren't. History will be ignored or altered to fit Agenda 21's requirements. Children will be taught to be narrow minded and prejudiced.

In short: education will be replaced with indoctrination. And since all teaching will be done via the internet, there will be little or no need for teachers.

This may sound extreme but the United Nations' Decade of Education for Sustainable Development aims to steal a generation of children and to teach them to put loyalty to the State above loyalty to family or country. It is no coincidence that children have been given the right to complain about their parents – and if they do so, they can be removed from their home by social workers.

The lead agency for the UN's Decade of Education for Sustainable Development is UNESCO and it aims to integrate the principles, values and practices of sustainable development into all aspects of education and learning, in order to address the social, economic, cultural and environmental problems we face in the 21st century.

As usual with the UN the targets are full of high blown language and light on practicalities. There is, for example, no mention of literacy or numeracy.

UNESCO identified eight themes for the Decade of Education, which was due to take place between 2005 and 2014 but which appears to have stretched out a little longer than that:

1. Sustainable urbanization
2. Sustainable consumption
3. Peace and human security
4. Rural development
5. Cultural diversity
6. Gender equality
7. Health promotion
8. Environment

Some folk might wonder what all these wonderfully meaningless phrases have to do with education.

The fact is that the 'new' education will teach new values too – with children being taught that the concepts of right and wrong are outdated and that everyone is entitled to be looked after. Education will be reorganised to teach children the importance of collectivism. A well-established aim is to destroy the moral fabric of society and to remove the concepts of respect and dignity.

The events of 2020 have clearly shown us that education as it used to be has no place in the future which is planned for us. Most school teachers couldn't be bothered to set classes on the internet while schools were closed. The Agenda 21 followers have no interest in promoting education for they know there will be no point to it. Exams will be made easier and easier and certificates given freely to one and all. Only the elite will be educated in the future.

Agenda 21 will create a new type of class division. Remember that in addition to changing education, the UN also plans to end national sovereignty, private property ownership, constitutional rights and democracy. Mobility will be greatly reduced since citizens will be relocated into 'smart cities' known as 'growth zones'.

Those fighting for the success of Agenda 21 deliberately want people to be ignorant (particularly about history and science), illiterate and innumerate as well as unquestioning. Education has been deliberately dumbed down and universities have been turned into diploma printing machines.

Today, surveys have shown that millions of children are unable to identify a cow or a robin. The appallingly low quality of British education hasn't just left children illiterate and innumerate but it has also left them ignorant, prejudiced, bigoted and narrow-minded.

A few years ago, an author called Robert Fulghum wrote a book titled, *All I really Need to Know I Learned in Kindergarten*. The book resonated with thousands who agreed with the title. Things are different now. Children can go through an entire school career without learning the basics. The one thing I learned at school ('absorbed by accident' is probably more accurate) was how to learn. Today, this is a rare skill.

Children have been taught to become tolerant to mediocrity, prepared to accept stupid senseless rules and unquestioning of waste and corruption by politicians and civil servants. Those under the age of 30 will have absolutely no future in the 'new normal' and yet they are the most accepting of the modern myths of Agenda 21. It is a war which has been won without a shot being fired.

Many children, and indeed all ages up to millennials, have no respect for anyone (other than the State), no imagination, no dignity, no resilience, no ability to think laterally (or 'outside the box' as it used to be called) no generosity of spirit, no sense of continuity, no sense of history, or their place in history, and, perhaps most important of all, no understanding of the joy of kindness.

To summarise, the Agenda 21 plan for education, which is being carefully followed by politicians and teachers everywhere, is to create ignorant, compliant and malleable children because ignorant compliant and malleable children will grow up to be ignorant, compliant and malleable adults who are too nervous and too fearful to question what is happening in the world around them. To disguise what is happening, exams are made easier and easier and diplomas and certificates are handed out to anyone who wants them.

Einstein (Albert)

'Three great forces rule the world: stupidity, fear and greed.'

Elderly

We live in a politically correct world but the elderly don't count. Every year hundreds of thousands are slaughtered by government decree. If a government had killed that many black protestors there would be an uproar. Commentators on the posh papers would be hysterical. There would be much talk of genocide. But these were just old folk, alone and abandoned in care homes.

Elderly patients in hospital are largely ignored by staff and left to starve to death, denied even water if they cannot get out of bed and fetch it themselves. It is common for elderly patients to be left in pain, lying in soiled bed clothes.

Old people are regarded as a burden which the governments have decided they cannot afford, and so the politicians will continue to authorise whatever methods are necessary to ensure that the number of burdensome old people is kept to a minimum. Look at what happened in the early days of 2020 when thousands of older folk were denied medical treatment and murdered by doctors, advisors and bureaucrats.

But sadly, caring, manners and respect have long been absent from our society. In the UK, the Government is throwing money at failing businesses, charities and the Arts – all deliberately destroyed by wicked economic policies designed to enrich the billionaires and change our world into the new normal – but nothing has been done to help the elderly whose miserly pensions force them to choose between freezing to death or starving to death, whose savings now give 0 % interest and who are constantly hounded by the dishonest and unscrupulous and deal breaking BBC to pay the licence fee.

Back in February 2011, an official UK report condemned the NHS for its 'inhumane treatment of elderly patients' and stated that NHS hospitals were 'failing to meet even the most basic standards of care' for the over-65s. Nothing was done to correct this.

It is no exaggeration to say that the NHS at large still treats the elderly with complete contempt. If animals were treated the same way there would, quite rightly, be an outcry. It used to be said that you can judge a civilisation by the way it treats its elderly so what does that say about our civilisation?

Caring is no longer an essential ingredient of health care that can be taken for granted and sadly we should be wary of being too trusting.

The problem is that if you are over 65-years-old your government wants you dead. And the Great Reset has brought this agenda to the top of the political wish list so it is now official Government policy to ignore the needs of the elderly. The only -ism that no one cares about is ageism.

The startling, sad truth is that ageism is today the acceptable face of prejudice, bigotry and discrimination. People who would not dream of expressing prejudice towards people of another race will quite happily express outrageously prejudiced views about the elderly. Individuals who regard themselves as entirely free of bigotry will merrily express bigoted remarks about the elderly without even thinking for a moment that they are behaving badly. And the desperately and determinedly politically correct who proudly consider themselves entirely free of any tendency towards discrimination will, apparently without regret, discriminate against the elderly without a second thought.

But it is, it seems, perfectly acceptable to abuse and mistreat anyone over the age of a certain age without recourse. It still staggers me that in the United Kingdom it has, for some years, been perfectly legal for doctors and nurses to murder anyone who can be described as 'elderly' and therefore regarded as an expensive and troublesome burden. And I find it difficult to believe (but it is a fact) that staff working in nursing homes are allowed to medicate the elderly against their will and without their knowledge; doping them with tranquillisers and sedatives in order to make them less troublesome to care for. The quality of care in nursing homes and care homes of all varieties is generally appalling. Patients or their relatives pay huge sums for squalid accommodation and sub-standard service.

It is the elderly who are, above all others, regarded as disposable and irrelevant. It is the elderly who have no rights. Sexism and racism are outlawed but ageism is not. Indeed, ageism is now a State sponsored prejudice.

Traditionally, the elderly were consulted and regarded as repositories of wisdom, knowledge and experience. Not now. Today, the elderly are assumed to be slow-witted, out of touch and stupid.

The ones who don't use the internet are regarded as irrelevant and disposable – not even any good for recycling.

The age at which citizens are officially regarded as nothing more than a cumbersome nuisance has been falling steadily for years. Today, anyone over the age of 65 is likely to be regarded as worthless. It has been repeatedly suggested that those over 65 should not be allowed to vote and that euthanasia for the over 65s should be made widely available (and involuntary

I haven't seen much sign of the celebrities who have appointed themselves the saviours of mankind and the environment, talking much about old people. They are too busy devoting themselves to the absurd, discredited pseudoscientific myth of global warming. The celebrity lefty luvvies who like to share their sympathy for foreign refugees and asylum seeking terrorists know that they won't get quoted in the papers if they tweet about vanilla white old people freezing to death or struggling to live on one tin of beans a week.

Celebrities line the streets in support of a politically inspired Agenda 21 support group called Black Lives Matter but they say and do nothing about the plight of the elderly – black, white or whatever.

And yet it is claimed that between 60,000 and 100,000 elderly citizens die of cold every winter in the United Kingdom.

Every year.

Despite this, the BBC recently had a headline which read: 'Low Tax on Heating Bad for Climate'. The story was, inevitably, based upon the views of a green global warming conspiracy group.

No one, it seems, gives a damn about the fact that if the tax on heating is raised then the number of elderly who die of the cold will doubtless increase. It is no good offering to give the poorest some financial help because, as everyone knows, the elderly will often not ask for financial support from the Government even if they are entitled to it. They think it demeaning to do so.

If 60,000 asylum seekers died of the cold, the liberal lefty luvvies would be twittering as fast as their fingers could fly. They would be appalled. They would demand action.

But the elderly are our oppressed and forgotten people.

In the UK, more than a million old people who have trouble surviving receive no help whatsoever. Nothing.

Moreover, a contact working in an English hospital tells me that elderly patients are deliberately put onto wards where the killer infection caused by the MRSA bug is endemic in order to get rid of them as quickly as possible.

Could this be one of the reasons hospitals seem apparently reluctant to take the simple steps that would eradicate killer, antibiotic resistant bugs?

In every conceivable way, the elderly are poorer today than ever before.

And yet our politicians, driven by Agenda 21, don't care. As far as they are concerned, the elderly are merely a nuisance.

What the politicians and the doctors and the nurses and the advisors forget is that one day they too will be old. By then they will have helped build a society in which anyone over the age of 40 is regarded as worthless and disposable.

Elections

Shortly after the conveniently available Emergency Bill was first introduced into British law in March 2020, the Government cancelled all elections. There was never any reason for this but Parliament agreed and that was that.

When will elections be held again? Or should the question be: will elections be held again? Or will all the parliamentary parties merely allow the present state of affairs to continue indefinitely 'in the national interest'?

Elite

The nanny state which has been created is run by elites who themselves regularly ignore the rules they have created for the rest of us.

Emerson (Ralph Waldo)

'He would be a man must be a non-conformist.'

End of the world scares

Spurious climate scares have been common for generations. So, for example, back on 24th June 1974, *Time* magazine (that's the silly rag which made Little Greta their person of the year in 2019) announced the coming of another ice age. We are still waiting for that one.

Scare stories always attract readers, viewers and listeners and the gullible will always believe what they read, see and hear. I fear that the current, fashionable global warming madness was inspired by ignorant lunatics with access to social media and too much time on their hands.

Predictions and forecasts made by global warming 'scientists' have been woefully inaccurate – consistently.

Back in 2007, the World Wildlife Fund told us that we had five years to save the world. The Global warming Hysterics told us that the English county of Cornwall would be a desert by 2010. In 2011, the International Energy Agency said we had five years to avoid Armageddon. In 2017, the United Nations said we had three years left, and in that same year the International Energy Agency also said we had three years left.

Some of these merry doomsters are relatively cautious and merely claim that our planet will be unliveable within a generation. Others are far more specific. Greta Thunberg recently announced that we had eight years left to save the planet. I don't think she explained why it was eight and not seven or nine years before the Four Horsemen would ride into view in their electric cars. It seems to me bizarre that a relatively uneducated girl with no scientific background feels able to be so dogmatic. Is it at all possible that someone is feeding her opinions, I wonder? An American politician called Alexandria Ocasio-Cortez is more optimistic. Last year she said we have twelve years left before something will happen. In 2013, a Cambridge professor called Peter Wadhams said that we had until 2015 before all the Arctic ice disappeared. Mind you, he was optimistic compared to Gordon Brown who, in 2009, taking a tea-break from buggering up the British economy, told us that we had just 50 days to save the planet. And in 2004, the readers of *The*

Observer were warned that by 2020 Britons would be living in a Siberian climate, though I'm not sure how they fitted that into the 'global warming' theory. Eleven years ago, Prince Charles said that we had eight years left to save the planet so you might imagine that the heir to the throne would be hiding in a cupboard feeling rather embarrassed since there is clearly now no point whatsoever in doing anything to oppose the terror which awaits. However, Charles is made of sterner stuff than most of us, and he is continuing with his scaremongering without allowing his past predictions to interfere with his latest proselytizing.

All this wild, scary stuff merely proves that the whole global warming/global warming thing is a fraud, an international scam of Brobdingnagian proportions. Despite the evidence, the mythmakers will doubtless keep going with their predictions. And, of course, making a prediction about the end of the world is a great way to get publicity and pick up more Twitter, Instagram and Facebook followers. The trick, it seems, is to pick a date a few years ahead and then hope that by the time we get there everyone will have forgotten what you said.

The global warming cultists remind me of that chap who, for 25 years, used to wander up and down Oxford Street carrying a board warning people to eat less protein.

It is my considered view that if Greta confined herself to walking up and down Oxford Street with a placard predicting the end of the world she would do far less harm.

Enemies

We are fighting a war for control of our bodies, minds and souls. Our enemies are using every psychological trick they know to frighten, to subdue, to oppress and to control.

To win any war you must first know who your enemy is.

Our enemies are legion and include:

a) The governments of the world and the politicians who are not in government but who would like to be.

b) The big, powerful non-governmental organisation such as the United Nations (and its offshoots such as the World Health Organisation).

c) The egocentric billionaires who have decided that they know best how the world should be run and who know they can increase their vast wealth by bullying us and controlling every aspect of our lives. Bullying, through fear and lies, is one of the most efficient ways to control populations.

Our enemies have been planning the fraud (which is no more and no less than a global coup) for many decades. The takeover of our lives may not yet have involved tanks and fighter jets but it is nonetheless a coup.

For the coup to be successful our enemies needed control. And for control they needed to 'own' the world's media.

This they have done; and so far they have done it most successfully.

Those newspapers, television and radio which make up mainstream media have been bought with massive amounts of advertising revenue. It is the biggest military operation in history, and the megalomaniacs behind it couldn't have even attempted it without the paid for support of the mainstream media, the faithful, obedient, slightly unexpected, endorsement of internet operations such as YouTube and the ever loyal assistance of a number of 'fake news' sites which have dedicated themselves to the demonization of those telling the truth.

Entertainments

Through absurd requirements, governments have deliberately forced the closure of theatres, cinemas and sports arenas. In the absence of evidence supporting these strictures it is difficult not to conclude that the closures were forced in order to damage morale and turn countries into harsh, post civilisation societies.

Having destroyed theatres, cinemas, concert halls and the arts in general, governments are now handing them taxpayers' money as gifts, subsidies and loans. The people who accept this money are damning their souls. When art is subsidised or paid for by the State, it stops being art and becomes propaganda – a part of the civil service, bureaucratic and dull, beholden to its political and administrative masters, afraid of originality and fearful of upsetting those doling out cash from the public purse.

Environmentalists

This is one of the words which changed dramatically in recent years. A while ago an environmentalist was someone who cared about nature and the environment, plants and animals and seas and fish. Today, these are usually the same people who believe in global warming. Most of them know nothing and care less about the environment. Nine out of ten are raging hypocrites who pay lip service to the notion of protecting the environment when really it is their plan to fly around the world promoting their views, to take over the planet and promote the Great Reset.

Equality and diversity training (also known as unconscious bias training)

This type of training (more a form of brain washing in reality) teaches individuals to question their own beliefs, assumptions and behaviour. These are replaced with forms of positive discrimination.

And so, members of police forces are desensitised and mentally reframed. Wives and family members have reported that police officers who have gone through diversity training become quite different; they become far more ruthless and aggressive because they no longer think like human beings. They become brutal, prejudiced and robotic in their determination.

Anyone who protests against the iniquitous activities of our oppressors is described as coming from the far right (even though the vast majority are not and many have no traditionally styled political affiliation or leaning).

The whole training is designed to suit Agenda 21 and leftist leanings.

ESG

ESG stands for economic, social and governance commitments. Those who obey the requirements of ESG must follow the politically correct rulings of the far left and, in particular, the enthusiasm of the global warming cultists.

Many big industrial companies, banks and investment companies have felt the need to announce their compliance with ESG. More and more are claiming that global warming is now no longer debatable, that they are committing their company/bank/fund to net zero emissions. Many surprising individuals have become lay preachers in the new religion of global warming. (Global warming is certainly far closer to a religion than a science.)

Investment companies and pension funds are refusing to invest in fossil fuel companies (regarding them as 'sin' stocks alongside tobacco, gambling and pornography). I suspect that one of two things will happen: either companies promoting renewable energy will, like electric car companies, soar in value or good sense will prevail when investors eventually realise that if we suddenly stop using fossil fuels then we will all die cold and hungry.

Eternal threat

When we win this war we must remain eternally vigilant. The people responsible for Agenda 21 will not go away. Like the baddie played by Alan Arkin in the movie 'Wait until Dark', the dark forces which have brought us new forms of oppression will remain active indefinitely.

European Union

The European Union was founded by Nazis immediately after the Second World War, although it was not known as that for a few decades. I have described the history of the EU in several books (notably 'The Shocking History of the EU') and in the first half of its life there is no doubt that the EU's founders and controllers were looking for ways to ensure that Germany won the peace, even if it hadn't managed to win the war.

In the second half of its life, however, the EU acquired larger ambitions and became a significant controlling force in the development of Agenda 21. The adoption of global warming as a raison d'etre, the introduction of recycling demands, the endless demands of a tinkering bureaucracy, the steady and deliberate destruction of small companies were all part of the Agenda 21 programme.

Euthanasia

Euthanasia is being talked about much more openly these days. It is heavily promoted by eugenicists though it is usually discussed in terms such as 'Do Not Resuscitate' or 'Nil by Mouth'.

Evidence based medicine (EBM)

It used to be customary for doctors to plan the treatment of their patients according to the evidence obtained from tests and investigations – matching that information against research results.

This is no longer the case.

In 2020, it became normal for prejudice and political instructions to take the place of good medical research and evidence based medicine.

There was little or no opposition from the medical profession as this extraordinary change took place around the world. Any doctor who dared speak up and protest was threatened with the sack – and with the loss of their licences to practice.

This change will, if not halted and reversed, mean that in future politicians and administrators will make decisions about treatment – and not doctors.

While writing this book, I discovered an old paper I had read but forgotten about. It is rather depressing and supports the conclusions I made in my book, *Paper Doctors* (which was published in 1977).

Entitled 'How evidence-based medicine (EBM) is failing due to biased trials and selective publication', and published in the 'Journal of Evaluation in Clinical Practice', the paper is a damning one. Evidence-based medicine is defined as the 'conscientious and judicious use of current best evidence in conjunction with clinical expertise and patient values to guide health care decisions'.

In other words, the aim is to provide patients with care based on the best, most reliable and most appropriate knowledge.

But there is a lack of evidence to suggest that EBM has resulted in health gains for patients. The paper suggests that the potential for improving health care has been thwarted by bias in the choice of hypotheses tested, by the manipulation of study design and by selective publication. (In other words, journals are only publishing research work which is helpful to drug companies. The research which criticises new products is never published.)

'Evidence for these flaws is clearest in industry-funded studies,' say the authors, who argue that the indiscriminate acceptance of 'evidence' produced by drug companies is 'akin to letting politicians count their own votes'.

The authors also point out that most studies are funded by drug companies and that 'clinical decisions based on such evidence are likely to be misinformed, with patients given less effective, harmful or more expensive treatments.'

The authors call for more independent research, and for the formation of more informed and independent bodies to assess the available research. And they suggest that research which is biased should be downgraded in value.

This paper was published in 2014. Nothing has changed. I am not surprised. I made many of the same points (and the same suggestions) back in 1977.

Facial recognition cameras

Facial recognition cameras are being used to track the movements of all citizens and to allow the police to make arrests of troublesome citizens. Just a few years ago the cameras were so ropey that an observer might, if they were lucky, be able to differentiate between

Margot Fonteyn and an arthritic elephant or between Elizabeth Taylor and Jack Nicholson. Today, facial recognition cameras have improved immeasurably and are getting better day by day.

Most worrying of all, it is claimed by those who operate them that they enable viewers to identify potential terrorists and paedophiles merely by looking at an image on a television screen.

It sounds like a science fiction movie.

But it isn't.

It's the new reality.

And it isn't difficult to see how this new reality is going to be used to control us.

In China, facial recognition surveillance cameras are used to catch jaywalkers and drivers guilty of motoring offences. A police facial recognition system takes photos of individuals (and, if they are in a car, the vehicle's number plate as well) and identifies individuals from their database.

Individuals who do 'bad' things are likely to be publicly named and shamed as part of their punishment. One fugitive in China was allegedly arrested in a crowd of 50,000 at a pop concert. Oh, and the cameras work at night too.

Finally, how's this for scary: facial recognition transactions are happening millions of times a day in China. You walk into a shop, glance at an LCD screen and you've bought whatever you looked at.

Fact checkers

Who checks the fact checkers? And what are 'facts' these days?

Most of the self-styled fact checkers are hired lobbyists promoting a particular point of view. Most have no experience of researching material and wouldn't know a fact if it leapt up and punched them on the nose. What they present as facts are usually opinions promoted by their sponsors.

Fact checkers are used regularly to oppose, belittle and demonise real researchers – particularly in the area of medical treatment and global warming.

False flags

The name 'false flag' comes from the days when naughty captains of sailing ships used to put up a flag suggesting that they belonged to an opposing navy. The innocent ship captains, seeing a replica of their own flag fluttering aloft, would merrily assume that they could safely approach to exchange cooking recipes and favourite holiday resorts with a fellow captain.

Then, suddenly, whoosh, a flurry of cannon balls would tear away their mizzen mast (I read the Horatio Hornblower stories when I was young) leaving them vulnerable to a quick and humiliating capture.

Pirates used to favour the same trick. Down would come the Jolly Roger. And up would go the Spanish or British flag.

History is full of false flag operations.

Remember the Trojan horse? That was an early false flag. There were false flag operations in ancient Egypt where Ramses was tricked. In Rome the church faked a document which gave itself the right to create the kings of Europe. In the 12th century, the church was at it again, this time inventing a character called Prester John who was used to trick the Europeans into entering into a war they had no hope of winning. Prester John was subsequently used for an astonishing five centuries without anyone smelling a rat.

From the 13th century onwards, the church blamed innocent people for everything which went wrong – including the weather. And since there was a little ice age for several centuries they had plenty of opportunity to hunt out people, call them witches and kill them. If the crops failed, the local witch (usually an unfortunate local midwife or nurse) would be blamed. If it was unduly chilly one winter then the witch would be burnt or drowned. If a plague killed a good many people then the deaths were blamed on local witches. Witch hunting was a popular profession and akin, its day, to the work done by Wikipedia editors today.

The Spanish-American civil war began when President McKinley told the Americans that the US Maine had been sunk in the harbour at Havana by a Spanish mine. The public outrage was enough to start the war. However, the captain of the Maine had insisted that the ship was sunk not by a mine but by an explosion in a coal bin. After the war, investigations showed that the captain was correct and that McKinley had lied. Tut tut. A politician lying. What a shock.

Hitler was a great believer in false flag operations. In 1933, the Reichstag building in Berlin, the home of the German Parliament, was set on fire. Hitler blamed communist agitators and used the fire to establish himself and his party in control of Germany. In 1939, Hitler arranged for German targets to be attacked and then told the Germans that Poland was responsible. And thus began the Second World War.

During that War, the Americans were outraged by the Japanese attack on Pearl Harbour which was, so claimed President Roosevelt, unprovoked and a complete surprise. Roosevelt was lying. He knew about the attack but wanted the Japanese to sink some ships and kill some Americans to provide an excuse for the Americans to join World War II.

It is very widely believed that the attacks on American targets on September 11th 2001 were arranged (or at very least known about) by the Americans. And both the Americans and the British lied about 'weapons of mass destruction' in Iraq as an excuse for invading that country. Colin Powell, George Bush, Tony Blair were just three of the most outspoken supporters of the Iraq war. All lied a great deal. And all politicians who supported or defended their lies were guilty of war crimes. The weapons of mass destruction scam was a massive false flag operation.

And then there was global warming – a huge confidence trick designed to control the people of the world and prepare them for Agenda 21.

At the turn of the century the big fraud was Y2K – when the world was told that computers would stop functioning properly at midnight on December 31st 1999. The claim was that computers would leap back to January 1st 1900 and that as a result there would be no electricity and aeroplanes would fall out of the skies. The fraud or false flag operation was created and maintained by software promoters who sold solutions and made $6 billion out of the nonsense.

Finally, in 2020 we saw the beginning of the biggest false flag of all time.

But you know all about that one, don't you?

Family

In a traditional society the family unit would have been the saviour of civilisation. But in many countries the family unit no longer exists. Those who follow Agenda 21 intend to get rid of the idea of the extended family. Children will be reared in centres rather than in homes.

The family unit is and always has been the basic building block out of which a society is built. For its own political reasons, Britain's Labour Government has done its best to destroy the family unit. And it has been enormously successful. Britain's tax and welfare policies provide financial incentives for lone parenthood. Marriage is penalised. Under the Labour Party's influence there has been a dramatic growth in the incidence of teenage pregnancy and a rise in the number of single parent families. Young men father children they have no intention of looking after. Young women deliberately try to get pregnant so that they can be given a home of their own and a weekly fistful of cash to spend. Half of all children are now born outside marriage. The Government has even introduced and promoted homosexual marriages. A government funded group produces a leaflet aimed at 13-year-olds which includes advice on 'how to be good at sex'. Sex lessons in schools include advice on anal, oral and digital sex for 12-year-olds. It is hardly surprising that one in ten women between 16 and 25 is now affected with chlamydia – a sexually transmitted disease which can cause infertility. The deliberate destruction of the family will mean that the elderly, the disabled and the weak will be left to die alone and uncared for.

Farms

There will be no place for traditional farming in the 'new normal'. Farms will be replaced with factories making food (including fake meat – which will be sold as 'meat' with no sign that it has been prepared artificially.)

There are serious plans in the UK to get rid of farmland. Boris Johnson has said that (in accordance with Agenda 21) he wants 30%

of Britain to be re-wilded. Since England is the most overcrowded proper nation in the world that is an absurd ambition for it will lead to even more overcrowded towns and cities. (Monaco and Hong Kong are probably more crowded but they don't count as nations. Singapore, which is a nation, is crowded.)

It has even been suggested that we turn 50% of our farmland into woodland. I have no idea why this has been suggested but the speaker probably has a penchant for eating twig sandwiches.

The United Nations wants to stop farming because of its bizarre, illogical and unscientific policies of 'sustainability' and 'biodiversity'.

Fear

Human beings suffer a good deal from fear. In the English language the word (and its associates) is used very widely and in places where it really should not be. So, for example, we say things like 'I'm afraid you didn't win..', 'I'm afraid I will be out next Wednesday…' and so on.

Fear is ingrained in our thoughts.

It didn't take much for governments and its psychology advisors to find ways to use fear to control the public.

We are being carefully, deliberately, systematically programmed to fear and to suffer. We are being filled to the brim with apprehension. It is the fear, in all its various shades of terror, which makes us susceptible to mental as well as physical suffering.

The fear of death encourages us to accept all sorts of insults and strange conditions. And so people who would, a year ago, have laughed at you if you had suggested that they wear a face covering all day long, will now happily cover their faces out of doors, indoors and even in the bath if they believe that doing so will reduce their chances of developing a terrible illness and dying.

Endless fear messages make people likely to believe anything especially if what they are being told might offer hope. Fear forces individuals to accept any instructions which they believe will free them from their predicament.

Governments are creating fear and then providing what they claim is the answer. It's the ultimate nanny state.

Feminism

It has been suggested (not without good cause) that the suffragettes were at the forefront of the idea to break down the traditional relationship between men and women. Certainly, feminism had a huge impact on society and was instrumental in creating a more pliable male population.

Final solution

Bill Gates has talked of a 'final solution'. He believes that the world is massively overpopulated.

Finance

It all begins, of course, with the Global Reset, as advertised by Prince Charles.

This doesn't include any provision for private property – unless you're already a billionaire or a member of the British royal family.

If you don't believe me check out the Agenda 21 promotional guff, as published by the United Nations. And take a look at Pope Francis's words on private property.

There are still people who think things will get better soon. They won't. Next year is going to be far, far worse than this year and it is going to be ever harder to break the hold the evil people have on our lives. If you are awake and you care about life, your family, your friends and your community then you have to do everything you can to stop these people and halt the Agenda 21 plan.

Fires

Global warming cultists believe that there are more forest fires today than ever before. This isn't true, though to try to make their claims come true the cultists are setting many fires themselves. This has two useful effects. First, it enables them to claim that the world is getting so hot that whole forests are suddenly bursting into flames. Second, when the fires spread to crops much food is damaged. This helps increase the number of people starving to death and helps reinforce the idea that farming is too vulnerable to be left to farmers and should be replaced with factory made food.

Flooding

Flooding will increase since environmental agencies now prevent landowners dredging rivers. The inevitable result is flooding. This is deliberate and is designed to force home owners into apartment blocks in the new cities – where flooding will never be allowed to be much of a problem. The flooding also helps make farm land unusable – thereby helping to lead the way to more factory produced food.

The building of new houses on flood plains is designed to impoverish those ambitious enough to want to own their own homes.

Food

There is plenty of food on earth. The problem is that much of it is in the wrong place. Look at what happened when the EU built its food mountains. The food was needed in Africa but the EU's agricultural policies meant that it got stored in areas where it wasn't needed. Tariffs on imported food, and the dumping of surpluses, together with corruption, have suppressed the development of food growing in what used to be called the 'Third World'. There is no doubt that much of the starvation in Africa was directly caused by the EU dumping food there with the result that local farmers simply could not compete and so went bankrupt.

The greedy billionaires want to get rid of farms (particular small ones) and replace the food they produce with artificial food made in their laboratories. Their long standing plan has suddenly become urgent since they do not want to waste a carefully created crisis. They are already selling laboratory grown meat as beef. There will be no label to show that the meat was grown in a laboratory. The plan is that every piece of food will be digitalised and identified and part of the 'internet of things'.

Suddenly, and belatedly, they claim to have realised that nutrition has a value in health care and they want to control our diet with legislation, advice and taxes (on sugary and fatty foods). Long standing medical tyranny is about to be extended and to become food tyranny. They are planning to introduce medically tailored meals and to extend genetically modified foods. The policy carried out with great success in India by Monsanto, for example, will mean that farmers will have to buy all their seeds from the big companies and it will be illegal to keep seeds from one year's crop for the following year.

There will be very few different varieties of foods and this will, I think, create unnatural susceptibility to disease. Some genetically modified foods (such as tomatoes and tobacco) will be grown containing drugs.

In September 2020, big food companies and supermarkets used campaigning and lobby groups to urge the British Government to adopt tougher rules on food production. This sounds splendid, even though it is rather surprising to see large food companies asking to be controlled more tightly with tougher legislation. The underlying aim, however, was (as it usually is in such cases) to make life impossible for smaller companies and newcomers. Large companies, whatever area they are working in, will always lobby for more legislation, more controls and bigger punishments because they know that they can afford to set up huge departments to deal with the legislative requirements whereas small companies, and newcomers, will be unable to do so. The European Union has for years created laws to suit the demands of big companies seeking to control their area of business.

Every day there is more news about how our eating habits are set to change.

Bill Gates is said to have developed a genetically modified cow which produces four times as much milk as an unmodified cow. Gates has also developed a special coating that can be put onto fruit to make it last longer in storage. I very much doubt if these modifications will be subjected to long-term clinical trials to see if they are safe.

Oh, and KFC is said to have developed a laboratory which can make chicken nuggets with the aid of a 3D printer. The Agenda 21 enthusiasts want to sell us GMO beef but don't want us to know that the stuff is fake. Gene editing has been made legal so companies can grow 'more hardy and nutritious varieties' of foodstuffs. In the UK, the Government has expressed its determination 'to liberate the UK's extraordinary bioscience sector from anti-genetic modification rules'.

Dr Frankenstein lives and is doing nicely, thank you.

Having one type of a crop or animal has always been dangerous – but that's where we are heading. Maybe our politicians should read about the Irish potato blight and the famine which ensued.

It is true that we need to re-evaluate the way our food is produced and used. A third of global farmland has been degraded by chemicals and pesticides and between a quarter and a third of all food is thrown away.

But it's worth remembering that there has been a surplus of food every year since 1980 – the famines which have killed hundreds of millions were caused by corruption, incompetence and poor food distribution.

The bottom line is that it is a myth that the world is short of food. The corollary is that it is a myth that the world is overpopulated. The problem with food is that most of the stuff is in the wrong place. The problem with people is that most of them are in the wrong place too.

Food infections

In the UK, 2.4 million people a year contract the norovirus (which causes diarrhoea and vomiting) from restaurants and take away food shops. Closing restaurants and other food outlets will result in a dramatic fall in the number of infections and reduce health care costs.

Foreign aid

Crazy UN rules mean that the UK gives financial aid to China and India – now two of the richest and most rapidly developing countries in the world. This is a part of a deliberate plan to make the UK poorer and to spread poverty equally around the world. (It is difficult to avoid the suspicion that this is also part of the punishment being meted out for having had an Empire.)

Freedom

We passed 'peak freedom' some time ago. Unless the people of the world rise up and take back their lost democracy and freedom we will never again be as free as we were a few years ago.

In 2020, the British were prevented from demonstrating or voting. Those querying the official line were denied access to the mass media.

We have to stand up for our freedoms or what sort of human beings are we?

Freedom means having choices and since we now have no choices we have no freedom.

Freedom means trust, honesty, honour, dignity, faith and an open media.

We have none of those things.

Freedom means democracy and a government of public employees who treat the public, their employees, with respect.

We don't have that.

I have spent most of my life writing about, and campaigning for, freedom. I realised a few years ago that the common theme running through my novels is freedom.

But unless we stand up and defend it, we will soon lose our freedom permanently.

Freedom of the press

There is no press freedom today. We are not allowed to debate important issues. The mainstream media does not allow discussion which questions the official line on anything. The irony is that our press freedom has gone not because tyrannical governments have taken it away but because journalists have sold it.

During World War II, Michael Powell and Emeric Pressburger produced a film called 'Colonel Blimp' starring Roger Livesey and Anton Walbrook. Churchill complained that the film was not very patriotic but Powell and Pressburger stood firm and the film was released in 1943. 'Only the English would have had the courage, in the midst of war, to tell people such unvarnished truth,' said Anton Walbrook, an Austrian. What a contrast with today's supine media.

But today, free speech has gone the same way as democracy. The oppression and the silencing of debate have been going on for a long time. The authorities (and their servants) deliberately libel and monster those who speak out and who discuss evidence which contradicts the official line. This is done in order to try to damage their credibility.

The odd thing is that doctors aren't allowed to talk about vital health issues but bankers and billionaires can make statements about health issues all day long.

In the UK, the Government has introduced an 'Online Harms White Paper', and government officials now target anything which they consider 'disinformation' or 'unacceptable content'. What they mean by these vague words and phrases is, of course, anything which does not toe the party line.

Regulators, powered by lobby groups, will be able to remove material from the internet, even if it is accurate and truthful, if it is deemed unacceptable to the authorities.

Universities (and their staff and students) have successfully silenced speakers whose views were deemed unacceptable to the few. Many subjects, it seems, cannot be discussed in public. Students have claimed that if they are subjected to unpleasant items in history they will be offended or hurt and that as a result, these topics should never be discussed. The BBC has apparently decided that global warming (to give but one example) can no longer be discussed because, they claim (without any justification) that the science has been settled and there is no reason for further debate which might upset those who believe in the global warming religion.

Some years ago I resigned from a well-paid column on a British Sunday newspaper because the editor refused to print a column questioning the validity of the Iraq War. I didn't believe in the weapons of mass destruction claims and I thought we were being lied to. I didn't see the point in writing a column if I wasn't allowed to express my honestly felt views. Resigning from that column on a matter of principle meant that I didn't get any more newspaper work. Editors don't much like columnists who have principles – and it cost me dearly in financial terms.

But that newspaper has been slowly dying since then.

The circulation fell by around 90% in the years which followed. Now, you could argue that the circulation fell that much because I left and I wouldn't stop you if you did but I wouldn't really believe it. And you could argue that the circulation fell because all newspapers are losing circulation and that's true. But this particular newspaper has lost a good deal more circulation than it should have done.

And I know why.

It is slowly dying because it lost its integrity. It doesn't stand for anything. It didn't respect its readers. And the readers saw or sensed that lack of respect.

It was, remember, HL Mencken who wrote that the relationship of a journalist to a politician should be that of a dog to a lamppost. And it was Theodore Roosevelt who, to paraphrase slightly, wrote that thinking there must be no criticism of the establishment is not only unpatriotic and servile but morally treasonable. Henry David Thoreau wrote his book, *Civil Disobedience* he meant it – and the original title was *On the Duty of Civil Disobedience*. Wimpy modern publishers usually leave off the first four words. Thoreau would regard them with contempt.

Furlough schemes

The furlough schemes which are so popular with millions around the world (and which ensure that people who cannot go to work are paid by the Government – or, rather, by taxpayers) will cost many billions of pounds. The cost to taxpayers will be phenomenal and will, inevitably, result in massive, unprecedented tax rises.

But I fear that the furlough scheme (in the UK promoted by a Chancellor of the Exchequer who is an ex-employee of Goldman Sachs) is designed not to help protect employees but to bring them under government control. The scheme may have seemed well-intentioned and generous but it was neither. Paying employees a hefty proportion of their income for staying at home and doing nothing, was introduced to force an increasing number of citizens into total dependency upon the State.

Under the Agenda 21 scheme, everyone will be dependent upon the Government for their income, their housing and their food. The furlough scheme is merely a large step in that direction: the provision of a state income for everyone.

The big companies which are receiving help from their governments are also becoming part of the State apparatus in whichever country they operate. This is all a step towards the strange mixture of communism and fascism that is favoured by the United Nations and its accomplices.

Similarly, grants and loans to small businesses and to the self-employed were all designed to increase the control of the State over as many of the electorate as possible.

The furlough scheme will morph into a Universal Basic Income for life, but with lower payments. The payments will be made to everyone but those with jobs will lose their tax free personal allowances and pay a higher rate of income tax. There will be no benefits payments or pensions, and those with eight children will just have to manage as best as they can on the Universal Basic Income.

During 2020, huge numbers of people took out home loans with the aid of their furlough income – seemingly regardless of the fact that they may well not have jobs or any income if the furlough scheme ends. Surprisingly, perhaps, banks seemed happy about this. I can't help feeling that this is part of the plan to bankrupt great swathes of the population. When interest rates rise, all those new home owners will find themselves unable to pay their mortgages. They will lose their homes, go bankrupt and have to accept a small rental apartment in one of the smart city tower blocks.

One of the aims of Agenda 21 is to widen the gap between the rich and the poor. The very rich are going to get ever richer and the middle classes and the poor are going to get ever poorer.

Remember: nothing is happening by accident.

GCHQ (Government Communications Headquarters

GCHQ in the UK has begun an offensive cyber operation to disrupt those opposing government propaganda. On 9th November 2020, *The Times* reported that 'It is not legally permitted to disrupt online content written by ordinary citizens.' (I assume that was a joke.) And the paper quoted a spokesperson as saying: 'You wouldn't get permission to go after cranks. People have a right to say batshit stuff online.'

General Medical Council

In the UK, doctors are controlled by the General Medical Council. Up until a few years ago, the GMC required doctors to pay a registration fee to keep their names on the medical register. (When I first qualified, there was no annual registration fee.) And then the GMC became much more intrusive. It introduced a revalidation scheme which seemed designed to force older doctors to retire completely – rather than working occasionally, or for a few hours a week. This had the inevitable effect of removing a huge number of experienced doctors from the available pool of doctors.

The GMC has also added a licence fee to the registration fee.

A decade or so ago doctors could lose their registration only for committing one or two fairly well understood sins: gross incompetence, having a relationship with a patient or acquiring a drug or alcohol addiction were the main reasons why doctors could lose their registration.

Today, doctors need a licence as well as a registration and licences can easily be taken away almost at the GMC's discretion. And so during the fraud, doctors were threatened that if they spoke out and disputed the official government line they would lose their licences.

This was not something that happened only in the UK – it happened all over the world and was clearly part of a well-organised and global plan to control medical practitioners. I know of doctors in France, Germany, Belgium and the United States who have lost their licences to practice or who have been threatened with losing their licences.

Genetically modified organisms

Messing around with the genetic structure of living things used to be called genetic engineering but it was quickly decided that this phrase was too frightening. And so genetic modification became the acceptable phrase and 'genetically modified organisms' the consequence.

It may all sound harmless enough, and the genetic engineers naturally claim that it's safe, but there is no independent evidence for their claims.

When you take genes from two living creatures and use viruses to force them together, the result is a GMO and, despite the promises of the politicians, the bureaucrats, the scientists and the companies making billions out of these products, no one knows what the long-term consequences might be. No independent tests have been done.

Scientists are now experimenting with people in the same way that they have formerly experimented with animals and plants.

I do not believe there is any evidence showing that GM foods are not dangerous.

How might they be dangerous?

They could increase food allergies. They might change the human body. They could create nutritional problems and digestive disorders. They might create new diseases. They could affect the liver and bring about changes in enzyme levels. And they might affect fertility.

Oh, and there is a very real risk that they could produce psychological symptoms such as confusion and aggression. They might result in a lower intelligence, anti-social behaviour and an inability to think critically.

I have been warning about genetic engineering for three decades (my book, *Food for Thought* which was first published in the 1990s contained a chapter on it, and in the 1980s I wrote a report on genetic engineering) and I am still not convinced that genetically modified food is safe to eat or, indeed, that any health products which involve messing around with genes are safe.

I am not alone in having these fears.

The American Academy of Environmental Medicine has asked doctors to advise patients to avoid GM foods.

But that is easier said than done.

For many years now attempts to stop the distribution and sale of GM foods have been a failure. Governments and bureaucrats have fought hard for the right of large companies such as Monsanto (in which software billionaire Bill Gates has a huge shareholding) to sell their products. And it is now pretty well impossible to avoid GM foods because GM crops have cross-pollinated with traditional crops.

Once a traditional plant is contaminated with a GM food which contains a patented piece of DNA, it becomes illegal to grow that traditional plant (or save its seed) without the permission of the owner of the patent. Obtaining permission usually involves paying a fee.

Genocide

It is difficult to avoid the conclusion that the various new restrictions were all deliberately arranged to kill off several million people – particularly the elderly, the frail, the disabled and the sick.

Georgia Guidestones

On a hilltop in Georgia, US there is a granite monument which has engraved on it in eight languages the ten guides. The monument is known as the Georgia Guidestones.

Although less than half a century old, the Guidestones are known to some as the American Stonehenge.

The first message on the stone is 'Maintain humanity under 500,000,000 in perpetual balance with nature'. This would involve culling around seven billion people and seems to fit with the depopulation plan openly endorsed by the British royal family and Bill Gates.

Gibson (Guy)

'Dull apathy and smug complacency seemed to be about to bring the British Empire tottering to its knees, if it didn't knock it out altogether.'
Wing Commander Guy Gibson VC DSO DFC was leader of the Dam Busters raid and an English hero.

Global warming

The global warming cultists still don't seem able to decide on a name for their movement (a word which is eminently suitable given its normal use to describe an opening of the bowels).

Back in the 1990s when the 100-year-old global warming myth was revived because of its political usefulness it was, as it had been since the days of Queen Victoria, called global warming.

(In fact, this nonsense goes back much further than the 19th century. As Adam and Eve wandered around in the Garden of Eden I suspect that after about a week or so, Eve probably turned to Adam and muttered something about it being rather hot. Adam, being the world's first cheapskate and not wanting to spring for some lighter leaves, probably replied: 'Oh, that's because of the global warming.')

As the years went by, the global warming theory was slightly buggered by the fact that the weather hadn't been given the proper script and there were real signs that the planet was getting colder and not warmer. The cultists responded by changing the title of their fraud to global cooling.

What the cultists obviously didn't realise is that the weather goes in cycles. All through history the climate has been changing. Sometimes the earth gets colder and sometimes it gets hotter and the cycles can last for centuries or even longer. Between the year 1200 and the middle of the 1800s, the world got so cold that that period is still referred to as the Little Ice Age. It had nothing to do with mankind making the world colder – it was just due to the vagaries of the weather.

And then, after a warm summer, the cultists changed the name of the new 'religion' to climate change in an attempt to avoid changing the name backwards and forwards every time the sun went behind a cloud.

The latest trickery is to remove old meteorological records so that new records can be announced. For example, there are plans to remove an old 'hottest' day record from long ago on the curious grounds that the meteorologist probably didn't read the thermometer properly.

The global warming fraud isn't science. It's a deadly mixture of tomfoolery, trickery and lies, prepared by individuals with a self-serving agenda and promoted by treacherous fools like Prince Charles who has steadfastly betrayed the British people and sold out to the Bilderbergers, the World Economic Forum and the evil cabal of billionaires.

The most important fact is that despite the nonsense spoken by global warming cultists there is no scientific evidence supporting their contention that the planet is getting hotter or that it is man's activities which are responsible. Dubious and self-interested claims from the United Nations don't count as evidence.

The truth is that even if the global warming cultists were right and the world was getting warmer, it really wouldn't matter a damn. Even their worst case scenario figures (which are false) show only that tides might be a few inches higher and temperatures a few degrees warmer. The end result would be a longer growing season and more food being grown. It simply isn't true that vast amounts of land would be under water. And it isn't true that animals would be threatened.

The global warming cultists, supplied with fake evidence by brigades of scientists who are becoming rich and famous by sustaining the myth, claim that there is too much carbon dioxide in the atmosphere because of all the people on earth. But volcanoes produce far more carbon dioxide than human beings who produce around 0.28% of atmospheric carbon dioxide. And carbon dioxide isn't a poison. Trees and plants live on it and the more there is the bigger the plants will grow.(Incidentally, chopping down trees to turn them into wood to be burnt in power plants, calling those wood chips biomass and claiming that biomass is a renewable form of energy is probably the biggest hypocrisy of all.)

The global warming fraud (or 'cult' as author Michael Rivero refers to it) is a crime against the whole of humanity.

It has been shown, time and time again, that there is no science except pseudoscience behind the global warming madness. It is a deliberate deceit, fake propaganda, a false flag as potent as the burning of the Reichstag. Indeed, belief in global warming has been accorded the status of a religion because it certainly isn't a science. The film 'An Inconvenient Truth', made by politician Al Gore, is still treated as a useful source of information despite a court ruling that the film contains numerous lies and distortions.

Global warming is being used as the excuse for a global takeover, and those who promote it most vehemently are being rewarded with the opportunity to make huge sums of money out of selling carbon credits.

The current global warming scam isn't a new one of course. Like most good scams this one has been around for a long time.

In 1817, the President of the Royal Society in London warned that there had been 'a considerable change of climate, inexplicable at present to us' and said that this would lead to changes in the accessibility of the Arctic Seas. It was nonsense, of course.

A century later, in 1922, the *Washington Post* warned that the Arctic was warming up, that icebergs were getting scarcer and in some places the seals were finding the water too hot.

In 1947, *The West Australian*, quoted a Dr Ahlmann, a Swedish geophysicist who was warning about a mysterious warming of the climate. And in 1958, the *Sunday Telegraph* in London warned that the climate is getting warmer.

Then the scaremongers suddenly went into reverse, and in the 1970s the experts warned that a new ice age could grip the world within the lifetime of present generations. Nigel Calder, a science writer, warned in a major television documentary on the BBC that the threat of a new ice age must stand alongside nuclear war as a source of wholesale death and misery. Calder claimed that the northern hemisphere had been cooling since 1950s and that the droughts in Africa and India were due to the 'little ice age'.

In 1975, *Newsweek* magazine ran a story called, 'The Cooling World' and predicted the beginning of dramatic global cooling which might well lead to a drastic decline in food production. They talked about economic and social adjustments on a global scale. (In 2006, over 30 years later, *Newsweek* published a correction.)

The bottom line is that politicians, journalists and experts are forever warning us of terrible things that are about to happen. The invariable rider is that they might well be able to save us from the terrible future which they predict, if we give them vast amounts of money, enormous prestige and a full page profile in the *Guardian* newspaper.

The BBC and other corrupt and blatantly dishonest news organisations now claim that global warming is accepted and need not be debated or discussed. This is a lie of course. (The BBC makes the same bizarre claim about almost all contentious scientific issues.)

Global warming is simply a pseudoscientific cult for self-important hypocrites and the people who promote the global warming myth are richly rewarded for their obedience while those who dare to question it are severely punished.

Governments, big industries (with a vested interest in the changes being forced upon us), ruthless lobbyists and, of course, the United Nations keep up the daily terror through a constant bombardment of lies, deceits and pseudoscience. It is, to use a felicitous phrase devised by my friend Dr Colin Barron, a seemingly unending example of 'death porn fear'.

The UK Government says that tackling global warming will require a host of new incentives, laws, rules, bans, taxes, appliance standards and institutional innovations. In November 2020, as the UK's economy fell apart, the Government announced another package of £12 billion worth of investment in green infrastructure such as cycle lanes. At the same time there was huge pressure for 'climate denial' to be criminalised and for those questioning the new cultish dogma to be prosecuted instead of merely being persecuted. (It is worth remembering that in 2015, former US vice-president Al Gore said that 'deniers deserve to be punished'. Gore was, of course, the presenter of an infamous video which has been proven to contain misleading pseudoscience.

Much the same is happening everywhere.

In the US, President Joe Biden wants to spend $2 trillion 'decarbonising the US economy'. The European Union has earmarked 30% of its $880 billion recovery fund for climate measures.

Today, it is estimated that 85% of all our energy comes from fossil fuels and the plan is to replace all this with solar and wind power. Both the EU and China have committed to achieving net-zero carbon emissions though this will, inevitably, involve a good deal of cheating, chicanery and lying.

The Economist magazine claims that the global plans will avoid the chaos of global warming and improve human health. It does not occur to the writers that it will be impossible to replace fossil fuels in a decade or so, or that doing so would destabilise the mid-East where nearly a billion people would suddenly have no means of support. There is no explanation of how human health will be improved.

As I explained earlier in this book, we are being encouraged to blame ourselves for destroying the planet. Guilt, they know, is a powerful and controlling force. They hope we will accept the constraints on our lives, the higher taxes and the poorer living standards as just recompense for our bad behaviour.

The Agenda 21 supporters have used the myth of global warming to terrify billions, and the global warming fraud (and it was and is a deliberate fraud upon the people) has been used ruthlessly to promote Agenda 21. The authorities we were taught to respect have betrayed us ruthlessly and without compassion or respect for the people they are paid to represent and protect.

Global warming started off as a harmless (if idiotic) pseudoscientific fad but has become the new secular religion; a cult. Politicians, bankers, industrialists, television personalities, pop stars and millions of ill-informed acolytes share the absurd belief that the planet is getting hotter because of man's activities and that soon the world will either be flooded so that there is no land left to sustain life or too hot for humans to inhabit.

Zina Cohen's book entitled, *Greta's Homework* contains 101 truths about global warming that everyone should read.

Goethe

'There is nothing more frightening than active ignorance.'

Goldman Sachs

Goldman Sachs, a bank which consists of a small army of spiritual midgets floating on a bed of sewage, is widely regarded as one of the disgusting companies on the planet. That wouldn't matter except for the fact that many alumni of the bank have been, and are, in positions of great authority.

Widely regarded as one of the most evil companies on earth (and memorably once described as a 'vampire squid on the face of humanity') the Goldman Sachs bank seems to specialise in producing bankers who, after getting rich as employees, move into what is usually (but these days inaccurately) described as public service. For example, in the UK, the Chancellor of the Exchequer and the Chairman of the BBC are Goldman Sachs alumni.

It was allegedly Goldman Sachs who advised the World Health Organisation that people should wear face coverings, regardless of the medical and scientific evidence. No one was much surprised when the WHO obeyed this instruction (and a similar one which came from a splinter group excreted by the World Economic Forum).

Goldman Sachs employees look at money in a different way to other people. Former Goldman Sachs CEO, Lloyd Blankfein is worth a billion dollars but has been quoted as saying that he considers himself well-to-do rather than rich.

Goldsmith (Oliver)

'Laws grind the poor, and rich men rule the law.'

Golf

Possibly, the most absurd, unjustifiable ruling of 2020 was that golf courses should be closed to golfers but kept open for walkers. Those in the golf course industry found it difficult to understand why the Government thought it acceptable for walkers to wander around golf courses without sticks and balls but unacceptable for walkers to wander around the same ground with sticks and balls.

The golf course owners were understandably concerned that the walkers might damage the putting greens and bunkers and that without any income from golfers they would be unable to pay for the necessary repairs.

Destroying sporting activities which require land is, of course, a key step in the Agenda 21 programme which wants to force everyone into cities – and to leave land outside to be abandoned. (Food will, of course, be prepared in laboratories and not grown on the land.)

GPs

From March 2020, the service provided by most GPs (family doctors) in the UK has varied between appalling and virtually non-existent. Could GPs really be so stupid as to believe the Government and its advisors? If they were then they had no right to be practising as doctors. Were GPs cowed by the Government's threats that anyone who spoke out would lose their job and their licence to practise? If that were the case then those doctors should have been hounded out of their jobs and forced to retrain as traffic wardens. Or were many of those doctors simply lazy; eager to grab a chance to enjoy a long, well-paid holiday from their responsibilities.

Whatever the truth, none of the doctors who failed to provide a full service seemed to give a damn for their patients' health safety.

The decline of the general practitioner can be judged from the fact that one GP told a woman she had cancer over a zoom consultation. Another GP wanted to sign a death certificate using a video link. When the daughter of the woman who had died refused, the GP said that he would only visit to certify death if everyone in the house (including the corpse) was suitably attired for the occasion.

Green

In political terms a close synonym for 'fascist'.

Green energy

Under instructions from the United Nations (and ever-active environmental activists driven more by enthusiasm, greed and a sense of misplaced righteousness than by science) governments everywhere are desperately eager to stop using fossil fuels and to invest more and more in wind-farms, biomass burning, solar farms and so on.

The resultant rise in electricity prices will be dramatic. There will be massive outages. There certainly will not be enough electricity to power all the electric cars being bought. (Everything, it seems, must be electrified but no one seems to worry about where all the electricity is going to come from.)

There is talk of decarbonising housing (at a massive cost per house) but at the same time the policies followed in 2020 mean that unemployment is going to soar and taxes will have to rise dramatically. The few people still in work are going to cry out in fiscal pain as they realise just what level of taxes they will have to pay.

Hand washing

The enthusiasm for hand washing is one souvenir of 2020 which is worth keeping. It has been known for many decades that hand washing is second only to penicillin in saving lives.

Health passports

Pro-Vaxx fanatics often argue that we should all be issued with health passports which show whether we have been tested and inoculated.

The idea is that we won't be able to travel unless our health passport is up-to-date and appropriately stamped – whether it's a bit of paper, a digital record kept on your mobile phone or something stored on a chip under your skin.

Health and technology groups are working rapidly to create a digital health passport for governments, airlines, employers and shops. They aim to develop an internationally accepted digital certificate. It's a small step to listing medical histories on a chip. Other groups are falling over themselves to create competitive systems.

All this is being promoted as a way to protect the world. Without your digital passport you won't be able to get on a plane, enter a building, go to a concert or do anything much. I suspect that privacy will be a distant memory.

Much of this was, of course, all planned long before the events of 2020 reared their ugly little head and created panic everywhere. It's 20 years since the CEO of Oracle apparently offered the US government a proposal for a national security database that collected everything possible to identify someone.

It won't be long before we are all expected to have an implant carrying all the required information, and it won't be more than a few months before the chip contains more than health information. It will be loaded with everything personal about us. Our personal implant will carry all our personal information, our financial details, our full medical record of course, our academic record, our criminal record and so on and so on. State employees and certain private sector employees will be able to read the implant. In due course automatic readers will check as we pass them that we have been properly tested.

Your health passport will contain details of what drugs you are taking – for your protection, of course. If you're a recovering alcoholic or drug addict then your passport will carry that information. And millions of people will be able to read it. If you have been treated for a sexually transmitted disease then those details will be in your health passport as will details of any mental illnesses you've ever had.

Everyone you meet in any sort of official capacity will have access to your health passport – whether it's a piece of paper or an implant.

We are all heading into a terrible, inhuman future where confidentiality will be merely a distant memory and where the intimate secrets of our lives will be assessed and judged by everyone in a uniform, everyone working for the Government and millions working for private security and management companies – including your employers. Oh, and hackers will doubtless help themselves to your private health information along with your email address, telephone number and internet passwords.

If you're happy with this total loss of privacy then that's fine – it's your choice.

How long will it be before the health passports they have planned turn into the identity cards that millions of Britons have already rejected?

They have, remember, been planning these health passports for years.

Health services in decline

In January 2020, I started to prepare notes for a book explaining why health care today is worse than it was half a century ago, and why, despite all the advances in technology, the health care available in the future will not be as good as it was 50 years ago.

The book got pushed aside by unforeseen events but today, it is even more clear that health care is deteriorating by the day and, having been writing about doctors, hospitals and medical treatments for many decades, I am now convinced that the majority of patients today are receiving worse treatment than was available in the 1950s.

There are some exceptions, of course. The very few patients who have had successful transplant surgery could argue, accurately, that back in the 1950s they would have died. And there are one or two new drugs available that are life-saving.

But those are exceptions. I'm talking about the quality of medical care available for 99% of patients, 99% of the time.

Even the good drugs, the antibiotics, are now often not as useful as they once were. Overprescribing and the wholesale, routine use of antibiotics on farms have meant that antibiotics which once saved lives are now often useless.

I qualified as a doctor almost exactly 50 years ago and after a year working in hospitals went straight to work as a general practitioner. I practised much in the way that doctors were practising half a century before that. If patients wanted a consultation they just turned up at the surgery during opening hours. I did a morning surgery and an evening surgery. I gave my own injections and took my own blood samples. I happily inserted catheters and syringed ears. Patients didn't have to make another appointment to see a care assistant with little training. If you couldn't get to the surgery you telephoned, or sent a message, and the doctor visited. If you needed help outside surgery hours you got in touch and the doctor would visit. Medical care was provided 24 hours a day and 365 days a year. Accident and emergency departments, called casualty departments then, were used largely for victims of road accidents, fights and fires. Why would anyone trek all the way to a hospital when they could have a doctor in their home within minutes? Patients who were elderly or frail or housebound or disabled were often visited routinely once every couple of weeks. District nurses drove themselves round their local community to dress wounds and check on patients discharged from hospital.

It now sounds like something out of a history book but I can't be the only one who can remember how things were and why they were better 50 years ago than they are now. It wasn't perfect by any means but it was a damned sight better than things are today.

Today, you're about as likely to get a home visit from a doctor as you are to win the lottery. And your chances of having a doctor visit you at home at night or at the weekend or on a bank holiday are nil – unless you live in a big city and have an arrangement with a private doctor who does house calls. Having a GP always available at the end of a telephone was reassuring; it was good to know that professional help was always available. If a patient had to go into hospital they knew they had someone they could trust if they didn't understand what was happening to them – they could speak to their GP or he would visit them in hospital to help explain things.

Everything has been going wrong for decades – but the slide downhill has accelerated recently. Medical care was never better than it was when people wore hats. Decency disappeared when bare heads became the norm. I'm obviously not saying one caused the other for that would be a simplistic example of post hoc ergo propter hoc, but it's an easy way to define a change. When medicine became more science than humanity the quality of care started to diminish significantly.

Fifty years ago, doctors always strove to keep patients alive. Today, 'Do Not Resuscitate' notices are placed on patients' beds as often as temperature charts. It has got so bad that I have heard reports that DNR notices are put on the notes of any patient over the age of 60 or even 45. Those youngsters who cheer this should be aware that in 10 years' time the age allowed could be reduced to 40 then, in no time at all, to 30. Remember the film Logan's Run in which 30 was the cut off end of life age.

The ethics committee at Great Ormond Street Hospital, once the standard for quality in the care of sick children, was reportedly criticised by a High Court judge for deciding that a nine-year-old girl should be 'managed' rather than 'treated' and for making this decision without talking to the parents. Lawyers representing the hospital had allegedly asked that Great Ormond Street Hospital not be named. I bet they did.

Today, elderly patients in hospitals are routinely left to die, unfed, unwashed and without fluids. In the UK, it's a government approved programme for the 'care' of the elderly.

The fraud perpetrated in 2020 gave hospitals the opportunity to shut down whole departments, many of which are still closed, and gave doctors in general practice the excuse to virtually shut down their surgeries. There was never any logical reason for this. GPs claimed that it would be better and safer to conduct all examinations by video rather than in person. It was even seriously suggested that young GPs found their work so onerous that they could not be expected to work more than one day a week – even though they were working 9 until 5 with an hour or two off for lunch. Patients who had serious symptoms were told that they could not be seen in person by a doctor or even a nurse.

The truth is that video consultations are pretty useless and very dangerous. You can't examine a patient by video. You can't listen to their chest or check their heart or blood pressure. You can't examine lesions properly. You can't palpate an abdomen. You can't look down throats or into ears. You can't even use your sense of smell – useful in the care of diabetics.

Hospital infections, too often untreatable, are now too common to be remarked upon. Fifty years ago, a ward sister or a matron would have forty fits if a patient on their ward or in their hospital contracted an infection or developed a pressure sore or any other sign of bad nursing.

Hospitals used to employ almoners whose job it was to make sure that patients didn't have to worry about anything. If an elderly patient was admitted to hospital as an emergency, the almoner would make sure someone went round to feed her cat. If a patient was worried about her bills being paid while she was in hospital then the almoner would deal with it. If you don't remember those days you probably think I'm joking but I promise you I am not. People working in health care used to understand the meaning of the word 'compassion'. Today, health care staff would probably laugh or sneer if you told them of such realities.

Even in small things, hospitals have gone backwards.

So, for example, many hospitals no longer allow flowers on the ward. The real reason is that they make a little more work for the staff. And the staff think that putting flowers into a vase is a demeaning activity. But for several thousand years it has been known that having flowers on a ward cheers up the patients and improves their recovery.

Similarly, when I was young, it was commonplace for someone to come onto a women's ward every day and do the hair and make-up of the patients. That doesn't happen anymore.

When I was a young doctor, all patients requiring hospital treatment were subjected to a full medical examination. They also had a full history taken. Woe betide any young doctor if a patient was seen by a consultant without there being a full medical history in their file.

How can it be an improvement to know virtually nothing about the patients you are looking after? Back in the 1960s we derided doctors who thought of patients as being 'the liver in the end bed' or 'the kidney problem in the bed third on the left'. But that is what health care has become once again.

Everywhere you look there are problems. Hospitals and general practices are managed by people who don't understand the first thing about medicine. In Europe, the EU has stopped doctors working more than a basic working week and so in hospitals there are frequently no doctors at all available at weekends or at night.

In the UK, the NHS has always been a money wasting machine. The amount now spent on the NHS is so great that if that money were simply handed out to the public, everyone in Britain would be able to buy themselves top level private health care. How can that be? It's simply because there are more administrators than hospital beds in the health service, and vast amounts of money is wasted on pointless bureaucracy. Like all large, bureaucratic organisations the last people to be fired are the bureaucrats themselves. They just keep hiring and building their empires.

The NHS is regarded worldwide as the pinnacle of socialised medicine. Many around the world look upon it with envy. But that is only because they look at from a distance: as observers rather than as consumers. The NHS has been a disaster in every possible sense. Most people who work for it say they wouldn't want to be treated in their hospital. The outstanding legal claims in the NHS had reached £85 billion before the fiasco hit and left patients untreated and uncared for. Untold thousands of people will be entitled to sue and demand huge damages as a result of the fraud.

Overall satisfaction with the NHS is low and falling annually. People complain of long waits, staff shortages, lack of money and money being wasted. It is a deadly tale of indifference, incompetence, greed, selfishness and weariness. The incidence of doctor induced disease (iatrogenesis) soars every year.

It has long been recognised, incidentally, that waiting lists of all kinds were and are deliberately created by doctors to enhance their private incomes. This is a weakness of a system which allows some consultants to work in the NHS and at the same time to have private practices. Their NHS income is the bread, butter and jam and the private income is the piece of cake. Consultants deliberately keep their waiting lists long because they know that this is the great selling point for private care. I once worked at a hospital where, during a consultant's annual holiday, a registrar and I worked hard and got rid of the waiting list completely. It wasn't particularly difficult. Naively we thought that the consultant would be pleased when he returned from his holidays. He was furious. 'Why the devil should people come and see me privately if they can be operated on tomorrow in the health service?' he demanded. He was the norm and not the exception.

Life expectation is falling for women, waiting lists are growing and waiting times are soaring, the amount of illness is rising constantly and the number of patients made ill by doctors has made iatrogenesis an epidemic – up there with cancer and circulatory disease as one of the three major killers in our world. One in six people in hospital is there because they have been made ill by doctors.

In half a century, the quality of medicine offered has slumped.

And there have been virtually no breakthroughs in the last 50 years. There are plenty of new drugs – but most of them are merely variations on long-established themes. Health care is now controlled by lobbyists working for big drug companies, and lies and myths rule our lives in a thousand different ways. The future, we are assured, is jabbing people with untested products. A jab for this and a jab for that. Drugs are going to be put into foods. The crisis has given drug companies the opportunity to introduce potentially deadly mRNA products.

Screening programmes are known to often do more harm than good but they are immensely profitable and so they are popular with businesses and doctors. Medical education is controlled by drug companies and so when doctors are looking for a treatment they think first of pills. Lifestyle changes rarely even figure in their calculations.

Long stay hospitals have been closed with the result that patients who need long-term care spend their days wandering the streets. Celebrities now promote health products and eating habits without having any knowledge or understanding of the harm they are doing. New regulations mean that small hospitals have closed with the result that patients have to travel for hours to visit a hospital.

Charities have become commercially linked with drug companies and use their lobbying skills to influence public policy in favour of their commercial partners. Food companies promote bad eating habits because they are more profitable than good eating habits.

In the UK it can, and does, take weeks or even months for X-rays and scans to be read and for blood results to be recorded, distributed and interpreted. It is for this reason, more than any other, that Britain has the worst cancer survival rates in Europe.

All things considered the modern history of medicine is a deadly tale of indifference, incompetence, greed and selfishness. All of this is important because it was long ago established that when a doctor is sympathetic and compassionate his or her patients will get better quicker – it's a human version of the placebo response which can add a quarter to a half to the effectiveness of a treatment. That has pretty much been lost.

In the UK, the only response to the chaos from the politicians and the collaborating public has been to demand yet more money for the health service, which actually has far too much money but just wastes most of it. Billions are wasted on unnecessary layers of administration and on paying too much for consumables.

When I published the prices the NHS pays for office equipment, washing powder and so on – and proved that the NHS was paying more for stuff bought by the ton than I would pay if I bought the stuff at a supermarket – the NHS responded not by dealing with the waste but by demanding to know where I had obtained the computer print-out containing the NHS prices. They were only interested in covering up the waste – not doing anything about it.

Complex financial schemes, private finance initiatives and absurd bonus schemes for executives have cost the NHS billions. It is hardly surprising that services are deteriorating and that some services, such as dentistry, are likely to be abandoned completely.

The future, I fear, is bleak.

Thanks to the fraud, health care is set to deteriorate even faster than before and the relationship between patients and health care professionals doomed to collapse still further.

Alternative branches of medicine will doubtless blossom and bloom. But for most people the future will involve telemedicine, preventive care and self-care. We all have to learn to look after ourselves and our loved ones.

Doctors haven't yet grasped this, but computer programmes will take over from medical practitioners. Back in 1984, a friend and I wrote the first home doctor programme for computers and ever since then computer programmes have been improving. They are now being fitted into robot physicians and surgeons. In ten years' time there will be very few jobs for human doctors. Students thinking of entering medical school might like to look for another profession. A career in plumbing might offer better prospects. I am being very serious.

This has not happened by accident. It is all part of the United Nations global plan for the future – Agenda 21. We are now living in the future they designed for us. And the plan, I believe, is that in the UK the National Health Service will deteriorate so much that it becomes hated and despised – in the same way that it was once loved and respected. Closing hospital departments has destroyed faith and trust in the health service (which is widely regarded now as the National Death Service) and made it easier for the Government to reduce the scope of the health service and introduce more private health care.

Unless we speak up, soon and loudly, the future will simply get bleaker and bleaker.

Health care is never going to be as good as it was last year. And last year's professional health care was worse than it was the year before that. Indeed, I firmly believe that professional health care today is, in many ways, worse than it was 50 years ago.

It will, of course, be important to kill private medicine too and it was, therefore, no surprise that during 2020 the British Government bought up all the beds in private hospitals – and left them empty.

We all need to lay in a stock of equipment for looking after ourselves. And we need to be able to use the equipment we own.

Heating

Governments are making log burners illegal. It will soon be illegal for people to chop down dead trees, chop up the trunk and branches, and burn the wood to keep warm. And gas boilers and central heating systems are being outlawed. This is being done to force people into apartment blocks in smart towns – which will be heated by electricity. The electricity will be obtained by burning biomass which will be obtained from chopping down trees in other parts of the world, cutting the trees into tiny pieces, transporting them thousands of miles and then burning them.

Henry (Patrick)

'Give me Liberty or give me Death.'

History

Anything which provides a connection with the past or gives us reason to be proud of our heritage is being removed. Statues are being taken down, books are being suppressed and discussion of the past silenced.

The University of Leicester recently announced that it would stop teaching Geoffrey Chaucer in favour of modules on race and sexuality. The English department was told that texts like *The Canterbury Tales*, *Mort d'Arthur*, *Sir Gawain and the Green Knight* and *Beowulf* would no longer be taught and that mediaeval literature would be banned. Viking myths and sagas, the role of the church and the state in literature – all gone. Nothing written before 1500 AD will be taught. *Paradise Lost* seems likely to disappear though the University of Leicester did agree that teaching on William Shakespeare would remain in place. It seems that Shakespeare isn't yet quite old enough to be banished.

Professor Nishan Canagarajah, the president and vice-chancellor at Leicester, said that changing modules was part of a long-term strategy to compete on a global level. He didn't specifically mention Agenda 21. Mr Canagarajah was born and educated in Sri Lanka. I wonder what would happen if an Englishman decided to eradicate much of Sri Lanka's cultural history.

Old buildings are being closed or demolished and areas of outstanding natural beauty are destroyed. In the UK, the National Trust is just one of many treacherous organisations which seem determined to eradicate our history and our culture.

And so, for example, the National Trust has linked almost 100 of its properties to colonialism – including the homes of Winston Churchill and Rudyard Kipling (both Nobel Prize winning authors). Members of the National Trust complain that the organisation is virtue signalling and jumping on the BLM bandwagon. Kipling's home has apparently been condemned because the British Empire was a central theme to his work (e.g. much of it was about India so that is a bad thing). And the Bath assembly rooms were named and shamed because the city was connected to wider colonial economies during the 18th century, and the rooms are in some way considered responsible.

Hitler (Adolf)

'What good fortune for governments that the people do not think.'
    '(People) more readily fall victims to the big lie than the small lie, since it would never come into their heads to fabricate colossal untruths, and they would not believe that others could have the impudence to distort the truth so infamously.'
    (Note: for the inadequately schooled, Adolf Hitler was a German politician, prominent in the 1930s and 1940s).

Hong Kong flu

The 1968 Hong Kong flu killed about the same proportion of the US population as the virus which appeared in 2020. The mortality rate was almost identical at 0.1%. There were no restrictions on movement. Hospital departments were not shut. The economy was not devastated.

Hope

There will always be hope, and as we struggle along in a world controlled by psychopathic fascists, we must try to see the bits of blue sky in the Gatesian grey. Occasionally, we must stop, smell the flowers and remember what a wonderful world God gave us.
    As we walked through a village during one gloomy period in 2020, we passed a café which had been allowed to open and which had a couple of tables outside. A woman was sitting alone at one of the tables. She was reading a battered paperback and had a pot of

coffee and a half empty cup in front of her. She looked up at us as we passed.

'Isn't it a wonderful day,' she said. 'It's a warm day and there's blue sky above. I've got a lovely pot of coffee and a good book.'

Hospitals

I doubt if I am on my own in no longer seeing hospitals as safe places in difficult times. I now see hospitals as dangerous. There is a risk that unnecessary and potentially hazardous testing will be done. There is the risk of being taken into an isolation ward and having a Do Not Resuscitate Notice applied to my medical notes.

I doubt if medical care will ever recover from the self-harm that has occurred in the last few months. But then, that was the intention.

Houellebecq (Michel)

'The whole point of bureaucracy is to reduce the possibilities of your life to the greatest possible degree when it doesn't simply succeed in destroying them; from the bureaucratic point of view, a good citizen is a dead citizen.'

House flies

The next time you wonder how evil scientists can be, remember that the ordinary house fly was used as a military weapon by the Japanese.

An entomologist called Shiro Ishii devised a bomb with two compartments. One contained a cholera infused slurry. The other compartment contained a batch of house flies. The bombs resulted in epidemics that killed 410,000 people.

Houses

Current policy is to knock down old houses (particularly Victorian properties) and to replace them with modern buildings which satisfy environmental and building requirements.

Sadly, the new houses are not as well-built as the Victorian ones. And because the houses are flimsy and badly designed they are cold in the winter and hot in the summer. They tend to fall down after a decade or two.

This is quite deliberate.

The Agenda 21 enthusiasts want all houses to be demolished so that we are forced to live in badly designed and poorly built apartment blocks in their smart cities.

It is the new future.

Human rights

Human rights have been steadily eroded. The Patriot Act in the USA after the 9/11 events and the emergency legislation introduced in the UK in March 2020 removed virtually all human rights. These are unlikely to be restored.

Humanity

Humanity is about kindness, respect, truth, dignity and honesty. None of these things figures in the world being prepared for us by the United Nations and those working towards Agenda 21.

Humour

Lefty luvvie Agenda 21 cultists have no sense of humour, do not want any humour in their lives and will, in due course, ban it because, in their eyes, it has no discernible function.

Hypocrisy

The most common symptom among those suffering from Global Warming Syndrome is hypocrisy. A study in late 2020 showed that climate experts and climate scientists fly more than any other type of expert – taking an average of five flights a year. Professors dealing with global warming take an average of nine flights a year – again this is more than other types of professor. And then, of course, there is Lewis Hamilton the racing driver. He spends his life flying round the world so that he can drive a car round and round in circles. But he's very concerned about global warming. If he really believes all the rubbish spouted by the global warming cultists he should just stay at home.

In 2020, Prince Charles, heir to the throne in Britain, was appointed hypocrite of the year for his total commitment to hypocritical behaviour. He was especially commended for taking a private jet (at a cost to UK taxpayers of £82,689) to speak about global warming at the World Economic Forum in Davos.

Charles, who constantly preaches sustainability and exhorts ordinary citizens to stay at home and avoid using aeroplanes, flies everywhere for convenience – usually at taxpayers' expense.

ICLEI

ICLEI (originally The International Council on Local Government Initiatives but now Local Governments for Sustainability) sounds like a boring organisation which someone thought up in the bath. It isn't boring but someone probably did think up the name while in the bath. And the name is deliberately boring. You hadn't heard of it, had you? And yet this organisation controls your life more than most organisations with which you are familiar.

ICLEI was set up in 1990, and it exists to bring Agenda 21 to local communities all around the world. It is a lobbying group and as Rosa Koire noted in her book, *Behind the Green Mask* it's rather telling that it was founded two years before the 1992 Rio Earth Summit where Agenda 21 was founded and approved. Maybe someone was thinking ahead.

ICLEI does all sorts of worthy-sounding things. For a fee it sells training programmes to governments everywhere and monitors community greenhouse gas emissions. And, more than anything else, it keeps the fear ramped up. It's a fear-porn specialist. We need radical solutions and accelerated action because we've all been 'driving too much, keeping warm and buying clothes'.

ID cards

War criminal Tony Blair pushed hard for these, as part of the EU's role in Agenda 21. The British people rejected them but they are now being resurrected as health passports and their main champion is Blair who wants us to have these ID cards to prove we are fit to travel by plane or train. The cards will also be necessary if we want to stay in hotels, eat in restaurants and so on. Blair will presumably suggest those who do not have ID cards are crammed into an unwanted building and destroyed with a weapon of mass destruction.

Illuminati

A name, which originated in 15th century, which is often given to people who consider themselves to be exceptionally enlightened. Illuminati are usually driven by money and power but may also be driven by power and money.

Immigration

Immigration policies were devised as a deliberate well thought out plot designed to disrupt society, break down nations, increase fear and create racism.

Nothing is accidental.

England is the most overcrowded country in Europe. Encouraging immigration on a massive scale is illogical and dangerous but was done on purpose to break down national barriers and to create racism – so that communities would be broken down

Immune system

Your body's immune system helps to protect you against infection. If your immune system – your inbuilt defence system – is in tip-top condition then you will be far less vulnerable to marauding viruses or bacteria. Your body will also be better able to fight cancer and it will also be more able to resist infection. Many things affect the efficiency of your immune system – including diet, stress, sunshine and medication. What you choose to eat can have a big effect on the strength and effectiveness of your immune system. People who are locked up and kept apart from others are likely to have poor immune systems.

Independence

Too much independence can destroy a career these days. Swimming against relativism can destroy a career in minutes. Independent, original thinking is very much frowned upon in today's New World Order.

India

India is collecting the largest biometric database in the world – holding data on 1.3 billion residents. The Indian government is scanning the eyes, faces and fingerprints of all citizens and connecting the data to welfare benefits, mobile phones and much more. The database also holds parents' names and bank account details. The poor must scan their fingerprints to obtain food. The elderly must do the same to get their pensions. The system is known as 'Aadhaar' and it is compulsory. The Indian Government will have complete control over its citizens. This scheme (the antithesis of freedom and democracy) is entirely in accordance with Agenda 21 and the plans of the United Nations, and it's coming soon to a country near you.

Infant deaths

The mortality rate among infants fell 30% during the period when people were put under house arrest. For example, the incidence of Sudden Infant Death Syndrome appears to have fallen noticeably.

Now what happened that could have had an influence?

Well, people didn't go to the pub.

It was illegal to sit on a bench in the park.

And, since doctors surgeries were pretty well closed, infants and children didn't have their regular inoculations.

So, which of those three do you think might have had an influence on the drop in the incidence of Infant Death Syndrome?

You might think this piece of news worth reporting in the national media. But you would be wrong.

Inflation

The only way that most governments dare to default on their debts is to create inflation – which removes the debts bit by bit. There is little doubt that governments around the world will create high inflation to help remove the massive debts they accumulated during 2020.

Younger people won't remember what inflation looks like so let me remind you that in the UK in 1974, inflation ended the year at 19% and in 1975 inflation hit 30%. (It's perhaps also worth remembering that income tax for private investors was 98% at the very top rate.)

When the British invented stamps in 1840, it cost a penny to post a letter – the stamp was, of course, known as the Penny Black. When I was a boy it cost tuppence halfpenny to post a letter. (That's around one penny in new money.) Today, as I write, it costs 76 pence or 65 pence to post a letter, depending on whether you want it delivered straight away or stored in a disused Cornish tin mine for a week before being delivered.

Around the world inflation has hit pretty high levels from time to time. In Hungary in 1946, prices were doubling every 13 hours. In Germany in 1920, the postal system had stamps ranging from 5 pfennigs to four marks. In 1922, they had a 100,000 mark stamp.

And in 1923, there was a 50 billion mark stamp. I collected these in the 1950s when I was a boy. I was thrilled to have a page full of stamps all worth billions of marks.

In August 2008, Zimbabwe issued a Z$100 billion note to keep up with inflation (then running at 2.2 million %). That was not, however, the highest denomination banknote produced in the last 100 years. In the 1920's, Germany had a 100 trillion Papiermark note. And in 1946, Hungary printed notes with a face value of 1,000,000,000,000,000,000 pengos (that's one followed by 18 zeros and it is known to its friends, if it has any, as a quintillion). One German I know recently pointed out to me that his father had taken out an insurance policy in 1903. Every month he made payments. The policy was for a 20 year term and when it matured, he cashed it and took out the proceeds. He used the entire proceeds to buy a single loaf of bread. A Berlin publisher reported that an American visitor tipped their cook one dollar. The family met and it was decided that a trust fund should be set up in a Berlin bank with the cook as beneficiary. They asked the bank to administer and invest the dollar. The price rises in inflation-crazy Germany became dizzy. A student at Freiberg University ordered a cup of coffee in a cafe. The price on the menu was 5,000 marks. He had two cups. When the bill came, the price for the second cup of coffee had risen to 9,000 marks. He was told that if he had wanted to save money he should have ordered both cups of coffee at the same time. The printing presses at the Reichsbank could not keep up. Factory workers were paid daily at 11.00 a.m. A siren would sound and everybody gathered in the factory forecourt where a five ton lorry waited. The lorry was full of paper money. The chief cashier and his assistants would climb up onto the lorry, call out names and throw down bundles of notes. People rushed to the shops as soon as they had caught their bundle. Doctors and dentists stopped accepting currency and instead demanded butter and eggs. When the Germans introduced a note for one thousand billion marks hardly anyone bothered to collect their change. It wasn't worth picking up. By November 1923, a single dollar was worth a trillion marks. People living on their pensions found that their monthly cheque would not buy a bun. People dependent on insurance payments were destitute. When traced back it is clear that hyperinflation in Germany started when Germany abandoned the gold backing of its currency in 1914. The Government borrowed to finance the war.

Inflation is usually something that happens by accident or through incompetence. However, the inflation that is coming is deliberate and it is going to impoverish everyone who isn't prepared.

And, of course, governments will lie about it.

In the summer of 2008, the official US inflation figure was between 2% and 2.5% but, if the American Government hadn't changed the way it measured inflation back in 1992, the official inflation figure would, during that summer, have been close to 9%. The real, practical inflation figure would have been even higher.

Inflation is an invisible tax. Although it is a boon for borrowers (the £250,000 borrowed to buy a house shrinks as a result of inflation) it is a curse for savers (the £250,000 pension fund shrinks in value and purchasing power as a result of inflation). Pensioners and others on a fixed income lose out because their buying power is constantly being eroded. Earners whose income doesn't match inflation (the real figure, rather than the false 'official' figure) also lose out. They may seem to be getting richer, as their income grows, but in reality they will be getting poorer. And everyone who pays tax will lose out. Tax thresholds do not usually rise with inflation. So stamp duty on house purchases affects an increasing number of people as house prices rise and the stamp duty thresholds remain the same. And since the point at which taxpayers find themselves liable for higher rates of tax tends to stay the same (or to rise nowhere near as much as inflation) the number of people paying higher tax rates is rising rapidly. You will probably not be surprised to learn that governments don't usually take inflation into account when helping itself to a share of your income. So, if you have a 6% income on your investments and tax rates are 40% you will pay 40% of your 6% to the Government. That leaves you with a 3.6% return. But if the official level of inflation is running at 5% then you are losing 1.4% a year. If real inflation is 10% you are losing 6.4% a year. You may think you are getting richer but in reality you are getting poorer.

How do you deal with coming inflation? Buy things that will retain their intrinsic value without decaying. Gold and good jewellery are traditional favourites.

There is a chapter on inflation in my book *Moneypower*.

Influenza

According to the BBC News website there were just 394 deaths due to flu in the UK between January and August 2020.

No one seemed to think this the slightest bit odd.

It did not apparently occur to anyone that in an average, ordinary sort of six month flu season the flu can affect one billion and kill up to 650,000 people.

In late 2020, the WHO announced that the flu had become rare and not seen in many parts of the world.

Informed consent

Doctors (and even governments) are legally obliged to provide their patients (and citizens) with all the available information before promoting or recommending any form of medical treatment. This is called the informed consent protocol. It is inconceivable that doctors or politicians anywhere would even contemplate trying to persuade patients to accept a drug therapy without first ensuring that they had been given all the necessary background information required to make an 'informed choice'.

And yet that is exactly what is happening now.

Suppressing the truth about treatments means that informed consent is an impossibility.

Insects

The Agenda 21 enthusiasts want us to eat more insects in the future. Indeed, insects will be a major part of our diet. In January 2021, the EU's food watchdog gave safety approval to human consumption of dried yellow mealworms (beetle larvae). Insects are now regularly eaten by humans in Africa, Asia and Latin America.

Intellectual property rights

According to Agenda 21 enthusiasts, intellectual property rights (copyrights and patents) are considered an obstacle to growth, since they give advantages and control to those holding the rights. However, what these people fail to understand is that abandoning intellectual property rights will mean the death of invention and creativity.

Interest rates

In the last few years, interest rates on savings have fallen to a level never previously known – not since money and banks were invented. Moreover, many banks and institutions have recently introduced negative interests – whereby people who have saved money have to pay a bank if they wish to open a deposit account. Traditionally, of course, savers were paid a small income on their money if they deposited it with a bank. The interest was a reward for thrift and for many a small deposit account with a bank, building society or some other institution was a valuable part of their pension fund.

Negative interest rates mean that savers, those who spend less than they earn and put part of their income away 'for a rainy day', or to help pay for a deposit on a house or as part of a pension plan, will be punished and their accumulated savings will shrink instead of growing. None of this is happening by accident. Those who are responsible for Agenda 21 want to take away our chances of acquiring a little wealth of our own because those who have some money (even if quite a small amount) also acquire a little independence. As we approach the moment when all deposits result in money going out of the deposit holder's account, rather than into it, the rate of interest being paid by institutions everywhere is crashing at an unprecedented rate. So, for example, in late September 2020, the British Government's savings agency, National Savings and Investments, announced that on 24th November 2020 the interest rate on its Income Bond would crash from 1.16% to 0.01%. This unprecedented fall made a mockery of the name of the investment since someone with £100,000 invested would receive an income of just £10 before tax.

None of this is happening by accident. Interest levels of 0% or below are designed to ensure that people have to spend their savings, sell their homes, downsize and impoverish themselves in order to stay alive.

Agenda 21 is supported by banks and hedge funds which are part of the global plan to impoverish the middle classes and bring everyone down to the same level. There is also a plan to prevent people leaving their money (either as cash, property, pension, investments or possessions) to relatives or friends or charities of their choice. The aim is to ensure that upon an individual's death all his resources will be absorbed by the State.

Low interest rates will be retained for as long as is necessary to ruin the wealth of all savers. Share accounts and pensions will be devastated – leaving only those with government pensions secure against poverty.

Later, when the savers have been financially destroyed, interest rates will be raised – probably quite dramatically to 10% or even more – in an attempt to control inflation and settle the economy. The result will be that most of those with mortgages will be unable to pay what they owe. They will lose their homes, and since the rise in mortgage rates will have pushed house prices down, most will be in negative equity when they are forced to sell. The result will be that they will be happy to move into one of the tiny flats built according to Agenda 21 in the large cities. Houses will be demolished on the grounds that they are not energy efficient.

An important, and widely endorsed, part of Agenda 21 is that no one should own anything. (It is not unreasonable to suppose that this rule will not apply to billionaires, politicians and Common Purpose apparatchiks.) Pope Francis has spoken out against private property.

Work is already underway to rob owners of their private property.

The number of laws and regulations making it nigh on impossible to sell many houses is growing rapidly. So, for example, home owners discovered some time ago that if they have Japanese knotweed growing in their garden, their house will be almost unsaleable. And more recently, flat owners have found that if their apartment is in a building which is clad with an inflammable material, they will not be able to sell their home until they have paid their share of removing and replacing the dangerous material. (This came after the Grenfell fire.) The whole building must be dealt with

and since the costs are extremely high, many flat owners are unable
or unwilling to find the necessary money for the required repairs.

Internet

The rush online which took place during 2020 was not an accident.
The acceleration in the number of people doing most or all their
shopping and banking online was the result of a deliberate plan.
Putting billions of people under house arrest was designed to help
destroy those bricks and mortar businesses which relied on
customers visiting their shops or offices.

There is no doubt that this rush towards lives run entirely on the
internet will continue in the years to come. The aim is not simply to
destroy businesses run offline but also to make us all dependent
upon the internet. The result of this dependence will be that we can
be easily isolated (by having our telephone connections cut off).

Everything that is put onto the internet is kept for ever by the
platforms owners. Facebook, for example, owns every piece of
information put onto its site; the company owns the copyright of
pictures and text. Even deleted material remains in the company's
servers to be used as the company sees fit.

Internet of things

As the 5G network expands, so we will all be increasingly exposed
to electromagnetic fields – which are known to damage the immune
system and cause neurological damage. (By 'are known to' I mean
'have been proven to').

Intersectionality

To the strange folk wandering through the byways of Agenda 21,
intersectionality (an ugly word if ever I saw one – as, incidentally,
are many of the words created by and for the Agenda 21 disciples) is
the theory that as individuals we are discriminated against and

oppressed by social identities such as race, sex and class. (They never mention age, of course, because old people don't count.)

Investment

In 2005, the United Nations devised its 'Principles for Responsible Investment'.

Banks, investment companies and pension funds largely ignored this nonsense but in 2020 (responding to the unscientific nonsense put forward by a young Swedish girl, a nonagenarian TV presenter and a member of the British Royal Family who travels everywhere by private jet – quite possibly with the lesser members of his entourage travelling in a second private jet) they started to fall over themselves to virtue signal and sign up to the UN principles, even though the intelligent ones admitted privately that the principles made no economic, business, scientific or environmental sense. It was merely mass hysteria. A modern version of St Vitus's dance. The Pied Piper of Hamlyn. The Music Man.

Jargon or buzz words

Public relations specialists and psychologists are constantly at work inventing and re-defining buzz words to promote Agenda 21. What these bits of jargon mean bears no resemblance to what they used to mean and what most people think they mean.

Jefferson (Thomas)

'When the people fear the government, there is tyranny. When the government fears the people, there is liberty.'

Jobs

The United Nations in 2020 said that 50% of all jobs are going to disappear and since it's the UN that produced the figure it's fair to say it was more of a forecast than a guess

Anyone looking for a job should perhaps concentrate on the world's fastest growing industry – the global warming fraud.

Johnson (Boris)

'It is time we had a grown up discussion about the optimum quantity of human beings in this country and on this planet.'

Journalists

Even by the end of 2020, many apparently intelligent journalists did not realise that what had happened during the year had been deliberate rather than accidental. Some blamed politicians and advisors for making mistakes (though none of what had happened was accidental or a result of poor thinking) and others genuinely seemed to believe that those questioning what had happened were merely conspiracy theorists. The quality of journalism plumbed new depths in 2020.

Judgements

We are all encouraged to make judgements about one another. If we buy something we are encouraged to give marks to the manufacturer, the retailer and, if the product was delivered, the person who did the delivering. Online we are constantly begged to give our views. Criticism is encouraged. If we have watched a video we can give a thumbs up or a thumbs down (in the way that the Roman citizens decided the fate of slaves in the amphitheatre). This rediscovered habit sometimes seems to be almost as cruel. Books and films are reviewed without being read or watched.

All this is training for our role in the new world of social credit.

The tragedy is that cowards will happily say in print, behind a nom de clavier, what they would never dare say to someone's face. That they are heartily encouraged to be hurtful is shameful and a reflection of our times. The young, the sensitive frequently find it too much to bear. Suicide is getting ever commoner, in part because of online abuse.

When comments are turned off (as they sometimes are, by video makers and so on who are exhausted, drained by the meaningless, ignorant abuse) these cowards cry censorship though truly only those with something real to say can be censored. The mindless abusers deserve to be eliminated in the same way that graffiti is removed from a wall.

Khayyam (Omar)

'The moving finger writes, and, having writ
Moves on, nor all your piety nor wit
Shall lure it back to cancel half a line
Nor all your tears wash out a word of it'

Kindness

We should be kind while there is still time.

Kissinger (Henry)

'Today, Americans would be outraged if US troops entered Los Angeles to restore order: tomorrow they will be grateful! This is especially true if they were told there was an outside threat from beyond, whether real or promulgated, that threatened our very existence. It is then that all peoples of the world will pledge with world leaders to deliver them from this evil. The one thing every man fears is the unknown. When presented with this scenario, individual rights will be willingly relinquished for the guarantee of

their well-being – being granted to them by their world governments.'
Henry Kissinger speaking at a Bilderberg meeting in France on May 21st 1992

Koire (Rosa)

'Agenda 21 is about destroying independence, culture, society, economy and human lives.'

Land

The Scottish government has already announced its intention to take land out of private ownership and into public ownership. There has been no talk of compensation. This is in line with the United Nation's Agenda 21.

Laws

The European Union always used to call them rules or regulations but in my book if I can be fined or sent to prison for not obeying a rule or a regulation then the rule or regulation is a law.

New laws are appearing rapidly. Some are local, some are regional, some are national and soon some will be international. Everything we do is now governed by legislation and the new laws are often enforced by private security firms. The reasoning is always the same: in a time of national crisis people must obey the laws.

Since the beginning of 2020, governments everywhere have been busy making new laws with unprecedented enthusiasm. These new laws, however, are not designed to protect people or property (the usual function of laws). Governments are no longer interested in arresting traditional law breakers such as murderers, thieves or fraudsters. Those law breakers act with impunity. Only around 7% of all crimes in England and Wales lead to anyone being charged – let alone convicted. Soft drug possession, and even dealing, have been effectively decriminalised. Only 5% of thefts lead to prosecution. Only 1.4% cases of rape lead to a prosecution.

The new laws which have been introduced are designed to control ordinary, law-abiding citizens. Police and prosecutors are taking these laws very seriously.

Leaflets

Those newspapers, television and radio which make up mainstream media have been bought with massive amount of advertising revenue.

So, we cannot use mainstream media to share the truth.

And our use of the internet is massively limited.

But the enemy is moving fast and, through its control of the mainstream media (which must now include much of the internet, such as YouTube) has a huge reach.

We need to move fast.

And we need to widen our reach. Things are never going to go back to the real normal unless and until we make that happen.

Distributing fact packed leaflets is an excellent way to help share the truth. It's something that worked well for Napoleon Bonaparte when he escaped from the Island of Elba and, faced with the French army, turned them from enemies to followers with a skilfully written leaflet.

Lefties

Lefty loonies are behind Agenda 21, Wikipedia corruption and the global warming cult nonsense.

Liberal

The 'term' liberal has been redefined by usage and now refers to a leftist extremist.

Licences and certificates

All those licences and certificates we need? They were planned years ago to disrupt and force us into living in fear. They were designed to be expensive and disruptive. If you don't have the right licence then you can't work. And then when you have one licence they want another and another. It's reminiscent of that scene in 'Horse Feathers' when Chico Marx persuades Groucho Marx that he needed to keep buying yet more tipster books if he were to succeed in his gambling ambitions.

Lies

Every few minutes another piece of madness darkens my day.

I discovered that we are advised that if we find someone who has collapsed and is not breathing then the first thing we should do is to put a cloth of some kind over the victim's face so that we, as Good Samaritans, reduce any risk of infection.

This seems rather like overkill to me since we have already established that the patient isn't actually breathing.

But, hey, I understand that the official policy these days is to kill patients who are frail, weak, disabled, elderly, injured or just plain nervous.

The media, of course, has poked and pushed and prodded at us all – printing every threat made by the politicians as if it had come down from heaven carved in stone.

'In several years sitting through every important debate in the House of Commons,' wrote former political correspondent Auberon Waugh, 'I never consciously heard anyone tell a word of truth.'

Waugh was enraged by the lies, the deceits and the manipulations of politicians.

'The role of journalists,' wrote Auberon Waugh, 'is to ridicule, humiliate and generally torment politicians, pour scorn on everything they propose to do and laugh at them when they do it.'

I wonder what Mr Waugh would think of the way the world's journalists have crept and bowed to the ubiquitous Mr Gates. I don't think there are any journalists left working in the mainstream media. There certainly aren't any at the BBC.

Topping it all are the stupid fake fact checkers who spend their days spreading nonsense around the internet and denying obvious truths. Most so-called fact checking is done by or for prejudiced organisations with a commercial agenda. And most of the checkers appear to be teenagers who don't know how to spell research let alone do it.

Life expectation

In the early part of the 20th century, millions of people lived in damp, cramped conditions and had very little decent food to eat.

Drug companies, and their many supporters in the medical establishment, like to claim that their products are responsible for improved life expectation since those days but the figures prove that to be a falsehood. Drugs have changed our lives in many ways but, with the exception of antibiotics such as penicillin, first introduced just in time for the Second World War, they have not had a major impact and it is not difficult to argue that many of the preparations put on the market have done considerably more harm than good.

It is, for example, difficult to claim that benzodiazepine tranquillisers have done anything to improve the quality of human life. Prescription drugs such as benzodiazepines, and some painkillers, are the causes of the biggest dependency problem in the world.

Even the good drugs, the antibiotics, are now often not as useful as they once were. Overprescribing and the wholesale, routine use of antibiotics on farms have meant that antibiotics which once saved lives are now often useless.

Doubters will, of course, claim that life expectation today is much greater than it was and that, therefore, medical care must have improved.

This is a fallacious argument.

If you look at the figures it is clear that life expectation rose over a century ago when the number of babies and infants dying fell considerably. A little over a century ago it was commonplace for a woman to have half a dozen babies but for only two of them to survive. It was these infant deaths which lowered life expectation figures. If lots of babies die before they are one-year-old then the average life expectation is brought down dramatically.

If one person dies at birth, and another dies at 100 years of age, their combined average life expectancy will be 50 years. But if most babies survive then the average life expectation rises equally dramatically. Back in Victorian times, and even earlier, humans who survived infancy and childhood commonly lived into their 70s, 80s and beyond.

The absence of relatively clean drinking water, and proper sewage systems, meant that serious infections were big killers in the 19th century. And it was infectious diseases such as cholera which meant that infant mortality figures were appallingly high. The death rates fell notably when fairly clean, uncontaminated drinking water supplies were introduced and proper facilities built for dealing with sewage. If you look at the figures it was not medicine which helped reduce the number of deaths from infectious diseases – the death rates were largely falling long before modern drugs and inoculations were introduced – but better living conditions.

And since the start of the 21st century, life expectation in most so-called developed countries has been falling not rising. Chronic diseases, mental illnesses, cancer and just about everything else have been rising. Infant mortality rates are no longer as good as they were. Dementia is endemic and childhood diseases such as ADHD and autism are commonplace. The incidence of diabetes (particularly maturity onset diabetes) and asthma and allergies have all risen.

Why?

Well, there are several simple answers.

First, the quality of food being eaten has fallen dramatically. And many people eat far too much.

Second, nearly everyone now takes prescription medicines, or over the counter medicines, on a daily basis. Side effects from the prescription medicines go unnoticed because doctors don't look for them and don't care.

Third, the number of carcinogens in our environment, in the soil, in the air and in our homes has risen.

Fourth, the amount of exercise most people take has fallen. Machines have made it easy for humans to sit around and take little or no exercise.

Fifth, the amount of stress has rocketed.

Sixth, drinking water is heavily contaminated with chemical pollutants and with dangerous residues of prescription drugs (including chemotherapy drugs, so dangerous that if spilt they have to be cleaned up as though they were nuclear waste) tranquillisers, sleeping tablets, antibiotics and hormones.

Seventh immune systems have been damaged by stress, poor sleep, poor diet and absurd inoculation programmes.

Light bulbs

People in Europe spend their days in artificial light produced by LED bulbs and the special new mercury bulbs forced upon citizens throughout Europe by the European Union. It is widely accepted that the incandescent light bulbs which were banned were far more relaxing than their replacements.

In another of its crazy attempts to 'save the planet' and prove itself to be stuffed full of environmentally-conscious bureaucrats and politicians, the EU decided to ban the sale of traditional incandescent light bulbs – the ones which have the tungsten filaments which dangle uselessly when the bulb has blown (or been dropped).

Consumers have been forced to replace old-fashioned light bulbs with new compact fluorescent bulbs (known as CFLs to the average acronym-happy eurocrat). These, they claim, use only a fifth of the energy.

There are, inevitably, a few problems.

First, the new light bulbs burn out faster if turned on and off a lot. So the bulbs will last longer if they are left switched on when no one is in the room. This wastes energy but reduces your expenditure on bulbs.

Second, the lighting produced by the new bulbs is so dim that most people won't be able to read by them. Angela Merkel, the German politician who put forward the proposal that we should all use these new bulbs, has admitted that because the 'energy-saving' bulbs she uses in her flat take some time to warm up, she often has 'a bit of a problem' when she is looking for something she has 'dropped on the carpet'. The result will be lots more people falling over and breaking limbs and lots more people suffering from headaches. The consequence will be that many people will simply buy more lamps and use two or three bulbs where they previously used one bulb.

Third, the new bulbs are much heavier than old-fashioned bulbs. This means that they will take more energy to transport.

Fourth, the new bulbs are much larger. They won't fit into all light fittings – so vast numbers of perfectly good light fittings will have to be thrown away.

Fifth, they cost up to 20 times as much as the old bulbs.

Sixth, the CFL light bulbs produce a much harsher, less relaxing light. Moreover, they often don't produce a nice, steady light (like an incandescent bulb) but flicker. They flicker at 50 times a second. If you try to read with one of the new bulbs there is a chance that your head will start to swim. Will the new bulbs trigger fits? I have no idea but I wouldn't bet against it. They will, at least, cause 'discomfort'. It seems pretty certain that the new EU-approved bulbs will cause migraines and dizziness.

Seventh, because they flicker, the new bulbs can make fast moving machine parts look stationary. How many limbs will be lost as a result of this?

Eighth, normal CFLs cannot be used with dimmer switches or electronically triggered security lights. Dimmer switches and electronically triggered security lights will have to be thrown away – wasting vast amounts of energy.

Ninth, the EU approved bulbs cannot be used in ovens, freezers or microwave ovens because they don't work if the temperature is too low or too high.

Tenth, the new allegedly low energy bulbs take ten times as much energy to manufacture as the old bulbs.

Eleventh, CFLs need more ventilation than standard bulbs and so cannot be used in any enclosed light fitting.

Twelfth, the EU-approved light bulbs use toxic materials including mercury vapour. This is a bit of a problem because the EU has banned products containing mercury vapour from landfill sites. Used CFLs will, therefore, have to be collected and disposed of separately. Experts advise that you telephone your local sanitation or refuse department if you wish to dispose of a used CFL bulb. The British Government has admitted that the bulbs contain mercury which is a deadly poison and has warned: 'If a low-energy bulb is smashed, the room needs to be vacated for at least 15 minutes. A vacuum cleaner should not be used to clear up the debris, and care taken not to inhale the dust. Use rubber gloves, and put the broken bulb into a sealed plastic bag, which should be taken to the local council for disposal. Unbroken used bulbs can be taken back to the retailer if the owner is a member of the Distributor Takeback Scheme. Otherwise, many local waste disposal sites now have the facilities to safely collect and dispose of old bulbs. You will, of course, probably have to drive to the disposal site (which will take up fuel and energy as well as time). You will have to do this every time a bulb is broken. There will almost certainly be a disposal charge because getting rid of dangerous light bulbs without being able to bury them will be quite a problem.

Thirteenth, to work at their best, CFLs must be kept on pretty well continuously. This means that if you are going to get the best out of your new EU-approved light bulb you will have to get used to sleeping with the light on.

Fourteenth, the new light bulbs which the EU is forcing us to use will aggravate a variety of health problems. Patients with lupus, an auto-immune disease, will suffer from many symptoms, including pain. Patients with light sensitive disorders will suffer more. The new bulbs could trigger eczema-like skin reactions and could produce skin reactions that lead to cancer.

Fifteenth, some CFLs need breaking in for about 100 hours before their brightness level stabilises. So, every time you install a new bulb you may have to put up with potentially serious health problems (headaches, tripping over) for 100 hours or so.

Sixteenth, CFL bulbs may interfere with the remote control for your television or other equipment – and may cause static noises on your radio or cordless telephone. One expert advises that if this happens you should switch off the light. Another has found that a cardboard tube fashioned from an old lavatory roll centre and glued onto the relevant, sensitive part of the television will minimise or eradicate the problem. (I do not recommend that you try this at home. Electrical appliances get hot. Bits of cardboard tend to be flammable.)

Lincoln (Abraham)

'Government of the people, by the people, for the people.'
(From Lincoln's Gettysburg address)

Magna Carta

The original idea of the Magna Carta was 'no taxation without representation'. (The people of Boston who didn't want their tea may have thought they were being original but they weren't.) The Magna Carta also introduced the idea of expelling from England all mercenaries who had come to England to do harm and introduced the concept of habeas corpus – where no one can be held in custody indefinitely without a trial. The Magna Carta gave the English people basic rights as individuals and gave England rights as a nation. Parliament was devised as a means of obtaining popular consent.

Malfeasance

Malfeasance (doing something illegal) particularly applies to public officials. It is defined as wilful and inappropriate action or the giving of intentionally incorrect advice.

The whole of the British Government's policy since March 2020 has been false. The house arrests were never necessary. The closure of hospitals and hospital departments was never necessary. The dumping of old people in care homes was never necessary. Around the world millions of people will die because of what seemed like mistakes.

But I don't think that they were mistakes. I don't believe those people died through simple incompetence.

None of the government's advice was appropriate. None of it is defensible.

The same is true of governments in the US and elsewhere around the world.

And though I am no lawyer it seems to me that there must be a case that our governments and their advisors should be taken to court and charged with malfeasance or misfeasance – whichever seems most appropriate.

In the UK, I hope and believe that within months our disreputable government ministers will soon be starting long prison sentences. Government advisors will also spend their last years making number plates or sewing mailbags. Staff at the BBC will not be immune since the BBC is in essence a state broadcaster and has a responsibility to provide fair and balanced information. The penalties for malfeasance or misfeasance can be very severe and involve many years in prison. Editors and news editors should prepare for a long stay at Her Majesty's Pleasure.

And lower level civil servants should be worried too. Defendants at Nuremburg learned that 'I was following orders' doesn't cut it as a defence. Thousands of snotty bureaucrats, brutal police officers and dancing health workers are going to have to acquire a taste for porridge.

In addition, I suspect, several million people will be entitled to take legal action for damages. Those who have lost relatives to this crime will be able to sue for millions. And those whose businesses have been ruined will also be able to sue.

Meat

I have for years argued that you cannot be an environmentalist and eat meat. I never expected this philosophy to catch on quite so suddenly.

Media

There is, sadly, now a huge amount of evidence showing that in recent years most branches of the mass market media around the world have been taken over to promote messages which suit governments, commercial entities and lobbyists working for them. It saddens me to write this for I have spent much of my life writing books, columns and articles and making television and radio programmes.

I no longer believe that any part of the mainstream media will ever again produce any proper journalism. Real exposes are a thing of the past. Even big book publishers have become embedded within the political establishment.

Despite this criticism, a few books have been published (usually by very small publishers) which show just how the media is now controlled and how the messages we read, see and hear often bear little resemblance to the truth.

Larry Beinhart's book, *Fog Facts*, which was published in 2005, is subtitled *Searching for truth in the Land of Spin* and the search he describes is a harrowing one. (Beinhart's novel, *Wag the Dog* was turned into a film with the same name starring Robert de Niro and Dustin Hoffman. It provides a magnificently ironic look at how the media can be used to deceive and manipulate.)

'One of the most disturbing trends in the years since 9/11 is that there no longer seem to be any consequences for political lying,' writes Beinhart. 'The secret Downing Street memo, secret and strictly personal, revealed – at the very least – that the head of British intelligence had been informed by his Washington counterparts that the White House was cooking the books on the information that they used to create a war in Iraq.'

And he adds: 'The failure of the media to take responsibility is the reason that political lying – especially in the soft-core, public relations style that misleads – has no penalties anymore.'

By 2020, it had become clear that the media was no longer merely complicit in allowing politicians to lie but it was actually contributing to the deceit, allowing itself to be used as a propaganda tool and no longer trustworthy in any meaningful sense of the word.

Udo Ulfkotte's book, *Presstitutes* is boldly subtitled *Embedded in the Pay of the CIA* and is an account of the way journalists are bribed and used as intelligence assets – receiving favours and speaking fees from those whom they please. It's a revealing story about the corruption of the mainstream media. The real point is that if journalists don't stay on message they can lose their jobs – and their perks. Ulfkotte's startling conclusion is that the entire political and media network has been bought. 'The greatest corruption is at the highest levels'.

'A paper that claims to be independent when it actually serves hidden interests is guilty of fraud,' writes Ulfkotte, who claims that media corruption may actually be worse than political corruption.

It is certainly not difficult to argue that media corruption is the most potent weapon in the hands of the politicians and billionaires attempting to force through the social credit and other hideous aspects of Agenda 21.

Ulfkotte's solution is quite simple: we should simply stop buying or using the material produced by corrupt publishing and broadcasting organisations. (In the UK, this means finding a way to refuse to pay the BBC licence fee – legally, of course.)

'When enough of us stop buying the products offered by these media houses, when we no longer click on their internet articles and we switch off their television or radio programmes – at some point these journalists will have to start producing something of value for their fellow citizens, or they're going to be out of a job,' writes Ulfkotte.

Medical ethics

There is no such thing as medical ethics or medical confidentiality these days. When I qualified as a doctor in around 1970, I was told that I could take the Hippocratic Oath if I wanted to. It was optional. I doubt if many modern medical students have any idea what the Oath contains. The General Medical Council (a quango masquerading as a charity masquerading as a government department masquerading as a private fee earning company) long ago decided that the Hippocratic Oath was out of date and should be tossed out so patients who think doctors still take the Hippocratic Oath (which contains the well-known phrase 'first do no harm') should know that the Oath was cancelled and that doctors no longer take it. Doctors are no longer allowed to respect patient confidentiality.

Mencken (H. L.)

'The urge to save humanity is always a false front for the urge to rule it.'
'The whole aim of practical politics is to keep the populace alarmed (and hence clamorous to be led to safety) by menacing it with an endless series of hobgoblins, all of them imaginary.'

Mental illness

For many years there has been a rising interest in the incidence of mental illness in Western societies. In the UK, the royal family (particularly Princes William and Harry) have talked of little else but their own mental health, their stresses and so on and they and other members of the royal family seem to feel that, although they have not bothered to go through any formal training, they are entitled to offer help to those with mental illness. Following their bizarre example, countless others are now offering their own versions of 'help' in online programmes, and small fortunes will doubtless be made by some of them.

Individuals have been encouraged to consider themselves mentally ill and to ask for medical treatment – invariably pharmacological in form. As a result the number of citizens addicted to mind-numbing tranquillisers and anti-depressants has been rising rapidly in recent years. In the late 1960s and early 1970s, the benzodiazepine group of tranquillisers became popular and fashionable among both prescribers and patients. It seems clear that this process was part of the overall plan to make a large portion of the population dependent upon drug companies and to numb them so that they became more subservient.

Microchips

Pet owners are accustomed to having their pets marked with an implanted chip. In some parts of the world it is illegal to have a dog which has not been microchipped. But the same thing is happening with people too. People in Sweden, Japan, Russia and even parts of America now have chips under their skin. The chip is usually put under the skin in the hand so that it can easily be waived under a scanner as form of identification – and to help the owner make purchases without using a credit card. In some cases, however, the chip is placed just below the hairline on an individual's forehead (and close to the frontal lobe) since the changes in body temperature which occur most notably in that area can be used to recharge the chip. In experiments, chips have been implanted which can be used to control or 'improve' the brain.

In the USA, the 1986 Immigration Reform and Control Act gave the President the power to force citizens to accept any type of ID (such as microchip) which is 'considered necessary'.

Middle classes

The people who will suffer most from Agenda 21 will be the middle classes. The rich will avoid the high taxes by moving to islands or large ships. The very poor (particularly those in Africa) will die unnoticed and un-mourned.

Mill (John Stuart)

'Over himself, over his own body and mind, the individual is sovereign.'

Mind control

There was much excitement among the easily excited (and fairly ignorant) when American billionaire Elon Musk showed how he could use a small remote control device to control an animal which had a receiver implanted in its head.

The surprise was that anyone took any notice of this.

During the 1950s, a Yale University psychiatrist Dr Jose Delgado examined mind control methods as part of the MK ULTRA program. It had been known for a century and a half that if wires are poked into the brain and an electric charge is passed through them, there will be different responses from different parts of the brain.

After his experiments, Delgado concluded: 'Physical control of many brain functions is a demonstrated fact…it is even possible to create and follow intentions…by electronic stimulation of specific cerebral structures, movements can be induced by radio command…by remote control.'

That was nearly three quarters of a century before Elon Musk conducted his much publicised 'breakthrough' experiment.

Indeed, if Musk or the journalists who wrote about his experiment, had done a little research they would have been able to read about Delgado's experiment in my book, *Paper Doctors* which was published in 1977.

This is what I wrote:

'In the 1950s, Dr Delgado of the Yale University School of Medicine showed that two cats, normally quite friendly, could be made to fight fiercely if electrodes implanted in their brains were given impulses. Even when it continually lost its fights, the smaller of the two cats continued to be aggressive when stimulated. In one dramatic experiment, Dr Delgado wired a bull with electrodes and then planted himself in the middle of a bullring with a cape and a small transmitter. The bull charged but was stopped by Dr Delgado pressing a button on his transmitter. The bull screeched to a halt inches away from its target. Dr Delgado has reported that: 'Animals with implanted electrodes in their brains have been made to perform a variety of responses with predictable reliability as if they were electronic toys under human control.'

'Similar experiments have been performed with human beings. The patients selected had all proved dangerous and had shown that they had uncontrollable tempers. By electronic stimulation, every patient was controlled. More detailed accounts of these experiments can be read in *Physical Control of the Mind* by J.M.R.Delgado.'

Today, of course, the receptors required for the control of the human brain do not need to be implanted surgically. Indeed, modern receptors are so small that they could be placed in the body via a far less intrusive method – an injection, for example.

Mindspace

The British Government Cabinet Office and the Institute for Government, funds a programme called Mindspace which deals with ways to use behavioural theory to influence public policy by creating incentives, using people's habits and taking advantages of the egos of citizens. The scheme is, of course, funded by the very people who are the targets – taxpayers and voters.

The Mindspace programme includes ways of promoting pro-environment behaviour and a 'good society'. This is, in simple terms, brainwashing. The Mindspace scheme is full of the sort of tricks used by advertising copy writers but taken much further along the line towards blatant manipulation and control.

The Mindspace policy came to the fore when the UK Government was desperate to find new ways to control public behaviour. It was thanks to Mindspace that millions of people were forced to adopt behavioural patterns which did them far more harm than good.

Mink

The Danish Government ordered the killing of 15 million mink over fears of a viral mutation.

I didn't realise that there were that many mink in the world, let alone in Denmark. What do they do with them all? Is there really that much of a demand for mink coats these days? I thought they were rather old-fashioned and that mink coat lovers would find enough second hand, or previously enjoyed, coats to keep them going.

The slaughter is all part of the plan to get rid of all domestic animals – both farm animals and pets.

Modern monetary theory

Those who believe in modern monetary theory argue that debt doesn't matter because central banks can always print as much money as they like and use taxes to slow things down if they suspect that inflation is growing.

The problem with this theory is that inflation always comes very quickly. By the time the economists, bankers and politicians have spotted a problem, it is too late to do anything about it. And inflation then runs away out of control.

Modern monetary theory will lead to chaos, hyperinflation and economic destruction. It is a tool in the hands of those promoting the Great Reset and Agenda 21.

Motor cars

The plan is to eradicate private motoring. The excuse for this is that private cars use up energy which cannot be spared. Motorists are blamed for damaging the environment and are, it is claimed, a major cause of global warming. There are huge taxes on buying a car, running it and fuelling it. Car parking becomes ever more difficult. It becomes increasingly difficult and expensive to take a car into a city. Toll roads are being introduced to make the cost of motoring ever more expensive.

In London, Sadiq Khan, the mayor, wanted to close roads, make more cycle lanes and make the English capital completely car free. Taxi drivers had fought hard against the ban. A judge found that the proposal did not take into account the needs of the elderly or disabled who 'could not be reasonably expected to cycle, walk or use public transport'.

The mayor of London also wants to widen pavements to ensure that pedestrians have more space.

Around the rest of the country, so called 'low traffic neighbourhoods' have been set up by councils as part of the green revolution intended to keep people separated in the long term.

Many of the changes which are already apparent are designed to make life unpleasant if not downright difficult for motorists. So, for example, town and city centres are filled with strange pieces of road furniture which create traffic jams (and, rather ironically, more pollution since stop-go motoring massively increases the use of fuel and the production of waste gases), speed limits are lowered to create more traffic jams (once again this causes vehicles to use up more energy), road taxes rise massively (except for electric cars, which still use the roads and which have been proven to require just as much, if not more, energy as cars using the traditional internal combustion engine) and so on and so on.

In the UK, the Government is planning massive changes to the Highway Code, including a hierarchy of road users to ensure that those who are believed to do the greatest harm have the greatest responsibility to reduce the danger they post to others. Car drivers will, for example, have to give way to pedestrians waiting to cross the road – wherever they may be standing – and new safe speed limits and distances will be imposed on motorists overtaking cyclists and horse riders. All this will slow everything down, reduce productivity and result in far more declining businesses. Just what the Agenda 21 enthusiasts are rooting for.

In late 2020, the UK Government announced that it was going to make it illegal to sell diesel or petrol motor cars from 2030. The previous, arbitrary cut-off date was 2040 and bringing this forward by a decade will be ruinous for car companies and those involved in the servicing and repair of vehicles driven by internal combustion engines.

The big question, however, is where does the Government think the electricity will come from. Huge amounts of electricity will be required to power all the electric vehicles it is expecting to replace petrol and diesel driven vehicles.

In fact, of course, there obviously won't be anywhere near enough electricity to go around. The UK is already on the edge of a major electricity shortfall, and electric cars use up vast amounts of electricity.

To deal with this problem, the Government will dramatically limit the number of private motor vehicles allowed and it will introduce massive road taxes on electric cars. By cutting the supplies to electric cars at unpredictable times, more and more drivers will be forced to stop using their vehicles. Existing petrol and diesel cars will be taxed out of existence. The impossibility of running a private vehicle will force people to move out of rural areas.

The long-term plan is to stop private vehicle ownership and to force people into towns and cities so that they don't need to travel to work or to the shops.

In February 2021, it was announced that motorists in the UK would be given £3,000 if they gave up their cars. The £3,000 would be available to spend on public transport, bicycles and electric scooters. The elderly and frail who have no access to public transport, and who are too unsure of themselves to ride bicycles or scooters, will simply have to stay at home or move into flats in cities.

Multiculturalism

Multiculturalism was introduced as an early attempt to destroy nationalism. The bizarre and unpopular millennial celebrations held in London were an early version of Agenda 21 – designed to help eradicate English nationalism.

Anyone who opposes multiculturalism is automatically denounced as a racist.

Murakami (Haruki)

'Everyone, deep in their hearts, is waiting for the end of the world to come.'

Named person

The Scottish Government has a policy called 'Getting it right for every child' (which inevitably has its own acronym – GIRFEC). The idea is to assign a state guardian to every person born in Scotland through its named person scheme.

Sadly for Agenda 21 cultists, this nonsense was blocked by the Supreme Court which showed a momentary and not entirely characteristic brush with common sense. The nonsense will doubtless return and will be revitalised.

The idea is that a named person, appointed by the State, will be a clear point of contact if a child or young person wants support. As each child grows older their contact will change, from a health visitor to a head teacher. In large schools it is likely that the head teacher will be the named person for more than a thousand young pupils. I feel sure that head teachers will welcome this extra responsibility.

Nanny state

The nanny state has been developing for many decades. The basic idea is to make us dependent on the State, to do what we are told, to accept that the Government knows best and that it is working in our best interests.

In Britain, the State now provides everything for over a quarter of the population, and this proportion is rising rapidly. There are millions of people who grew up in a household where the only source of finance was the State.

As an aside, the Scottish Government also wants to introduce a new Hate Crime and Public Order Bill which will make virtually all commentary, criticism and humour illegal.

Nationalism

There is no place for nationalism in the New World Order. Our new controllers, the ones who are planning a world government, will eradicate all signs of nationalism as both irrelevant and dangerous. Agenda 21 is specifically opposed to nationalism.

And so, for example, campaigners who would vote for an independent Scotland and renewed membership of the European Union are voting for two complete opposites. I wonder how many Scottish voters understand this. It appears that no one at the Scottish

National Party has worked this out since the SNP seems to be keen to promote Agenda 21 ideas, to support the European Union and yet at the same time promote Scottish independence. However, if Scotland rejoins the EU then Scotland will be no more than a region within the EU. Whatever happens, if Agenda 21 succeeds there will never be an independent Scotland.

Individual nations, however big or however small, will soon be gone. Not even the most patriotic of citizens will be able to save them.

In a very short time there will be no flags, no nations, no anthems. There will be one world, one flag, one anthem, one army, one government and one leader.

New normal

People have been taught to believe that things will go back to normal if they do as they are told. But things will never go back to normal unless we overthrow the people who are trying to force through the new normal. The new normal they have planned for us will consist of 2020 repeated endlessly.

Niemoller (Martin)

'First they came for the socialists, and I did not speak out – because I was not a socialist. Then they came for the trade unionists, and I did not speak out – because I was not a trade unionist. Then they came for the Jews, and I did not speak out – because I was not a Jew. Then they came for me – and there was no one left to speak for me.'

Nil by mouth

The letters NBM stand for 'Nil by Mouth' and that's now one of the commonest signs you'll see on the bed of an older patient. It's part of the official, legal and government-approved Liverpool Care Pathway, and it means that the patient is being officially starved to death. It's the dehydration which probably causes most discomfort of course.

When the letters NBM are put on a patient's chart, or at the end of their bed, it usually means that a doctor or a nurse (probably only half-trained) has decided that it is time for that patient to die –by being starved to death or killed by a lack of fluids. Decisions of this type used to be made by a team of experienced doctors. Today, these decisions are made by junior doctors or nurses.

According to the UK Statistics Authority, 345 patients in British hospitals and British care homes died of thirst during the first part of 2020.

Non-governmental organisation (NGO)

You're probably not going to believe this, but a non-governmental organisation is a non-profit corporation that is independent from government control. NGOs sit comfortably between governments and private companies. There are pretty well no controls over what an NGO can do and although they aren't supposed to make a profit, the staff do very well, thank you very much. Huge salaries, huge pensions and huge expense accounts make life very good for the employees of most NGOs. Employees sometimes don't pay much, if anything, in tax (though they're supposed to be caring for the world and ostensibly trying to make it a better place).

Mind you, United Nations staff don't believe in paying tax either.

Offence

We are being taught that we must take great offence at even the smallest slight. This is so that very few people dare to speak their mind and we are all constantly afraid of causing offence and getting into serious trouble.

Oil

The global warming cultists want us to stop using oil (and other fossil fuels).

They want to prevent us using oil for several reasons. They want to stop us travelling and they want to keep us trapped in new smart cities. By pretending that fossil fuels are causing global warming, they can persuade us that in order to save the planet we must no longer use oil, coal or gas. Stopping the use of oil will have a number of other advantages. It will push up prices generally (and therefore impoverish those who own property or have savings), it will damage pension funds and investment accounts (impoverishing the middle classes) and it will, paradoxically, help wreck the planet by forcing us to rely on electricity (which cannot be made easily or efficiently by wind or solar power). Banning oil will also force us to use more biofuels –fuel made from food. Turning more of our food supplies into fuel will speed up the rate at which starvation reduces the world population.

Pressure groups working with the global warming cultists (many of whom have no understanding of the consequences of their actions) are trying hard to force big oil companies into abandoning fossil fuels and using their income to put up solar panels and other nonsenses. Two of the world's biggest oil companies, Shell and BP, seem embarrassed and ashamed to be selling oil. Both are spending much money on 'green' sources of energy (which will probably be expensive and fruitless) and abandoning oil exploration programmes.

If the pressure groups succeed in forcing oil companies to stop taking oil out of the ground, the result will be disaster – with no transport on road, sea or air and billions of deaths due to starvation and cold.

Global warming mythologists use every opportunity to warn investors that oil, gas and coal in the ground will become 'stranded assets' since there will be no role for fossil fuels in the 'new' world. However, the fossil fuels will only become 'stranded assets' if billions of people are prepared to starve or freeze to death.

There is, I fear, a misunderstanding about how important oil is, and has been, to every aspect of our way of life.

Our modern civilisation is built on oil. Oil gave us cheap energy. And cheap energy gave us our wealth, our progress and the complexity of the world we live in. Oil gave us modern farming.

The absence of oil will take away our wealth.

However, instead of drifting back to a 19th century life, where fields were ploughed by horses and local communities made their own decisions, we will find ourselves living in a real nightmare: a complete collapse of society. Just as previous civilisations have completely collapsed, throwing their worlds into barbarism, so the same will happen to us. Our children will live in their history – a history no longer taught in schools.

To the Agenda 21 supporters this will not be a disaster. It will be success.

Operation lockstep

In 2010, the Rockefeller Foundation (which, like so many organisations, describes itself as a major philanthropic society) organised a scenario planning exercise. It wasn't secret but it wasn't terribly public either.

The lockstep scenario was one of four scenarios presented by the Rockefeller Foundation, and it dealt with a zoonotic viral pandemic that killed millions of people around the world. The Lockstep described 'a world of tighter top-down government control and more authoritarian leadership, with limited innovation and growing citizen pushback.'

In what was effectively a war game, the new virus killed 20% of the population and had a deadly effect on industry, tourism, economies and supply chains. Shops were closed and empty for many months. China imposed mandatory quarantines and sealed its border and these policies saved many lives. Western countries were too lax and there were many more deaths. Around the world, political leaders ordered their citizens to have their body temperature taken at public places such as railway stations and shops. At the end of the pandemic the control measures which had been introduced were kept and intensified to prevent a future outbreak. Citizens around the world gave up their privacy and accepted mandatory biometric IDs – all in order to be safer and to regain some of their lost stability. States became more controlling and political leaders were free to introduce new laws as they felt appropriate. Millions were imprisoned in their homes and mandatory health screenings became commonplace.

It is difficult to find much difference between the scenario the Rockefeller Foundation dreamt up and what happened as a result of the fraud of 2020.

The Foundation even foresaw that there would be sporadic incidents of conflict as individuals who had lost freedom, status and opportunity objected to the new laws. There was also a rise in post-traumatic stress. Medical martial law was introduced in many countries and there was an increase in what was called 'syndromic surveillance'.

The scenario described here is extraordinarily similar to Event 201, a planning event coordinated by the World Economic Forum, the Bill and Melinda Gates Foundation and the Michael Bloomberg School of Public Health at Johns Hopkins University's Center for Health Security in 2019.

Event 201 centred on a pandemic which was said to kill 65 million people and seemed to imply the need for much 'help' from large corporations.

Both scenarios involved the loss of democracy and freedom in a world with behavioural, medical and digital surveillance and control and, of course, the introduction of mandatory treatment in a feudal world where the State had all the power and the individual had none.

You could, of course, argue that these scenarios were merely well thought out predictions. But if they had been just that, wouldn't you expect the organisers to have promoted them at the time and to have been proud of their foresight?

Orwell (George)

'During times of universal deceit, telling the truth becomes a revolutionary act.'
'Like all other modern people, the English are in process of being numbered, labelled, conscripted, 'coordinated'. But the pull of their impulses is in the other direction, and the kind of regimentation that can be imposed on them will be modified in consequence.'

Other deaths

In the UK, between March and September of 2020 the incidence of a number of serious diseases rocketed. And the deaths from those serious diseases also rose dramatically. The number of deaths from diabetes rose by 86%. The number of deaths from bowel cancer went up by 46%. The number of deaths from breast cancer went up by 47%. The number of deaths from prostate cancer rose by 53%. All these extra deaths were partly a result of hospitals or hospital departments being closed and partly a result of the fact that the Government and the media had created so much fear that people were frightened to seek medical help or enter a hospital.

Outcome based education

The aim of 'outcome based education' is to indoctrinate children to accept life in what is, in effect, a global collective with the community the only thing that matters. Children are taught to be obedient, to work in groups, to see themselves and their parents as a threat to the planet on which they live, to reject confrontation, avoid thinking and control their imaginations. Young people learn to be dependent upon government benefit schemes (such as the furloughing schemes introduced in 2020) and to take a completely different attitude to their parents towards work, property, belongings and ambition. Students are taught to give the correct answers to tests – and never to think for themselves or to be creative. Young people are taught to accept the communitarian idea and to abandon individual rights.

Overpopulation

The myth that the world is overpopulated has been popular for decades. The truth is that the world is perfectly capable of providing enough food for a population of more than seven billion. The problem today is not a shortage of food but the fact that the food is frequently in the wrong place with the result that food is frequently wasted in some countries while millions starve in other parts of the world. Food production could also be increased by introducing better, simpler farming methods. Indeed, it is easier to argue that the world is under populated than that it is over populated.

The Agenda 21 followers believe the world needs far fewer people – and would like to remove 90% of the global population.

However, once individual nations start reducing their populations, how will the individual leaders trust one another?

Say, for example, that every national leader agreed that to start with he would reduce his country's population by a modest 50%, how would they all know that the other leaders would do as they had promised? After all, politicians are not known for their honesty or their reliability. And arms reductions have never proceeded smoothly.

What if someone like President Putin of Russia decides that while every other leader is reducing their population, he will only pretend to reduce the Russian population? That could give him a huge advantage over other countries. He could end up with a population bigger than the rest of the world – and total control.

Incidentally, the individuals arguing that the world is over populated do not appear to have taken their own warnings very seriously. Prince Phillip, Prince William, Bill Gates, Boris Johnson and Stanley Johnson have a good many children between them. Indeed, thanks to Boris's contribution, there seems to be some confusion about the grand total of children fathered by these men. Boris Johnson is reputed to have fathered numerous children (by an unknown number of women) and, like most who believe the world is over populated (such as members of the British royal family) Johnson is a hypocrite who clearly thinks that it is other people who need culling.

Paine (Thomas)

'The harder the conflict the more glorious the triumph. What we obtain too cheaply, we esteem too lightly. Tis dearness only that gives everything its value.'

Paretsky (Sara)

'True villainy lies in betrayal, torture and violation of the spirit.'

Password storage

As we accumulate yet more online contacts, so the number of passwords we have to remember grows beyond Topsy's wildest expectations. We are advised, of course, to use different passwords for all our accounts, and this can lead to bewilderment not to say downright confusion since we are also advised not to write down our passwords.

There are, however, online APPs which enable individuals to store all their passwords in one convenient online storage place on the cloud.

The world has always needed a steady supply of complete idiots and it is my hope that the young people who use these services will continue to do so.

Hopefully, this will keep the conmen busy enough, and rich enough, to leave the rest of us alone.

Pensions

Old people are considered to be surplus to requirements, a nuisance and a drag on the global economy. Britain has the poorest state pension system in the developed world, and young campaigners in the UK are working hard to make sure that the pension becomes even more inadequate. When winters are cold, thousands of elderly people have to choose between buying sufficient food or keeping their homes warm. Inadequate pensions ensure that around 60,000 old people die of the cold every winter in Britain.

It was reported, at the end of 2020, that the year's events (specifically the deaths of so many elderly people) had saved the

British government £600 million in pension payments and had saved companies £60 billion in pension payments.

Pets

There is absolutely no place for pets in the 'new normal'. Pets will not be allowed in the smart cities since they are a distraction and a sign of 'ownership'. Moreover, they are regarded as likely to spread disease.

Meanwhile, the law forces pet owners to microchip dogs.

The innocent may believe this is so that their dog can be found if it strays. But does anyone believe their government cares about such things? The microchips enable the authorities to keep an eye on the whereabouts of the owners as much as of the dogs. And the officially mandated micro-chipping is, of course, a sign of who really 'owns' and controls the animal.

Philanthropy

Modern billionaires like to be seen as philanthropists without the pain of actually giving away any money. So for example, in 2012, Elon Musk of Tesla said he pledged to give away half his wealth during his lifetime. In 2018, he promised to sell around $100 million of Tesla shares every few years for charity. But his major disbursements will only begin in 20 years' time.

Bill Gates is widely regarded as a philanthropist. However, his donations cement his control over world health matters.

Plan

Apart from killing people, and thereby helping to reduce the size of the world's population, what was the point behind the deliberately arranged hysteria, and carefully orchestrated panic, of 2020?

The answer, of course, is simple.

The plan was to disrupt our lives and redesign the world to suit the Agenda 21 lunatics, and to please the billionaires who are still greedy and want to be trillionaires.

The plan was to alter the social fabric of every country in the world, to ruin the financial security of everyone not already a billionaire or on the list of accepted individuals (members of the British royal family, Tony Blair were clearly on the 'accepted' list), to abolish private property, to destroy health care, to eliminate privacy and to terrorise the world into accepting a new world order.

The very rich will, of course, be exempt from the rules. As an early example of this, in late 2020, the UK Government announced that it would exclude hedge fund managers and city deal makers from the quarantine rules.

The Agenda 21 cultists want to reinvent education – they want to stop learning and just test, test and test. For now, schools are going to be turned into prisons. Have you ever wondered why new schools and universities have such high gates and walls? It's to keep pupils in – not to keep intruders out. In the future, education is going to be controlled through the internet. Closing schools was part of that plan. Teachers who voted to keep schools closed were doing precisely what the billionaires wanted them to do.

They want to control movement and stop us travelling. We soon won't be able to travel anywhere. How much longer do airlines have? (Private aeroplanes will boom as the elite continue to travel wherever and whenever they want to go.)

They want to put an end to private cars. And although they may let a few of us operate electric cars, they have already threatened to cut off electricity supplies to those using electricity to power private vehicles. Train and bus services are doomed.

They want to store us in tiny apartments in high rise towers in big cities. They want to close the countryside to us and keep rural areas empty.

Our food will be made in laboratories, not grown on farms for they want us to stop eating food grown the old-fashioned way. I haven't eaten meat for over 30 years and I have campaigned for decades to stop animals being farmed for meat but I am desperately concerned about the changes being made to our diet. How safe will all this new food really be? I have real doubts about the safety of genetically modified food but unless we grow our own food that's what we will be forced to eat.

They want to change the way we work – with millions of jobs being handed over to robots. Those training as doctors, lawyers and teachers have a decade's work ahead of them at best. They will all be replaced by computers and the internet.

They want us all to be dependent upon the State with everyone receiving a fixed weekly wage – just enough to live on.

They want us to be jabbed regularly – to keep us under control, to make us sicker, to sterilise us and certainly to boost drug company profits.

They want to remove ambition and hope from our minds. They want us to learn to blame ourselves for everything that goes wrong. People who feel ashamed are easier to control.

And, more than anything perhaps, they want to reduce the world population by 90% or so. Hospitals have been putting 'Do Not Resuscitate' notices on patients over the age of 65 – or in some places over the age of 45. The elderly and the sick are going to be culled. Billions are going to have to die though I have a suspicion that there aren't going to be many politicians or billionaires lined up in the world's morgues. Isn't it convenient that restrictions in Africa are going to kill countless millions? That will give the depopulation programme a good start.

They want to introduce a global social credit, such as has already been introduced in China, so that we are penalised if we misbehave and rewarded if we do as we are told. We will be penalised for what we eat, how much we spend or even who our friends are. Everything we do will be watched and assessed.

They want to crush and destroy all opposition. Demonstrations will be banned. Political parties will be closely controlled. And the media (including the internet) will allow only 'accepted' content.

They want to eradicate national sovereignty. (In Europe they have been using the European Union to do that for many years).

They want to increase the role of the State in raising children.

They have been planning all this for many decades.

Police

The attitude of the police towards those protesting against the loss of democracy and civil liberties, and the exaggerated political response to the events of 2020, has changed. It has changed dramatically and it has changed all around the world. It is impossible not to believe that this is planned.

The police are now roughing up peaceful protestors who are opposed to the loss of their freedom. (It is notable, however, that those protesting about black lives or the global warming myth are treated with respect. When black lives matter protestors are violent or destructive, the police stand back – even taking the knee in deference. When global warming cultists stop traffic for hours, the police talk to them, dance with them, pose for photographs and generally make it clear that they are with them and their cause.)

If an old lady protests about the loss of her freedom, she is likely to be man-handled roughly and tossed into the back of a police van. Once arrested she will be kept for hours – even though it may be patently clear to everyone concerned that she has broken no law and cannot possibly be charged with anything. The odd thing is that when the police have been busy arresting citizens protesting about the loss of their freedom, they seemed neither concerned about their own health nor the health of the individuals they were manhandling.

The police are hired to protect the public but they have been encouraged and ordered to betray that trust. How many brave policemen and women really signed up to arrest 70-odd-year-old ladies who have broken no law and done no wrong other than to stand up against a totalitarian government which is determined to destroy the people who put it in power? It seems to me that when there are nearly 30 police officers involved in making a single arrest of an unarmed, unthreatening citizen, maybe the police have become a trifle confused.

Moreover, I fear that the police have made a huge personal and professional mistake. They have become foot soldiers for the forces of evil.

I doubt very much if anyone has explained to them the price they and their family will have to pay for the decisions they have made or been bullied into making.

If the police knew anything they would understand that there is a huge political power play in action. And they are not going to be immune.

If they think that by beating up a few brave, old ladies they will be able to win themselves a place at the table when the Global Reset is put into place then they are seriously deluded. They are merely fodder in a war they don't understand.

Their actions will leave them isolated from the community. They do what they are ordered to do but the new world they are helping to create will mean that there is no health care for them or their families. Their children will, if they survive, grow up uneducated and working as slaves. They will have little or no money. And they will have no jobs.

What the police do not realise is that they have absolutely no future; they are merely being used to assist the greatest conspiracy in history and help create a climate of fear and obedience. I suspect that most, if not all, cannot yet see that, when they have served their purposes they will be fired. If any police officer thinks that the Rothschilds, the Roosevelts, the Rockefellers, the Gates, the Musks and the royal family give a damn about them then they are, I suspect, sadly, badly wrong.

There will be no place for the police when the Great Reset has occurred. They will be replaced en masse by snitches and sneaks, robots and drones and, when force is required, the military.

It's already happening of course. The police themselves have stupidly helped the Government encourage snitches to tell on their neighbours. And in China, the model for our new normal Great Reset, the scary model for the society we will soon be living in, the authorities are already using robot policemen. Drones are in operation everywhere.

And if the protests lead to civil disobedience – which is what the politicians really want – then it is clear that the police will be pushed aside and replaced with the military. It will be time for bullets – rubber or real – and the average copper will be sent home to watch it all unfold on television.

I wonder if the bullying coppers have been told that they will all be redundant within a year or two – if things go according to plan, the Agenda 21 plan.

And so what will the policemen do then when they are not
selected to be among the 500 million remaining on earth, when the
depopulation plan so favoured by Bill Gates and the British royal
family is finally put into place.

I doubt if the police have been warned that they won't have jobs
in two years, and that, indeed, they don't have any sort of future.

If the police want any sort of future, they should arrest the global
warming cultists (all of whom are fighting for the tyranny of Agenda
21 though most of them don't realise it and aren't bright enough to
realise just how they are being manipulated) and help and encourage
those fighting for freedom from this tyranny.

Political correctness

Political correctness is destroying our freedom. We have become the
new puritans, demonising those who dare to question the official line
on anything. As Udo Ulfkotte put it: 'We are the heirs of the Puritans
who had a nasty habit of picking on little old ladies, demonising
them and then burning them at the stake.'

Disney has blocked children from watching the films *Dumbo*, *The
Aristocats* and *Swiss Family Robinson*.

The Aristocats is considered unsuitable because it features a
Siamese cat which viewers have complained might be seen as a
stereotyped portrayal of Asian people. *Dumbo* is banned for children
because several of the characters working in the circus are black
workers. *Swiss Family Robinson* is out because it may contain
'negative depictions and/or mistreatment of people or cultures'.

Politicians

Honest politicians are now as rare as hens' teeth or mares' nests. So
many politicians are on the fiddle that you could make a dozen string
orchestras from the members of the House of Commons alone.
Around the world there is no group of professionals as determinedly
dishonest as politicians. There are more politicians in prison (as a

percentage of the total) than lawyers, doctors, journalists or estate agents.

Pope Francis

Pope Francis said in October 2020 that the year's crisis had proved that economic policies had failed to produce social benefits. There was, of course, no evidence for this. Nor is there any evidence proving that communism has produced social benefits or that communitarianism will improve the world.

Pope Francis also said that private property cannot be considered an absolute right.

This is rather hypocritical since it comes from a bloke who is looked after by a number of servants and a private army. He also has his own country. Naturally, this nonsense fits very neatly into Agenda 21. Incidentally, those doubting the enthusiasm of Pope Francis for the United Nations' Agenda 21 should note that the pontiff has blamed capitalism for the 'fragility of world systems'. He has also described property rights as a 'secondary natural right', in accordance with the UN's demonization of private property ownership and enthusiasm for its quasi communistic politics.

Population

The global population growth has been falling since the 1970s. The reason is believed to be a rise in male infertility. Scientists seem puzzled by this but I believe there are two causes.

First, the evidence shows that drinking water supplies contain quantities of oestrogen. The oestrogen gets into the drinking water from the urine of women who have taken the contraceptive pill. Sewage companies discharge their 'treated' water into rivers from which drinking water is obtained. It is not possible to remove the oestrogen from the water before it is pumped into the fresh water system.

Second, there is some evidence that drugs, especially those given by injection, have been used to control population growth.

Positive discrimination

The most obvious and significant racism in the UK is that created by positive discrimination. The same is true of sexism.

In the arts, theatre, television and publishing, positive discrimination means that women and non-white participants are heavily favoured. Within the BBC, diversity is all that matters but diversity there is defined as offering favouritism to those who are not white, male or old.

I noticed in October 2020 that the *New Yorker* magazine writes Black (as in 'a Black man') but white (as in 'a white seventeen-year-old'). I am quite unable to see how this overt and rather pathetic act of adjectival racism does anything but offend, discriminate and build racism.

I am not sure whether the editors there realise it but using initial capitals for some words is a trait favoured by lunatics when writing letters to newspapers and celebrities. (As in 'I am going to Shoot and Kill Everyone on Wednesday'.)

Postal deliveries

Since the plan is to force everyone to live in smart towns, it won't be long before rural postal deliveries are stopped. Those living in the countryside will be forced to drive into their nearest town and queue at a postal sorting office in order to pick up their mail. The absence of public transport, and strict controls on motor cars, will make this nigh on impossible for the elderly, the frail and the poor.

Power cuts

When are power supplies going to be cut? There is no doubt that it will happen on a big scale. The only question is 'when'?

The power grids will stop working.

The politicians will, of course, blame Russia, North Korea, Iran or China. Or, maybe, if they're feeling imaginative they will blame a bunch of irritable hackers from Mars or hidden deep in the bowels of Uranus.

But that won't be true.

When the power cuts occur, it'll be a global shut down and it will be planned.

When could it take place?

Well, the months of December to March would do the most damage to the Northern Hemisphere. And taking out Christmas would be popular among the doom laden gloom-makers who want to remove all joy from our lives. It would take us another small step towards eradicating Christianity. And without power supplies, the cold weather would kill off hundreds of millions of unwanted old folk around the world. Since they control the weather, it wouldn't be difficult for them to give us a few storms and some really cold weather.

Look around your home and think about it.

We have become totally dependent on electricity.

Without it we will have no light and most heating systems won't work. Food in refrigerators will spoil. Supermarkets and shops will have to shut because even if they have generators, they'll run out of fuel because fuel pumps need electricity. Naturally, there will be no TV or computers. There will be no internet and mobile phones, and iPads won't work because you won't be able to charge them. Cash machines won't work and banks will shut so you won't be able to access your money.

There will be chaos on the roads and looting in shopping centres as rioters look for food. Without street lighting, cities will be dark. Without traffic lights there will be accidents galore. Petrol and diesel vehicles will travel as far as the fuel in the tank will take them. Electric vehicles won't move an inch.

The civil disobedience will be widespread and so governments will bring in martial law.

So, now is the time to work out how you'll cope if there is a major power outage that takes weeks to mend. Could you cope without electricity for a month? How would you manage without electricity? How would you keep warm? Do you have food stocks?

You don't think any of this could happen?

Well, not long ago I'd have agreed with you.

But did you think they'd shut down hospital departments, shops, businesses and schools for no good reason?

Did you think they'd put us all under house arrest?

The people who have created and managed the world's biggest fraud will stop at nothing to get what they want: a reduced population, a world government and total control.

It is, I think, time for a little thinking and planning for a simpler way of living. Maybe it would be wise to stock up with tinned food, torches and radios with a supply of batteries. Old-fashioned dial telephones which operate on a landline should still work, so if you and the people you care about each have one then you should be able to communicate. Carrier pigeons won't be any good because people will catch them and eat them.

If you are prepared for a power shut down and it doesn't happen then you've lost nothing. But if you aren't prepared you could lose everything.

Predictive programming

There has been a good deal of predictive programming in recent years. The Big Brother programmes on television encouraged viewers to become accustomed to the idea of being constantly under camera surveillance – and to obey orders, however bizarre they might be. And the TV programme called 'I'm A Celebrity Get Me Out of Here' seems to have been designed to accustom us to eating insects – and making do without the comforts to which most of us have become accustomed.

Preventive medicine

Agenda 21 supporters have agreed that medical practice should in future consist primarily of preventive medicine programmes. This does not, as you might suspect, consist of a programme of health education – with dietary advice, advice to cut down alcohol consumption and to stop smoking tobacco, mixed with screening programmes and advice on taking regular exercise. Instead, medical practice will, in future, be built around a series of treatment programmes. At the moment, children have several dozen jabs before they reach puberty. (The precise number varies from country to country.) In future, this sort of programme will be extended to adults who will be expected to have many jabs every year. Those who refuse or fail to attend a clinic will lose points and be punished according to the 'social credit'.

Prince Philip (Duke of Edinburgh and father of four)

'In the event that I am reincarnated I would like to return as a deadly virus, to contribute something to solving overpopulation.'

Principles for responsible investment

This is a United Nations piece of virtue signalling which requires investment companies to ignore their responsibilities to investors but to consider 'environmental, social and governance factors' when making investment decisions.

In practice, this means that investment companies can ignore their primary responsibilities by claiming that they are obeying the UN's Agenda 21 aims.

Some of the companies which have signed up to these 'principles' are among the worst in the business – with appalling performance and outrageous fees. No one bothers to assess them according to their fairness, competence and decency if they sign up to the UN's nonsense.

Privacy

Privacy is going, going, shortly to be gone. Webcams, CCTV and social media have banished privacy. We are tracked, traced and tested. We zoom in and out of each other's homes because we are told it is better that way. It's certainly better for the people spying on us. When we chat through the internet they can spy on us all the time. They can read your emails (however much you try to hide them). So now they know everything about you, and your life is not yours any more.

Electronic eavesdropping, phone tapping and monitoring of financial records mean that privacy is a memory.

In the UK, some school children are already being asked to report if their parents are questioning the official government line. They are also asked what TV programmes their parents are watching and what online sites they visit. The aim is clearly to identify dissenters so that they can be dealt with. This is much the same sort of thing that happened in Nazi Germany and in East Germany after the end of World War II.

The private, personal details of people who are told to self-isolate but fail to do so are being passed to the police.

Profiteering

A number of organisations have done well out of the restrictions and the fear. National newspapers (such as the *Daily Telegraph* in the UK) have hidden vital information behind a pay wall. Some individuals have also done well by providing websites which turned out to be extremely profitable. (For the record, none of my video channels was ever monetised and we took no sponsorship or advertising on videos or the website. My last two books, published in autumn 2020, were made available free as PDFs.)

Progress

There is a commonly held misconception that progress is always a good thing and that change is invariably for the better. What happened in 2020 is proof, if proof be needed, that this is not always true. The changes which took place were neither progressive nor temporary: they are regressive, and unless we have the strength and the determination to oppose them, they will be permanent.

We are all accustomed to the vicissitudes of life, the unexpected hazards which leave us feeling as if someone has dropped a two ton weight on our head or, as PG Wodehouse might have put it, socked us on the back of the neck with a stuffed eel-skin.

Bad things happen and just as light bulbs always go at the most inconvenient moment (we've just turned on the light so of course it's inconvenient) so the dramas which punctuate our lives invariably arrive when we're busy with something else.

But that was then and this is now.

The vicissitudes which destroyed 2020 were not accidental or God given. They were deliberately manufactured by people whose evil is greater than that of any others in history.

We have been bullied, lied to, manipulated and threatened by people who are, in my opinion, the most crooked and contemptible human beings in history. The architects of the false plague of 2020 are wicked, and those who have supported and protected the fraud are also guilty of the greatest of crimes. Their well-documented cold-blooded aim is to deliberately diminish the quality, value, meaning and sanctity of human life. They want to control every aspect of our lives and to take our freedom, our democracy and our right to free speech. This is the Great Reset, the new normal, the new world order of which Prince Charles and others speak with such enthusiasm.

The collaborators, the ordinary men and women who have obeyed the indefensible and the unsupportable, must also take their share of the blame. 'I was just following orders,' was no defence at Nuremburg and it will be no defence when doctors, nurses, policemen, administrators, journalists and others stand trial for their part in the global genocide.

Psychological warfare (psy-ops)

Under the advice of mind control experts and warfare specialists, governments are using many techniques to attack and control their own populations. There are a number of traditional military techniques which it is important to understand.

First, they want to suppress the truth. Suppressing and distorting the truth is nothing new, of course, and politicians have been adept at it for years.

They give contradictory instructions to confuse and to create social disintegration. None of this is an accident. On the contrary, everything that has happened has been deliberate.

Governments have been using a massive number of psychological tricks to control their citizens. Military psychologists, trained in warfare techniques, have been let loose on the public with disastrous results. All normal activities have been suspended (apparently unpredictably) to create confusion and fear. We have been threatened with death and told that while others are a danger to us we are a danger to them. Various repetitive rituals such as using hand cleansers and clapping the NHS have been used to control our behaviour. We have been pushed and cornered and forced to do only what we are allowed to do. We have been told that we must sacrifice our freedom to save our lives. We have been disorientated and forced to submerge our identity into the community. Families and friends have been divided to separate and isolate us and make us more accessible for reprogramming. Debate has been forbidden and the facts have been distorted to support the official line. Obedience is everything, and many have been turned into collaborators with the hope that if they do as they are told then one day they may be allowed to return to something approaching normality.

Sometimes psy-op techniques are rather more intrusive. In their book, *Illuminati Agenda 21* Dean and Jill Henderson report that 'Major Michael Aquino was an army psy-ops specialist in Vietnam, where his unit specialised in drug-inducement, brain washing, virus injection, brain implants, hypnosis and use of electromagnetic fields and extremely low-frequency radio waves.'

Implants (put into the body as 'chips') will be promoted as a way to gain great intellectual prowess without any effort. They will be sold as a way to improve physical and mental skills, to eradicate all pain (both physical and mental) and they will doubtless be accepted, with enthusiasm, by millions who fancy the idea of being able to speak six foreign languages without any effort.

Public private partnerships

Public private partnerships (known as PPP or 3P) have been widely introduced around the world and were created by the United Nations' Sustainable Development policies. The idea is that taxpayers' money is mixed in with corporate money to build and maintain massive, expensive and rather grandiose projects designed to stimulate economic development.

These projects are frequently extremely profitable for everyone except the public and the taxpayers.

Pubs

In the UK, pubs and restaurants have been given automatic permission to sell takeaway food and alcohol until 2022 – suggesting that forced closures are expected to last at least that long. In the end, of course, pubs will be forced to close permanently and restaurants, cafes and hotels (particularly those in rural areas) have very little future. There is no place for any of them in the world envisaged by the Agenda 21 cultists.

Quarantine

In the year 2020, the rules about quarantine changed constantly from day to day and from country to country – proving without a shadow of doubt that the quarantine regulations were directed not by scientists but by politicians. In the UK, the Government announced that hedge fund managers and others important in the world of finance would be exempt from quarantine regulations.

There were rumours late in 2020 that quarantine camps were being prepared in some countries. It was said, not without cause, that the camps would be used to house dissidents, those who questioned the official line.

It was fairly widely agreed that the camps would, in reality, be extermination camps where people who died would be officially classified as suffering from the disease of the moment.

Queues

The length of queues everywhere will increase.

Shops will cut back on staff (to reduce costs) and the rules will mean that some shoppers will have to wait outside in the cold and the rain before being given the opportunity to go inside, purchase a pair of socks and queue for the opportunity to pay for them.

No one quite understands why the new rules mean that staff in banks, postal sorting offices and so on, have to work shorter hours, but the result is that there will be much longer queues during the hours that these premises are open.

Racism

Amidst all the talk about racism in Britain, no one seemed to notice that the ethnic group least likely to go to university is white British. If there is racism in Britain then it is whites who are the victims.

There are many who believe that 'Black Lives Matter' protests and campaigns were supported by billionaires, politicians and the police in order to increase racism and close people's eyes to the millions dying in Africa from starvation as a result of the restrictions.

The Agenda 21 plan is for six and a half billion people to die. The first millions will die in Africa of starvation caused by the policies introduced in 2020.

Reagan (Ronald)

'The nine most terrifying words in the English language are: 'I'm from the Government and I'm here to help.''

'Freedom is never more than one generation away from extinction.'

Recycling

Recycling must go down in history as one of the greatest and most successful confidence tricks. It was designed as a training programme to force citizens to be compliant and obedient to the State.

The recycling programme was always a conditioning programme, designed to force individuals to become compliant. In the UK, for example, most of the carefully sorted recycling was transported abroad to be buried in landfill, burnt or just dumped. In 2017, China announced that it would no longer be the world's dumping ground, and British waste was sent instead to Malaysia, Vietnam and Thailand. Other waste from Britain has been found in dumps in Eastern Europe. (Trying to recover waste plastic is costly and uses a huge amount of water and energy.)

Reducing carbon dioxide levels

Thanks to Agenda 21, governments everywhere are committed to reducing carbon dioxide output to round about 25% below 1990 levels, or reducing them by 40%, or maybe reducing them completely. These absurd and impossible demands are passed on to local governments which have no choice but to accept them.

The thing is that no one knows what carbon dioxide levels were in 1990. Or what they were in 1989 or 1979. No one was measuring those levels back then.

And no notice is taken of the fact that your town or city may now be twice as big as it was in 1990.

The result, of course, is that, in a desperate attempt to keep up with the Agenda 21 demands, your town, city or village has to cut transport, cut industry, change farming practises and alter everything about your life. Building permits will be affected by the need to keep reducing carbon dioxide levels. Property companies won't be allowed to build nice little houses with good solid walls, well-built kitchens and pleasant gardens. Instead they will have to build towering blocks of flats made out of thin cardboard. And no one will be allowed to have a garden.

In the world of the 'new normal' everywhere will look the same. Hotels will all look identical because they will all be built and furnished according to the same Agenda 21 rules. Quirky bits of architecture have to be pulled down (regardless of any historical or architectural value) and cycle lanes must be marked off even if a road is barely wide enough for two small cars. There will be no more crackling log fires in country pubs or hotels.

Regionalisation

Back in 2002, I wrote a book called, *England Our England* in which I discussed some of the ways in which the European Union was attempting to destroy the United Kingdom in general and England in particular. This was, I explained, all part of a plan to destroy nationalism and sovereignty.

An essential part of the EU's political programme was the dividing up of the UK into a number of regions. Plans were put in place to develop regional parliaments. Scotland was already designated a region (and given a little parliament of its own) and the same thing happened in Wales and Northern Ireland.

Ironically, the nationalists in Scotland and Wales thought that their new parliaments were an important step on the road to independence. What they failed to realise was that their new parliaments were exactly the opposite of independence: they were part of a plan to turn the whole of the UK into a series of regions which would be subservient to the central bureaucracy of the EU in Brussels. There were to be nine regions in England though the south east of England was destined to be a region with part of France – proving, if there was ever any doubt, that this was a plan to destroy England and create a series of regions throughout the European countries.

The Labour Government tried to 'sell' the idea of regional parliaments to the English people and tried to start the process by opening a parliament in the North East of England. However, the voters (who were never told that the plan for a regional parliament was part of a plan to break up England) rejected the idea as just another level of unnecessary bureaucracy. The only part of England to be turned successfully into a region was London which now has its own parliament or assembly.

Those regions were the first step towards globalisation and a world government.

Remembrance Day

In November 2020, the British Government introduced restrictions just in time to prevent the marches and meetings traditionally held to commemorate Remembrance Day. Was this merely an accident? I think not. It is far more likely that the plan was to remove another piece of British history and to take away a part of the nation's self-respect and cultural identity.

Renewables

When you see global warming cultists claiming that renewables now make up a hefty proportion of our energy source, you should remember that by far the biggest 'renewable' source of energy is biomass – by which is meant wood.

In the UK, the biomass which is burnt is mostly in the form of wood pellets which come from trees in North America. The trees are chopped down, turned into pellets and then shipped to the UK to be burnt.

Biomass is one of the least efficient, most polluting sources of energy on earth. It is, however, the darling of the global warming cultists – who know little and understand nothing.

Reset

Klaus Schwab and Prince Charles talk constantly of their plan for a 'great reset'.

What they mean by this is that they will tear down everything we hold important and then rebuild the world in a way that suits them, gives them lots of power and makes them even richer.

Who are they? Well, the list is a long one but you won't be far out if you start with Prince Charles, Tony Blair, George Soros, Klaus Schwab and Bill Gates and then mix in a variety of assorted Rothschilds and Rockefellers.

Add in the usual Bilderberger enthusiasts and stir to taste.

Reshaping

This quote appeared in the *Guardian* on 16th September 2020. The author was someone called Mohamed El-Erian. 'We must use the … crisis to reshape our society and economy. Now is the time to look to lock in trends and conditions that will reshape our society and economy for the better over the long-term.'

Which trends and conditions of the 'crisis' would you like to lock in?

And which do you think would reshape our society and economy for the better?

The *Guardian* newspaper has financial links with the Bill and Melinda Gates Foundation.

Retrojecting

This ugly word means projecting 21st century attitudes onto the past. It is because of retrojecting that statues are being removed if the person immortalised can now be accused of having led a less than blameless life. If you parked your hansom cab on a double yellow line in 1874 then your statue will be dragged down by vandals while the police stand by, exhausting their repertoire of non-violent physical skills by kneeling and cheering at the same time.

Right wing

Anyone who opposes the very lefty Agenda 21 brand of totalitarianism and fascism is marked as 'extreme right wing'. If you question the principles of communitarianism (the modern version of communism) then you must be extreme right wing. (If you are right wing then you must be extreme right wing.)

Risk/benefit

In theory, risk/benefit means assessing the risk of a particular activity and then making a judgement about the advantages, disadvantages and dangers. These days, those in authority have turned the idea of 'risk/benefit' on its head. And so, governments want to ban domestic log burners in which the owners often burn fallen branches or chopped up dead trees but want to replace power stations dependent on oil, gas or coal with power stations dependent on burning wood which has been taken from trees grown in another country and transported thousands of miles by boat and lorry. This is, for some inexplicable reason, supposed to be better for the environment.

And the principle of 'risk benefit' is turned on its head, in even more dramatic terms, by insisting that in order to protect themselves from a disease with a low mortality rate, all citizens must avail themselves of an experimental medical treatment which is known to be of very doubtful benefit but also known to be exceedingly dangerous.

Rivero (Michael)

'Politicians seek to gain wealth and power and authority by taking something that occurs naturally, transforming it and promoting it as a crisis, and then selling the population a solution in exchange for higher taxes and increased authority over their lives.'

Robots

It is a myth, enthusiastically accepted, supported and promoted by the intellectual classes, that the only people whose lives are threatened by robots are blue collar workers. While it is obviously true that most factory workers will find themselves replaced by robots (something that has been happening for decades) and that most administrators and bureaucrats will be replaced by computers, the people who are most at risk at losing their jobs are those in the professions. It is difficult to see why there will be any need for doctors or lawyers in a decade's time. Computers make excellent diagnosticians, and robots can perform even complicated surgery more effectively and more speedily (and with fewer deaths) than human surgeons. Now that doctors and nurses have abandoned their caring role and taken on a colder, clinical approach to their work, it is even more certain that they will be replaced by robots which (or who) can be trained to be compassionate, thoughtful, considerate and caring.

And lawyers? Well, even a modestly sized computer will be able to hold more legal information than any bewigged head, and there can be no doubt that it will not be long before robots will replace solicitors, barristers and judges.

Teachers too have no professional future. Teaching will be done online. The world will need one geography teacher, one history teacher, one mathematics teacher and so on. The rest will either be retrained or simply made redundant.

On the other hand there are some jobs which it will be difficult to replace with robots. Plumbers, able to struggle under sinks and behind lavatories, and electricians, capable of wriggling along in lofts, will remain in demand for some time. I suspect that other building and renovation specialities will remain in the hands of humans.

Rockefellers

'Some even believe we are part of a secret cabal working against the best interests of the United States, characterising my family and me as internationalists and of conspiring with others around the world to build a more integrated global political and economic structure – one world, if you will. If that's the charge, I stand guilty and I am proud of it.' – *David Rockefeller in his 2002 autobiography 'Memoirs'.*

Rousseau (Jean-Jacques)

Rousseau, when writing about the 'Social Contract', claimed that men are basically good and that it is government and laws that make them bad. If he was right then it stands to reason that the more government there is, and the more laws that are made, then the worse people will become. The EU, which has produced hundreds of thousands of laws, has enraged millions, and I do not doubt that as a result of the many laws which exist we are now all lawbreakers.

Royal Family

I used to be a royalist. No more. I believe that sensible folk should boo and hiss whenever they see a member of the royal family. They should wave pea shooters or two fingers, rather than hands or hankies. The modern royals exhibit greed, self-importance, hubris and hypocrisy but absolutely no sense of responsibility, loyalty or respect towards the people who pay for their rock-star lifestyles.

Britain's royal family has played an enthusiastic part in the plan to make the British people accept Agenda 21. Prince Charles has for many years been a keen advocate of the global warming myth, busily flying around the world to attend global warming conferences. Charles's two sons, William and Harry have also been keen supporters of the same myth. Queen Elizabeth II, the reigning monarch, was notably absent during the months in which the 2020 hoax started to build towards a climax.

The astonishing thing about Charles is the hubris, the certainty that he, a man who has never known any of the normal worries of the world, an intensely over-privileged member of an arrogant over-privileged family, thinks he understands the global warming cult and knows best how the world should be managed.

He, like the rest of his family, has betrayed the British people and the people of the Commonwealth.

His son, the Duke of Cambridge is also blessed with copious quantities of hubris and appears to be a world class hypocrite. He has stated that there are too many people in the world – but he has three children. He flies constantly but claims that 'global warming is irrefutable'. Just how or why he knows this to be the case he has not bothered to share with us. As always with the royal family it is a case of 'do as I say, not as I do'.

If the royals understand that the myth of global warming was devised as an excuse for Agenda 21 then they are traitors. If they don't understand then they are gullible fools.

We should get rid of the existing royal family completely. We can confiscate their estates and provide them with rented accommodation in a high rise block of flats.

But that would leave us with the danger of having a president and so, to avoid that dire eventuality, we should have rotating royals. This could be arranged via a weekly lottery. Punters entering the lottery could, as one of the prizes, have a chance to win being king and queen for a week.

The temporary holders of the royal offices would do the usual hand waving and opening of cupboards, envelopes and approved buildings – and then, at the end of their week, go back to their usual lives. The confiscated royal estates could be used to fund this simple operation so there would be no drain on taxpayers.

Candidates for the role should be stupid, vacuous, vain and have a grotesque sense of entitlement. Almost any successful reality television 'stars' would be suitable for these roles.

Rupert Bear

'Trolls never do any good to anybody.' (*Rupert Annual 1969*)

Rural living

Agenda 21 has no room for people living in the countryside. They will force people out of the country and into their smart cities by banning cars and public transport, cutting electricity and telephone supplies to rural areas (in the UK, despite many promises, there are still huge areas of countryside without any cell phone coverage and many other areas with intermittent or pretty useless coverage).

Broadband coverage in rural areas is often miserable and likely to remain so.

Other measures will be to stop doing road repairs in rural areas and to leave communities without fresh water supplies for long periods. Requests to take water from springs and boreholes are being denied, and house owners asking for permission to build septic tanks will find many difficulties put in their way. The end result will be to force down rural property prices and to force those living in the country to move into one of the new tower blocks in a designated city.

In the suburbs there will be taxes on gardens too.

The UK Government has announced that 30% of the UK is to become 'wild'. It would be impossible to do this without confiscating much farmland, many areas of outstanding natural beauty and a great many private gardens. Surprisingly, perhaps, residential gardens take up 4.8% of UK's land whereas industrial and commercial land takes up only 0.4% of the available land.

Safety

The instinctive human need for safety and security has been enhanced by constant threats and scares. We have been encouraged to accept any law which we believe will make us safer and help us avoid any risk.

The fear tactics have created a global population of hypochondriacs.

Scanners

AI scanners are being used to supply data to the authorities. The scanners identify individuals who do not keep sufficient distance between themselves and others and, when used with facial recognition cameras, enable the authorities to arrest 'those whose reckless selfishness is alleged to be endangering mankind'.

Schools

Since February 2020 I have pretty well lost touch with what is possible in this upside down world.

I do not, for example, understand why so many apparently sane and fairly sensible people should be so overwhelmed by manufactured fear and manipulated misinformation that they have lost touch with reality. Why do so many people feel safe only if they are told exactly what to do for every minute of the day? When did so many people lose their humanity and their good sense?

For example, I know of absolutely no medical reason for primary school children to wear face coverings or to be forced to keep apart from one another.

If I had a child at a school where the authorities were planning to force CIA torture techniques on children I would want to ask a lawyer to warn the teachers that I would hold them legally responsible for any physical or mental harm caused by their woeful ignorance.

I would point out that children in China have already died as a result of obeying the new rules.

All teachers who support these absurd and entirely unnecessary nonsenses are guilty of child abuse. And it's no good them saying they were obeying the Government or their union. It was no good for the Nazis at Nuremberg and it's no good for teachers today. Nor is ignorance any excuse. Any teacher who thinks that children are seriously at risk from the over-marketed virus is too stupid to be teaching finger painting let alone anything more sophisticated.

Why is this happening?

The only explanation I can think of is that the plan is to close all schools and force all professional teaching online. Exams will be set, taken and marked online. Anyone who doesn't bother to attend classes will simply stay ignorant. The aim of education will be to enable pupils to pass examinations and to learn how to perform simple, work tasks.

The Agenda 21 plan is to get rid of teaching as a profession and teachers seem surprisingly keen to collaborate in their own destruction. Young people who are planning a career in teaching should think again and look for some other way to earn a living.

Schwab (Klaus)

Klaus Schwab, the founder and executive chairman of the World Economic Forum, and whom some regard as a dead ringer for Dr Strangelove, has a knighthood. I would now believe anyone who told me that Queen Elizabeth travels everywhere by broomstick. She betrayed her people by not speaking out about the European Union, and her family has furthered that betrayal by supporting the Great Reset and the intended slavery of the British people.

Schwab wrote a book called, *Shaping the Future of the Fourth Industrial Revolution* and subtitled *A guide to building a better world.* It should have been called 'Nightmare on Your Street'. It seemed to me to be at the same time impenetrable, arrogant, ignorant and badly written (I found it well supplied with split infinitives) and yet the scariest book I have ever read. I was so horrified by the contents that I had to keep struggling on.

Here are a few quotes to give a flavour of the book:

From a section headed 'Altering the Human Being':

'The lines between technologies and beings are becoming blurred and not just by the ability to create lifelike robots or synthetics. Instead it is about the ability of new technologies to literally become part of us. Technologies already influence how we understand ourselves, how we think about each other, and how we determine our realities. As the technologies…give us deeper access to parts of ourselves, we may begin to integrate digital technologies into our bodies'.

And these from a section about agriculture:

'To feed the world in the next 50 years we will need to produce as much food as was produced in the last 10,000 years'.

(So what? The population is bigger and we have better farming techniques.)

'…food security will only be achieved, however, if regulations on genetically modified foods are adapted to reflect the reality that gene editing offers a precise, efficient and safe method of improving crops.'

(And where did that nonsense come from? Who says gene editing is precise, efficient and safe?)

And from a section on neurotechnologies:

'Neurotechnologies enable us to better influence consciousness and thought and to understand many activities of the brain. They include decoding what we are thinking in fine levels of detail through new chemicals and interventions that can influence our brains to correct for errors or enhance functionality.'

(If that doesn't scare you, nothing will.)

Scott (Walter)

'Breathe there the man with soul so dead,
Who never to himself hath said,
This is my own, my native land.'

Scottish National Party (SNP)

The SNP closely follows all Agenda 21 principles. For example, the SNP plans to criminalise inflammatory publications such as the Bible and most (if not all) newspapers.

Self-programming computers

Billionaire and general bad egg Elon Musk is reported to have claimed that human beings must merge with artificial intelligence systems if they are to compete with self-programming computers.

There is, of course, an alternative: simply slow down the development of computers and insist that they are used as tools and no more.

But that doesn't seem very likely.

Meanwhile there is hope.

Would a computer write this book?

No, of course not.

Self-publishing

Since truth became a dangerous commodity it has become necessary for many authors to publish their own work. Traditional publishers will not risk upsetting the establishment by publishing any author who tries to share inconvenient truths. The close down on the truth has been incredibly well-planned and efficiently managed.

Naturally, the shills and thugs and trolls use the term 'self-publishing' as a term of abuse – implying that because an author only self publishes because his or her work is unworthy of publication rather than because self-publishing is the only way round the censorship which now abounds.

So, when the Wikipedia page which carries my name was taken over by mindless morons in the service of the fascist state, I suddenly became described as a 'self-publisher' and a 'blogger'. (For the record I have no idea what a 'blogger' is, although I have written articles for my website since long before Wikipedia was born.)

Sadly, even self-publishing has become increasingly difficult.

One major platform, which has published over 100 of my books (most of which had previously been published by mainstream publishers) now refuses to publish books by me which deal with the infection. (Oddly, however, that same platform will publish books on these subjects by other authors. Indeed, one thief stole the transcripts of my videos from my website and published them under his own name. He put my picture on the cover of the book but takes all the royalties himself. The platform allowed this.)

For the record, my books have been published by dozens of mainstream publishers in the UK and by mainstream publishers in 50 countries (in 25 languages) with many bestsellers around the world. But as far as Wikipedia is concerned I am a self-publishing blogger.

The ignorant editors at Wikipedia are clearly unaware that many of the world's most renowned and successful authors have, from time to time, published their own books.

Sewage

A new national smart sewer network is being put in place in the USA to predictively analyse American sewage? They say this will enable them to spot virus outbreaks. But what else are they going to be measuring – and why?

Shakespeare (William)

'If this were portrayed upon a stage now, I could condemn it as improbable fiction.'
'Hell is empty. The demons are everywhere apparent.'

Shaw (George Bernard)

'All progress depends on the unreasonable man.'

Smacking

The smacking of children has been made illegal in Scotland. This is just one small step towards the State taking over the 'ownership' of all children – much as was forecast by Aldous Huxley. (Scotland is the 58th country in the world to ban smacking in the home, also giving children the same rights as adults.)

It is traditionally considered the responsibility of parents to teach their children old-fashioned things like respect and good behaviour but the Scottish Government has, at a stroke, removed the parents from the equation and appointed itself the guardian of every child. (The Scottish Government has form as far as this is concerned since a couple of years ago they tried to impose the idea of guardianship on all children.)

Taking responsibility from parents, and giving it to the State, is one of the many tenets of Agenda 21.

The majority of doctors and psychologists and behavioural specialists believe that modest and controlled physical punishment is an essential part of child upbringing – and far preferable to the far more damaging psychological punishment which involves withdrawing affection from a child for (sometimes) long periods of time.

Dr Benjamin Spock, probably the most famous paediatrician of all time, and certainly the most influential, began his career by opposing physical punishment but changed his mind, and his advice, in later life and agreed that modest and controlled physical punishment (a smack on the hand, for example) was far preferable to the alternatives.

Small businesses

The Agenda 21 plan is to see small businesses destroyed by the introduction of many new laws. The laws will be easily dealt with by large companies which can hire specialist departments to deal with additional complications. In the world of Agenda 21, everything will require a licence and permit – and obtaining these licences and permits will be difficult and expensive. Doubters should remember that the EU did everything it could to kill off small businesses.

Smart

The word 'smart' (as applied to meters, cities and so on) is often applied to anything which removes all your rights and privacy, and gives those rights to the Agenda 21 cultists.

Smart cities (smart growth zones)

Part of the Agenda 21 plan is to move all citizens into huge (or 'mega') cities. China has already started doing this. People are forced from rural and suburban areas into high rise flats. This is all rather reminiscent of the highland clearances.

Citizens from rural communities will be forced into the smart cities by a complex combination of positive and negative incentives. There will be grants, tax credits and housing benefits to persuade people to move into cities. And in the countryside, rural properties will be condemned, seized and demolished. The building of new roads and railway lines and sewage treatment facilities to serve the new cities will be used as an excuse for confiscation and demolition.

Re-wilding plans will also be used to force people out of the countryside as will huge dams. In China, the Yangtze dam displaced millions of people from rural areas to smart cities.

In addition, there will be very few or no rural services with fire brigade, ambulance services and postal services all being ended in rural areas.

Poor broadband will make it increasingly difficult for people to live in rural areas as more and more of our lives become dependent upon the internet. Rural roads will be left un-mended and bus and train services to rural areas will be cut even further. Farms will no longer be needed as naturally grown food is replaced with artificial food made in factories. Bill Gates' plan to block out the sun will damage farming.

In the UK, the plans are already well in hand to create these smart cities.

Under cover of 2020's manufactured crisis, the Government introduced new planning legislation. Development in England will in future be concentrated on brownfield sites in 20 selected cities in the Midlands and the North. Building will only be allowed in places such as Birmingham, Bradford, Leeds and Stoke. These are to be the new, smart cities. Once land has been declared 'unprotected' it will enjoy a 'presumption in favour' of planning permission. This marks the end of local democracy.

In January 2021, it was reported that seven of the largest cities in the UK were experiencing a property boom.

Those commentators who have noticed this dramatic change in the way England is organised have been rather indignant but, as far as I know, none of them has noticed that this is connected to the Agenda 21 plan for smart cities. Indeed, these are largely the same commentators who regard those of us worried about Agenda 21 as 'conspiracy theorists' and then dismiss us as 'discredited lunatics'.

The Agenda 21 supporters claim that the smart cities will give us a healthier way of life. We will be able to walk or cycle everywhere we need to go. We will not need to travel because there will be nowhere to go outside our city and since all cities will be the same what would be the point in going to another city? Pollution will drop because no one (except the bureaucrats who will need to travel about to make sure we are being obedient) will have a motor car.

Apartments in the high rise towers will be cheap to rent because they will be small (and poorly built). There will be little need for energy for heating. No one will have a garden so there won't be any need to waste water growing grass, flowers or vegetables. The weather will be controlled so there will never be any snow or ice. It will rain at night. There will be no police and no crime because everyone will be watching everyone else to make sure that they behave, and drones and robots will be watching us all to make sure we report any law-breaking we observe.

Smart meters

Homes are being fitted with smart meters which are allegedly being introduced to help consumers save money.

However, although a smart meter is extremely unlikely to save more than a few pennies, it might kill you. The risks to human health are so real that in France, a court ordered the removal of some smart meters because people had been made ill by them.

Moreover, it now seems that a new sort of smart meter will have to be installed in the near future. So existing smart meters will have to be removed and, presumably, dumped.

In the UK, the Government is reviewing plans to give electricity companies the power to cut off electricity supplies without warning or compensation. A particular target will be users of large amounts of electricity in homes. Electric vehicle charging points and central heating systems are particularly likely to be targeted. Smart meters will make it easy for electricity companies to cut off electricity supplies to individual homes. Dissidents will find that their electricity supplies disappear.

Sneaks and snitches

For several decades now people have been trained to abandon basic human behaviour and to sneak and snitch on their neighbours, relatives and friends to the tax authorities, the social services department and the police. They have been encouraged with cash payments for their treachery.

Today, in addition to encouraging people to report neighbours or family members who break laws in any way, the police have published advertisements inviting people to report family, friends, neighbours and workmates who they suspect of having been 'radicalised' into expressing opinions at variance with those of their government.

It is clear now that this was all preparation for the future social credit.

These days snitching and sneaking is organised and professional among companies everywhere. If you buy a new television set the retailer will tell the TV licensing gestapo what you've done. If you buy a few chickens so that you can let them run around in your garden and lay fresh, free-range eggs, the person who provided you with the chickens will be 'encouraged' to tell the 'authorities' and someone from the chicken licensing gestapo will come to your home and, if it is for some reason considered inappropriate for you to keep chickens, kill the birds you have bought.

Social credit

A few years ago, in a book of mine called, *The Game's Afoot*, I wrote that the Chinese Government was giving people marks according to behaviour. The social engineering (citizens being ranked and rated according to their behaviour) began in earnest just over a decade ago.

'The Government,' I wrote in some amazement, 'will measure people's behaviour in order to decide what services they are entitled to. Anyone who incurs black marks for traffic offences, fare dodging or jay walking will find that they are no longer entitled to the full range of public services and rights. Moreover, internet activity will also be used to assess behaviour. Individuals who do bad things on the internet (or whose searches are considered questionable) will find themselves 'black marked'. Researchers from the International Monetary Fund have called for internet search history to be tied to credit scores. Individuals who have 'responsible' jobs will be subjected to enhanced scrutiny.'

It was called a social credit score and I wrote then that it was likely that Western governments would soon follow suit.

And they are now doing so with great enthusiasm. It might not have obviously reached your town just yet but it will.

China has led the way because the Chinese system is more efficient than anything the West can offer. The Chinese Government has control over everything and the people don't have much control over anything.

It works very easily.

Everyone starts off with so many points.

And a smart app on every phone measures behaviour and helps the authorities decide whether or not you are a good citizen.

There are, of course, video cameras absolutely everywhere watching to see whether you cross the road at the wrong time, smoke in public, throw down litter or do anything considered anti-social or inappropriate. If you talk to the wrong sort of people you'll find your credit rating goes down. Stand and talk to me, for example, and you'll get black marks.

China has one camera for every two people and they're equipped with facial recognition technology that can pick an individual out of a football crowd in less time than it takes to say 'surely they can't do that!'

Supermarket computers watch to see how much you spend on alcohol, cigarettes, sweets and fatty foods. You'll lose points if you spend too much on the wrong sort of food.

Local authorities measure how much recycling you put out, and cameras in the bins will tell computers how much food you've thrown away and how much excess packaging you've had to discard. Eating meat or consuming unacceptable foodstuffs will result in a severe loss of points as will putting too much refuse into public bins. Facial recognition cameras in bins will see and punish you and reduce your food credit.

In a way, social credit scores are already here in the West though up until now they have been introduced slowly and surreptitiously.

In the UK for example, drivers of more expensive motor cars have to pay a special, massively increased tax to use a motor car on the roads. That's a blatant punishment for spending 'too much' on a motor car.

On the other hand, citizens who drive electric cars do not have to pay anything towards the building, maintenance and repair of roads. They are exempt from the tax because they are 'good' citizens. Their cars use the roads just as much as cars which are powered with petrol or diesel but they are exempt.

Drivers of petrol or diesel powered cars are punished for being 'bad' citizens and must pay ever-rising annual taxes to pay for the roads. The system ignores the fact that electric cars have been proven to be no better for the environment than petrol or diesel powered cars. And drive your car into a city and you'll have to pay a special penalty.

So what can we expect?

If you live in a house that is bigger than you need then you will be marked down as socially undesirable and your taxes will rise. If you have spare rooms you'll be punished. If you do a useful job and give money to charity you'll get extra points. If you criticise the Government then you'll lose points.

When you're away from home, the authorities will, of course, know where you are all the time.

Indeed, if you behave badly you won't be allowed to go far from home. If you haven't obeyed all the health regulations you won't be allowed to travel on public transport, fly anywhere or go abroad.

If your social credit rating goes down you won't be able to borrow money, buy a house or book a decent room in a hotel.

If your rating goes down too far you won't be allowed to go into hospital, and if you get taken to hospital by accident they'll slam a Do Not Resuscitate notice around your neck before you can say 'what's that for?'

You'll receive bonus points if you live in a tiny, modern, poorly built flat with thin walls and absolutely no privacy but you'll lose those points if you keep a pet or complain about anything.

If you spend too much on clothes or shoes your rating will go down, and saving money will mark you out as guilty of something or other and you won't be able to hire a car, get a promotion at work, use a gym or get your children into a school with textbooks.

If you are a lot of trouble you'll find that your internet speeds will slow to a crawl and if you have your own business and talk back to council officials, you won't get any help with planning problems or be able to obtain any official government contracts.

If you don't dress appropriately when out in public, or are spotted crossing the road when the lights are against you, then you'll be photographed and your picture displayed. If you have a row with a neighbour then your pictures will be put on a billboard near your home and you'll be shamed. If you are late with your taxes you'll be marked down for regular audits, your business will be inspected once a week and your picture will appear on a shame board on the internet. You'll find it impossible to obtain licences, permits and loans you might need.

In restaurants, the cameras will study your manners and eating habits and the amount of food you leave on the plate. All of these things are likely to result in damage to your social credit rating.

Snitches, sneaks, police officers and over-compliant government employees will mark you down for any sin of commission or omission.

And by now you probably think I'm making this up and I wish I were but I'm not. We're not talking about the far distant future. We're talking about the very near future. Indeed, much of this is already happening in China.

You'll receive points if you give blood, lose points if you associate with people with low scores, be punished if you spend frivolously or criticise the Government on social media.

Not having the correct number of children, being overweight and owning land will result in a loss of social credit points. (Note that in the UK the Office for National Statistics has already claimed that childless women will be a burden on the State because they'll have no one to look after them).

Not having a smart meter in your home will result in a loss of points as will any example of civil disobedience. Chronic sickness, mental illness, being old and being disabled will lose you points as will being arrested (it doesn't matter whether you are found guilty).

Having too big a carbon footprint, being middle class or white or asking too many questions will all result in a loss of points as will being too protective of your family.

You'll lose social credit points if you cause someone 'identity harm', say something that makes someone feel uncomfortable about who they are, where they are from or what they look like – or don't say something that causes them to feel good.

If you show any micro-aggression, are accused of exhibiting 'white privilege' or alleged to have stirred up hatred you'll be punished. If you are reported to have behaved in a threatening or abusing or insulting manner you will be in trouble as you will if you communicate threatening abusive or insulting material to another person.

Your intention will be irrelevant. There is no need for a guilty verdict. The complainant only has to say he was hurt. Writers, actors or film or stage directors could be charged if anyone finds any of their material offensive. Shakespearean plays won't appear much in the future.

You probably think I'm really kidding now. But I'm not.

In the UK, the police now define a crime or incident as hateful based on the perception of the victim (and not on the intent of the offender).

Naturally, the police and politicians have been encouraging citizens to snitch on those breaking laws.

You can get into serious trouble for playing loud music or having trees in your garden. (Strangely, trees are regarded as bad, despite their value in getting rid of carbon dioxide, because they may interfere with communications.) There will be no place for aesthetics or nature in the new world order.

What else will be bad?

Eating on public transport, missing a medical appointment, parking in the wrong place, missing a job interview and jaywalking will all lose you points and make your life more difficult.

If you think I've gone mad you should know that cybersecurity experts have discovered that 32% of adults between 25 and 34 in 21 countries (a total of 10,000 individuals) have already had difficulty getting a mortgage or loan because of their social media activity. And so far around 4.5 billion people around the world use the internet and most have social media accounts.

Moreover, a fairly scary survey found that two thirds of individuals are willing to share information about themselves or others to get a shopping discount while half are willing to do so if it helps them skip queues at airports. One in two individuals says they are happy for the Government to monitor everyone's social media behaviour if it means keeping the public safe.

Of course, it will be impossible to find out what your social credit score is, to find out exactly how scores are made up or to correct any error. And scores will be changed in real time. So you could join a queue thinking you are entitled to hire a car or board a train and find, when you get to the front of the queue that your rating has changed and you can't do either of those things.

Governments, big companies and local authorities are already gathering information about you from facial recognition cameras, biometric studies at airports, drones, surveillance planes and social media. This is the technocratic state in full fly. Using a silly name on social media will provide you with absolutely no protection. They know exactly who 'stinkyfeet' really is and they know the name, address and inside leg measurement of 'bumfluff'.

You can forget about privacy, freedom or rights.

We will soon all be living in China.

If one person in a family breaks the law, the whole family will be punished.

Taking an active part in a religious ceremony will result in punishment. You may, for example, be sent to an education and training centre where the inmates study political propaganda.

Every time you give information online, they are storing up information about you, your views, your personality and so on.

And there are so, so many ways in which your social credit score can be adversely affected.

If you drop rubbish in a public place you will be shamed and will lose points. In Thailand, tourists who drop rubbish in a national park must give their name and address. If they leave rubbish behind they are in trouble.

All this is known as social engineering. It's something politicians have been trying to do for many years since, when it works, which it does, it gives them complete control over the population. There is no longer any need for politicians to worry about opposition or criticism.

In China, citizens who do 'good' things for the State, and their community, are rewarded by having their photographs and names on a local wall. This is exactly what I remember seeing in East

Germany in the 1970s. And back then people vied with one another to please the State and win a place on the wall.

So, again, if you want to know the sort of society you and your children will live in then look at China now (and East Germany fifty years ago) where what people do, say and think is being monitored.

But our future won't be so free and easy as life in China is at the moment.

We are moving rapidly into a dystopian, digital dictatorship.

Good behaviour will be rewarded and bad behaviour punished. But who defines what is good and what is bad?

'Geotracking' is the new normal now. Your financial records are combined with your criminal record, academic record, medical record and shopping patterns. They're keeping an eye on the type of friends you have, the videos you watch, the people you date or marry or meet.

This is Big Brother on speed

In the brave new world, those with a low credit score won't be able to move an inch.

People who speak out about corruption, or who question the propaganda will be punished. If they are fined then their fine will be higher because they are seen as bad people.

And it's already all happening.

Computer games are training us for our future.

I'm banned in China because I wrote a column for a Chinese newspaper which was considered unacceptable. My books in Chinese were instantly removed from sale.

I leave you with this fact.

There are public loos in China which won't let you in without first checking your face and identifying you. Only then will the machine dispense the small quantity of loo paper you are allowed.

How many sheets will you be allowed if you have a low credit score? Two? One? None at all?

You may be smiling now.

But see if you're still smiling in twelve months' time.

Meanwhile, governments everywhere are using fear and ridicule and brainwashing and indoctrination techniques to force you to accept social engineering.

Special Branch

Under the Covert Human Intelligence Sources (Criminal Conduct) Bill in the UK any intelligence service will be legally able to commit whatever crimes they fancy. They will be allowed to murder British citizens without fear of their being any reprisals or consequences. Who can they kill? David Kelly? Oh no, they killed him already. Princess Diana?

They can kill you – if you don't behave yourself. They can kill me – if I write a book or article, or make a video, criticising the Government. As if I would do such a thing.

Incidentally, I could find no mention of this Bill on the BBC website – though it is probably the most important piece of legislation since the Magna Carta was signed.

Spies in the home

Some new television sets can film and record what the TV's viewers are saying and doing. The films and recording continue even when the TV is switched off and can be sent off to the 'authorities'.

It has been reported that Alexa (the oh so useful and ubiquitous voice) can record questions, comments and conversations. I believe this to be true.

Worse still, it was revealed in early 2021 that children are to be used as spies against their parents by state agencies. The Covert Human Intelligence Sources bill will allow teenagers to spy on their parents and it will authorise them to commit crimes. More than 20 state agencies in the UK will be allowed to use children as undercover agents. These child agents will be able to glean information that could be used to protect public health or national security or to help collect taxes. Older children (16 and 17) could be recruited to spy on their parents if they were suspected of being involved in crime or terrorism.

Sport

There will be no place for sport in the new normal. Both professional and amateur sport will be outlawed as unnecessary and irrelevant and a waste of essential resources. Parks, playing fields and golf courses will be allowed to go wild. The only sports allowed will be eSports (though without the live spectators).

Starvation

The world's new unelected leaders believe that the world is massively overpopulated. They wish to deal with this by reducing the number of babies being born and by increasing the number of people dying. In the Ukrainian genocide (known as the Holodomor) which took place in the Ukraine in 1932-33, around 12 million people are believed to have died of starvation.

It seems certain that food and water shortages are going to be used to rid the population of the several billion individuals who are considered surplus to requirements by a cabal of billionaires.

Statues

Statues are being removed all over the world because of complaints by Black Lives Matter protestors.

For example, in Exeter in England there is a campaign (which may well have succeeded by the time you read this) to remove a statue of a British war hero.

Campaigners want to remove the statue to General Buller, who won the Victoria Cross, because he is said to represent patriarchal structures (e.g. he is male) and 'negatively impacts on anyone who doesn't define themselves in binary gender terms'.

The campaign to remove the statue has nothing to do with General Buller, of course. It is part of a wider campaign to destroy our history so that we can all become of the new world order of slaves.

Stockholm Syndrome

The Stockholm Syndrome is a condition in which hostages develop a psychological attachment to their captors. The term originated in 1973 when four hostages were taken during a bank robbery in Stockholm, Sweden. The hostages refused to testify against their captors and, indeed, defended them.

In 2020, it was difficult to understand why so many members of the public were acting like cowards, behaving obediently and accepting the blatant nonsense they were being fed. In the end, I came to the conclusion that having been filled with fear they were accepting the instructions of the authoritarian figures in government. It was a form of mass hysteria; a new version of the Stockholm Syndrome.

Suicide

In the US, a survey of 5,412 adults for the CDC showed that 41% had reported at least one adverse mental or behavioural health problem but among the 17-24 year olds the figure rose to 75%. Anxiety, depression and suicidal thoughts were commonplace. Over 10% of adults had considered suicide in the 30 days prior to being questioned.

In late October 2020, the London Ambulance Service in the UK revealed that they were dealing with 37 suicides or attempted suicides each day. In 2019, they were dealing with 22 suicides or attempted suicides each day. It is reasonable to assume that the increase in the number of people trying to kill themselves, or killing themselves, was a direct consequence of the events of 2020.

Suppression

Those who doubt that the events of 2020 were planned might like to reflect on two things.

First, everything that happened was global. So-called mistakes occurred in many countries.

Second, there was a clampdown on discussion, debate or the publication of news relating to the events of 2020.

Sustainable

This is the most dangerous and destructive word in the world. You will see it everywhere. 'Sustainability' should be approached with great caution. It invariably precedes the arrival of trouble, penury and hunger. 'Sustainable development' means oppression, suppression and a complete lack of freedom or democracy.

Swinburne (A.C.)

'There are worse things waiting for men than death.'

Talking to plants

Prince Charles believes that talking to plants helps them grow. What he probably doesn't realise is that when he speaks, he breathes carbon dioxide over his plants. And plants live on carbon dioxide.

Charles wants a smaller global population.

Does he realise that if there are fewer people, there will be less carbon dioxide.

And if there is less carbon dioxide, there will be fewer plants or smaller plants.

And, therefore, there will be less food available.

And more starvation.

Charles appears to be an idiot and may well be. He is also immensely dangerous.

Taxes

The huge debts incurred in 2020 will mean that taxes will have to rise dramatically. There will be many new taxes introduced. And because the income raised through taxes won't be enough to pay off government debts, confiscation programmes will be introduced. Taxes will soar and will help enrich the billionaires and impoverish everyone else.

Confiscating personal property (houses, land, vehicles and so on) fits nicely with the Agenda 21 plan to ensure that the State owns everything and individuals own nothing.

Billionaires and members of the royal family will not be affected by the new taxes and confiscation programmes.

Teachers

'The pupils know something is not quite right,' said a school-teacher commenting on the fact that her students were being forced to obey a variety of scientifically unjustifiable regulations.

Teachers betrayed their pupils during 2020. They kept schools closed when they need not have been closed, they demanded that pupils covered their faces, they insisted on pupils keeping a distance from one another (when they should have known that the measures they were demanding would serve absolutely no useful purpose but would cause long-term psychological damage), they insisted on school closures (when the closures were entirely unnecessary and merely did irreparable damage to the education of millions of students) and they allowed the installation of Wi-Fi in school classrooms when they should have been aware of the existence of evidence proving that Wi-Fi and cell phone systems in schools would do irreparable damage to the health of pupils.

Technocracy

A now prominent political philosophy which promotes the idea of scientists running the world.

Telephones

Try to find and buy an old-fashioned dial telephone which does not rely on electricity. If there is a major power outage you will still be able to communicate with others who have similar old-fashioned telephones.

Television

'Our job is to give people not what they want, but what we decide they ought to have.'
Richard Salent (Former President CBS News in US)

Temporary

Temporary measures (as introduced by governments) are never temporary; they invariably become permanent. The so-called temporary measures will remain to remind us that we are in danger and should therefore be ever-fearful. The hypoxia caused by covering mouth and nose will, of course, make citizens ever more stupid and accepting, thereby conditioning them and preparing them to accept future tyrannies.

Terra Carta Pledge

Prince Charles has urged businesses to sign the Terra Carta Pledge to put the planet first. This nonsense is part of Agenda 21's plan for a 'sustainable' future. It will be interesting to see if Charles decides to do his bit for a sustainable future by putting an end to his peregrinations around the world by private aeroplane.

Terror

Terror is always used to intimidate, to gain power, to push through laws and to usurp human rights. The advocates of Agenda 21 have used a campaign of terror (and its antithesis and regular companion 'fear') to drive their evil agenda.

Terrorism

On 2nd July 2020, I defined terrorism as using intimidation and violence in the pursuit of political aims.

There can be no doubt that governments everywhere have been using intimidation to pressurise us into being scared of their fashionable version of the flu bug.

And there is no doubt that governments are using violence to oppress their citizens.

My conclusion is that our governments are terrorists – it is our duty to oppose them, to defeat them and to ensure that they are punished. If we don't stand up for ourselves they will continue to oppress us with what I long ago described as intellectual terrorism.

Test and trace apps

These remarkably badly designed applications are collecting private and personal information from millions of gullible citizens. The information will be shared with the police and, doubtless, the tax authorities.

Many individuals are reported to have given false names and details when required to give personal information when entering cafes, pubs, restaurants, churches and other buildings. In late October, during the Welsh autumn restrictions, two pubs were closed because customers had given fake names and details. The authorities became suspicious when 479 people called M. Hancock attended one public house in a single week. Suspicions were aroused still further when it was discovered that all had given the number of a disused telephone box in Cardiff as their contact number. On the other hand, 1,543 people who had given their name as Jones really were called Jones.

I am told that some individuals are so determined not to give their personal details to strangers that they have had fake visiting cards printed. Such cards do not cost much, I am told, and when offered as evidence of identification, look satisfactorily official.

In view of the real physical risks involved, before you accept any test which involves a physically invasive procedure you should write down the date and time, the place where the test is being performed and the name of the person doing the test. You should also make a note of the qualifications of the tester and under whose authority they are performing the test.

Few people seem to think it odd that they have to be tested regularly to see if they have acquired an allegedly dangerous disease. It would seem reasonable to assume that someone who had a deadly disease might have noticed that they have symptoms. And since the infectious symptoms associated with the disease are pretty much the same as the flu (coughing and sneezing) it would seem rather likely that sufferers would be aware of the condition. (As an aside, how can you spread a disease if you don't have the symptoms which are recognised as the methods by which the disease is spread? At least one major study has shown that asymptomatic transmission does not occur.)

The Trilateral Commission

The Trilateral Commission, founded in 1973 by David Rockefeller and Zbigniew Brzezinski, was created as a new international economic order. It was, perhaps, the forerunner of globalisation. The developing short-term aim was to abolish national, state and personal sovereignty, to reform global trade, to introduce mass surveillance, promote the internet of things, roll out extensive cellular networks and, perhaps most significant of all, to censor all opposition, to demonise all critics and to stamp out all debate of these issues.

The ultimate aim was to lead to a technocratic world.

The country now regarded as closest to the ideal is China where communism has been the stepping stone to the 'new world order' also known as communitarianism. In the rest of the world socialism and far left liberalism have provided the necessary political framework for the progression of Agenda 21.

Thermal scanner

A thermal scanner is a completely useless device held by a person dressed in the sort of costume popularised by astronauts, but with a plastic apron added. The instrument is held a few inches or a foot or so from the forehead of the subject and used to measure the temperature. Thermal scanners are widely used to 'diagnose' specific diseases though in truth, in this regard, holding a doughnut near to the subject's head would provide equally useful information.

Truth

'Truth is like poetry. And most people hate fucking poetry.' (*from the movie 'The Big Short'*)

Twain (Mark)

'It's easier to fool people than to convince them that they have been fooled.'

Two tier society

A two tier society is coming fast. The top tier will consist of those who have been jabbed. The lower tier will be those who have not been jabbed. This will divide families and friends more dramatically than traditional divisions, and the divide will be permanent. This will be a class system and those in the lower tier will be a definite underclass. They will be outlaws.

UN and carbon emissions

The United Nations has requested individual nations to reduce their carbon emissions by 25%. Those countries which agreed to what was, in practice, a demand, abandoned their national sovereignty to an unelected, unofficial world government. There was never any scientific evidence to support the theory that global warming exists (whatever the cause) or was a significant threat to mankind. But despite the lack of evidence, limits were placed on economic development, standards of living were reduced and fossil fuel power generators were closed – all to fit the aims of Agenda 21.

United Nations

The United Nations was originally set up with the goals of ending world hunger and achieving peace on earth. It was set up in 1945 but since 1959, the John Birch Society in the USA has fought (without success) to take the USA out of the UN – claiming (quite accurately) that its true goal was to set up a world government. The UN has created its own army and has pushed for a world tax.

Today, the UN is recognised as a corrupt organisation which has done much harm (for example, its record on bribery and favouritism and the Iraqi oil for food scandal). Unelected individuals (mostly appointed as a favour or a reward) run the organisation and its subsidiaries (such as the World Health Organisation) and the UN's aim appears to be to deprive the world's population of independence, freedom, democracy, privacy and dignity and to impose a totalitarian rule. Their plan was always to use fear to control the world's population and to use political correctness and false health and safety regulations to frighten people and to promise them a world free of risks –albeit free of freedom. The cult of global warming has been used to promote the UN's aims.

The UN's plans include the reform of education, and re-designing it to dumb down teaching and to produce semi-literate, semi-numerate citizens. Agenda 21 also plans to replace traditional medical care with an endless series of inoculation programmes.

To achieve its aims the UN needs to eliminate sovereignty, nationalism, individualism and all human ambition and motivation. It was because of its opposition to nationalism and sovereignty that the establishment was so opposed to Brexit.

(Many of those who supported the EU did so out of a misunderstanding of the aims of the European Union. Not a few wanted the UK to stay in the EU because they were worried that if Brexit went ahead they would not be able to purchase Italian shoes or French wines quite so readily.)

The UN long ago gave itself rights and powers it was never intended to have.

It has given itself authority over the world's climate, the environment, health, safety and education and it has told national, sovereign governments what plans they must put in place and what time frame they must follow. The UN has 17 specific goals and 169 subsidiary goals. These sound wholesome until you dig down and find out how it is intended that the goals are achieved, and what the mealy mouthed platitudes really mean.

The UN, which follows an agenda which most of us would regard as communist (though it is communist with Luciferian overtones), wants wealth and technology to be redistributed and private property to be put into the public domain. Their aim is collectivism; putting the Global State or World Government (as run by or through the United Nations) above all individual human rights. Bizarrely, the UN has blamed the world's woes on patriarchy. There has never been any attempt to explain this claim, or to provide any evidence in support of the allegation. The UN appears not to believe in evidence or science, preferring to make its judgements without such distractions.

The myth of global warming is used as the framework for this takeover and is the excuse for controlling education, a massive programme of confiscation, relocating people into centralised mega, smart cities and a huge programme of depopulation. The UN has become extraordinarily adept at capitalising on tragedy (whether real or man-made) and uses tragedy as yet another excuse for increased government intervention.

At the 1992 summit in Rio de Janeiro, there was a call for sustainable development and local councils and community activists were recruited to demand that environmental policies be initiated. However, these policies were manipulated at global level.

Aggressive recycling policies have been introduced with fines on councils and individuals introduced (in the EU through the European Union) to force them through. The recycling programmes were never practical and much of the carefully sorted material has been exported to be buried or burnt. Indeed, the recycling programme was never about recycling – it was always about control.

The policies have, of course, been global.

In California in the USA, home owners were threatened with jail if they cleared the brush around their homes because doing so would endanger a local species of rat which lived in the brush. The resultant fires destroyed millions of dollars' worth of homes. The rats moved away because of the fires.

In the UK, well-built Victorian homes were demolished and replaced with poorly built modern homes (built to poor modern standards). This was all part of the programme to force people into relocating into flats in smart cities.

The destruction of local businesses (which reached a zenith in 2020) and the absurd environmental rules (built upon the nonsense of global warming) were also designed to force individuals into smart cities.

I have seen one report which states that the UN (which is most decidedly not in any way a democratic institution and which has no elected officials) has around 3,000 employees. This seems a trifle on the light side since the secretariat alone has 41,000 employees, and the total number of people being paid by the UN is considerably higher. The Chief Executives Board for Coordination gives figures for 2012 of 30,723 plus 52,596 (2012 seems to be the latest available figure) and this doesn't include subsidiaries such as the World Health Organisation or the peacekeeping force (which comprises of soldiers from individual countries).

There are many perks for UN employees. So, for example, if UN staff are required to pay tax on their salaries and emoluments in the country where they are working then the General Assembly will reimburse staff so that they pay no tax. This seems rather strange for an organisation which is attempting to force a communist approach to life onto the rest of the world and which is promoting a 'better' and 'more sustainable' society.

During the Iraq War, the United Nations banned many imports into Iraq. The UN's ban included medicine, blood and other essentials (such as water purifiers) and as a result one in ten children died before their first birthday. American attacks had pretty well destroyed Iraq's sewage and water treatment systems, and the absence of water purification substances meant that contaminated water had to be drunk. American bombing had also destroyed the Iraqi power grid but the sanctions prevented the importing of the parts needed for repairs. The absence of food meant that parents sometimes had to choose between children – keeping one alive rather than seeing two children die of starvation. The total number of children dying as a result of the UNs sanctions is not known but believed to be greater than 1.5 million.

The United Nations is, without a doubt, an evil organisation. The plan is to create hell on earth.

Universal basic income

The idea of governments paying their citizens a universal basic income has been around for a long time. It is now getting closer to reality. In the UK, the benefits system and the tax credits system are already providing a universal basic income for millions. Furlough schemes are accustoming citizens to accepting a regular pay cheque from the Government. Providing every citizen with a monthly payment would cost a good deal of money but it would save billions currently wasted on administration and fraud.

I used to regard a basic income as a good idea.

In my book, *Bloodless Revolution* I pointed out that if the State paid us all a citizen's basic income, this would free everyone from exploitation, eradicate the need for unemployment or welfare benefits, ensure a much fairer tax system, eradicate poverty, end involuntary prostitution, do much to reduce crime levels and encourage people to work (in order to increase their income).

The citizen's basic income would stop people feeling resentment about their neighbours who didn't work. And it would allow the Government to find more productive employment for the vast army of bureaucrats involved in administrating the huge variety of State benefits. The saving to the nation would be phenomenal. Millions of man-hours would be freed for more creative enterprises.

In the UK, social security payments currently cost the nation well over £200 billion a year. Paying the bureaucrats and administering the payments costs half as much again. With ten million pensioners, the state pension scheme costs at least another £60 billion (and the numbers are rising fast) and administering the nation's pension scheme costs billions more. Pensions and other payments to former civil servants and public sector workers also cost billions.

Giving every adult in the country a lifetime income of, say, £10,000 a year would be cheaper than our current state pension and benefits programme. And it would be simpler and fairer and better both for individuals and for the State.

But things have changed.

Today, the universal basic income is being used as a form of control over the population.

Regretfully, I no longer think it is a good idea.

Veganism

Do you think it's an accident that veganism has suddenly become popular? It isn't. They don't want us eating animals. It takes up too much time. It's a slow, messy process. They want us eating the food they are making in laboratories. Some of it will, of course look and taste like meat.

I happen to be ovo-vegan (I do eat free range eggs) but it's my choice.

I don't approve of people being forced to behave in a particular way – even though I might approve of the end result, the means is unacceptable.

Vertical farming

Vertical farming is a silly name for factory farming.

(The followers of Agenda 21 constantly change the nomenclature they favour. So, for example, they changed 'global warming' to 'global cooling' to 'climate change'. Many of the words and phrases they use are devised by psychologists and then altered if they do not serve the correct purpose.)

Vitamin D

Vitamin D deficiency is very common among the ill – especially those who have infections.

Locking people indoors massively increases the risk of vitamin D deficiency, and the symptoms and health risks of vitamin D deficiency are massive.

Vitamin D deficiency doesn't just increase the risk of contracting an infection, there is also an increased risk of heart disease, asthma, cancer and dementia. Plus there is evidence that a low vitamin D could result in high blood pressure, diabetes and multiple sclerosis.

Moreover, individuals who have dark skin already have a risk of developing vitamin D deficiency because the presence of so much melanin reduces their skin's ability to make vitamin D when exposed to sunlight.

Vitamin D is essential (as are all vitamins) and without it our bodies simply do not function effectively and cell regeneration is less efficient. And again, here's the vital bit, vitamin D is an essential vitamin for preventing infection.

For most people the most important source of vitamin D is sunshine. People who stay indoors for much of the time are deprived of vitamin D and more likely to suffer from viral infections.

You can get some vitamin D from fortified foods but for most people, shut away indoors, the answer is probably taking a vitamin D supplement.

Voice recognition

Banks and other large companies are now inviting customers to record a phrase or two in order to identify themselves.

Voice recognition is sold as a method of avoiding fraud and a way of helping customers protect themselves.

This is nonsense, of course.

Banks never do anything to help their customers protect their privacy. For decades now their ethos has been directed towards the opposite.

The aim, of course, is to create a profile for each one of us – combining facial and voice recognition software and then connecting that to credit ratings and so on.

War

It is no exaggeration to say that we are at war with our own governments.

Our governments want to destroy us physically, mentally and spiritually.

Their aim is to make us so weakened and so frightened that we will do everything they want.

Remember: everything that has happened was meant to happen. Everything about the 'new normal' is designed to create and exploit suspicion, to create fear, despair and hatred. These all weaken the spirit of the people.

The aim is to turn us all into victims – but victims who are responsible for our own fate. They tell us that it is our fault that the world is in a terrible state and so we must be punished. We must have all responsibility taken from us and others, wiser and with a broader view, will take charge of every aspect of our lives.

Concepts such as dignity, trust, respect are now regarded as old-fashioned, out of date and too reminiscent of the Empire of which we must now be ashamed, and the Victorians who must be regarded as criminals.

Water

You might think that your tap water is clean, fresh and good to drink. But you'd be wrong if you thought that. Tap water is fine for washing but it's not good for drinking. Saying this immediately classifies me as a lunatic. But read on.

First, it has probably had fluoride added to it. The authorities have been adding the stuff to drinking water since the middle of the 20th century. The claim was that it kept teeth healthy. This was nonsense. Even the WHO has said that there is no difference in tooth decay between the countries which add fluoride to drinking water and those which do not. Fluoride does, however, cause a good many long-term health problems – including cancer.

Second, much drinking water is taken from rivers into which treated sewage has been deposited. Now, I am perfectly prepared to accept that the treated sewage pumped into rivers doesn't contain bits of loo paper, used tampons and so on. They've been filtered out. But the residues of prescription drugs such as tranquillisers and antibiotics haven't been filtered out because they can't be. And there has for years been clear evidence that rivers, and therefore drinking water, contain female hormones (from the contraceptive pill).I first wrote about this in the 1980s and there is a summary in my book, *Meat Causes Cancer – More Food for Thought*. There is also evidence that contaminants of drugs usually given by injection may be found in drinking water.

Wealth tax

The much mooted wealth tax (to help pay for the costs incurred in 2020 and the following years) will not be paid by the wealthy (who will go into tax exile) but by the middle classes aiming to acquire a little bit of wealth for themselves or their children.

Weaponisation of radio frequencies

The Russians and the Americans have been experimenting with 'energy' weapons for nearly a century. In America, a program called HAARP (High-Frequency Active Auroral Frequency Program) was set up in 1933 and experimented with the weaponisation of radio frequencies. This work is being continued today.

Weather

The weather is already being controlled.

Did you think it is a pleasant coincidence that big events such as the Olympic Games and royal weddings always seem to be blessed with good weather?

And now that a company which includes the ubiquitous Bill and Melinda Gates Foundation as investors is planning to block out the sun, we can look forward to a very peculiar weather pattern in the future.

Moreover, now that we know that our governments are trying to control us and kill many of us, we can be sure that they will weaponise the weather – using heat and cold to destroy crops and using storms to damage electricity supplies.

Webster (Daniel)

'I fear that they may place too implicit a confidence in their public servants, and fail properly to scrutinise their conduct; that in this way they may be made the dupes of designing men, and become the instruments of their own undoing.'

What the world will look like

The proponents of the 'global reset', 'the new world order' and so on, have very definite views on how our world will change to suit their own demonic purposes. They have, not surprisingly, been reluctant to share this view with the people they intend to rule. Nevertheless, this book contains a pretty fair indication of the sort of world, and life, we might expect if things continue to go their way.

White supremacy

Black Lives Matter demonstrators haven't noticed that their main financial and spiritual supporters, and the leaders of Agenda 21 are all white men of a certain age.

It perhaps hasn't occurred to the demonstrators that when the much promoted great reset takes place it will be black people in Africa who will be the ones who will die in the greatest numbers

Wi-Fi and cell phones

Children are exposed to thousands of hours of Wi-Fi radiation when they are at school. And, since most homes are fitted with Wi-Fi, and a wide variety of computers, cell phones, tablets and other electronic equipment, the Wi-Fi radiation exposure continues when they go home.

As far back as 2008, schools in Switzerland, Germany and England had begun removing Wi-Fi from schools. But although France, Belgium, Spain, Australia, Italy and Israel have all removed or reduced Wi-Fi or cellphone use in schools, other countries (such as England) has increased.

The countries which removed or reduced Wi-Fi or cellphone use did so because there are many peer-reviewed studies showing that EMFs can cause serious health problems – particularly in children. (The younger the child the greater the vulnerability. The bone marrow of a child's head absorbs ten times more radiation than an adult's head.)

The Council of Europe has warned about the risk of installing routers in schools and in 2011, called for a ban on Wi-Fi and cell phones in schools.

In July 2020, the Russian Government recommended the banning of Wi-Fi and cell phones in elementary schools on advice from the Medical Department of Russian Academy of Sciences and the Russian National Committee on Non-Ionizing Radiation Protection with the Russian Health Ministry. It had been determined that Wi-Fi can damage the DNA, cause cancer, produce developmental changes and also result in endocrine changes and neuropsychiatric effects. The Russians have been studying electromagnetic fields for longer than anyone and have for decades been assessing their value as military weapons.

In 2012, UNICEF found that Wi-Fi in schools led to an increase of 85% in central nervous system disorders and an 82% increase in blood and immune system disorders. There was also a 36% increase in epilepsy and an 11% increase in psychological problems. It is noteworthy that insurance companies won't give cover to cell phone companies for any damage called by phones or Wi-Fi.

The WHO has confirmed that electromagnetic fields are carcinogenic and more so for children who have developing bodies and thinner skulls

The irony is that there is no scientific evidence that global warming is real, manmade or a serious threat to life on earth but governments everywhere are busy taking action as though there were. On the other hand there is serious scientific evidence to show that EMF is dangerous to human health but governments are doing absolutely nothing to deal with the problem. On the contrary, they are encouraging schools to fit more, ever more powerful Wi-Fi equipment.

And school teachers are complying with zeal; boasting of installing ever more powerful equipment in their schools and drowning their pupils in electromagnetic waves. In Charleston, USA, schools boasted that they had cranked up the Wi-Fi cycle so that people in houses nearby could use it. In the UK, headmasters and headmistresses have delighted in boasting that their school has better coverage than any other establishment in the neighbourhood. It's like hangmen boasting about who can hang criminals at the greater rate.

Wikipedia

I have had a Wikipedia page since Wikipedia was first introduced. It always contained inaccuracies and it was obviously written by amateurs who didn't understand the first thing about journalism, and didn't know much about research. Several times I asked Wikipedia to take the page down but they wouldn't. Ironically, the reason given was that I was considered to have achieved too much to be removed. Curiously, the things for which I was considered notable have been removed – but not the page.

So, for a couple of decades the page sat there. Some of the stuff on it was reasonably accurate and some wasn't. After all, almost anyone can write and edit a Wikipedia entry and some entries are put together by kids for fun. (An American teenager edited apparently nearly half of the pages on the Scots Wikipedia. He started when he was 12 and it was years before anyone noticed that he'd been writing a good deal of drivel.)

Anyone can write and edit a Wikipedia page except a living individual who is the subject of a Wikipedia page. Crooks, rapists, paedophiles, lunatics, bigoted Klu Klux Klan members and 12-year-olds are all allowed to become Wikipedia editors. Many are deep state globalist technocrats, trans-humanist fascists, and lying, cheating global warming fakery enthusiasts.

Some editors mean well and are a credit to the original idea, others are just cowardly, little weasels who hide behind silly pen names and use the site to promote their political prejudices and pet theories. Many, I fear, are probably underachievers, full of opinions but never able to persuade the real world to take notice of them.

And it's perfectly possible to pay editors to improve a Wikipedia page – for a nice fee, a Wikipedia editor could probably make even Tony Blair look like a saint.

And then on March 18th 2020, I was stupid enough to make a video.

Almost immediately my Wikipedia page was changed dramatically.

Within hours there were Nazi war criminals who had better Wikipedia pages than I did. Everything I had ever done that could be considered remotely useful was removed. And the page was filled with an array of clever but deceitful distortions of the truth. It is official policy to insult, smear and demonise anyone who questions the establishment line and Wikipedia is one of the weapons.

So, for example, I suddenly became a discredited person.

Why?

Because someone at Wikipedia decided I was.

I have filing cabinets full of thousands of reviews and interviews and no one has ever described me as discredited – until Wikipedia, or an editor, decided I was.

But when a small newspaper in Scotland quoted Wikipedia, the Wikipedia editors put the Scottish paper down as a source for their defamatory comment. A neat little vicious circle.

Overnight, I became a conspiracy theorist too though I rather feel that the conspiring is being done by the people I was criticising.

Manipulated truths and deceits used to disappear when a newspaper was turned into chip paper. Today they last for eternity.

Someone dug through decades old internet pages and found that I had been criticised by something called the Advertising Standards Authority in the UK. What Wikipedia didn't bother to mention, though they should have known, was that the ASA is a private organisation and that when they received a complaint about me I sent them two dozen scientific references in support of my claim that meat causes cancer. The ASA, who had received a complaint from the meat trade, refused to look at the references and simply announced that I had been censured. The same thing is true of the Press Complaints Commission – they too refused to look at scientific references before reaching a conclusion.

Other decades old bits and pieces of nonsense were adapted, edited and published with the sole aim of discrediting me. It seemed to me that the page contained more garbage than the average dustbin. Wikipedia says my theories have been discredited but only by Wikipedia and a few drug company trolls. My writings about AIDS were intended to be reassuring and were all scientifically accurate. At the time I was writing, the public was being told that AIDS would kill everyone.

And so it goes. It has never occurred to Wikipedia editors to ask why, if I really were, in their words, a discredited pseudoscientist, I still have a Wikipedia page.

The last time I looked, I saw that they'd deleted details of the successful campaigns I'd run, the TV and radio series I'd made, the voluntary work I'd done with great joy and they had deleted the list of my books – over 100 of them. They deleted the fact that I'd written columns for many leading national newspapers – and dismissed me as a self-published author, slyly omitting to mention that I've had books published by dozens of leading publishers in the UK, the USA and around the world – and translated into 25 languages. They managed to mention that I had left *The People* newspaper but failed to mention that I'd resigned because the editor wouldn't print a column I'd written criticising Britain's involvement in the Iraq War. They say I can't practice medicine but ignore the fact that retired doctors aren't entitled to a licence. A large number of references to articles which were complimentary were simply deleted as were quotes praising my work. I'm accused of being a pseudoscientist and that's a libel which is used to discredit anyone who dares to question the establishment view.

The aim, of course, was simply to demonise me, to dissuade people from taking any notice of my books, articles and videos and to dissuade other doctors from speaking out.

That was the real point of it.

Wikipedia has become a potent weapon in a new war of oppression and disinformation, and in its political bias is now threatening our very freedom and promoting the elite at the expense of ordinary citizens. It is as reliable and trustworthy as the BBC – which is to say not at all. I've been proved absolutely accurate since March 2020 but truth and facts don't matter in this alternative world.

And I'm not the only one to have been targeted, of course.

Anyone who speaks out against the new establishment gets the same treatment. They remove all the individual's real achievements and replace them with anything they can find which can be edited in such a way to discredit the person concerned.

The Wikipedia site may have started out with good intentions, though the idea of allowing amateurs to write and edit an encyclopaedia was always a trifle flaky and dependent on goodwill and honesty, but until recently it seemed pretty harmless and occasionally useful

So who is behind it all?

Well, I know the names of some of self-styled editors. Some seem weasely or cowardly and appear to be driven by jealousies, prejudices and bigotry. They mostly hide behind silly code- names. Some are undoubtedly working for government agencies but others are not difficult to identify. They edit with the zeal of a fanatic; libelling me behind the scenes a good deal. One claims that the 2016 election and the Brexit referendum were swung by Putin. Mixing arrogance with ignorance, he describes himself as a member of the left wing thought police – which seems very accurate. Another 'editor' (who manages to misspell his fake name) has published strange and revealing political mutterings on a site called Reddit. This editor also wants to remove a Wikipedia page which deals with a series of 15 books I wrote about a GP in a village in Devon. .

Even those who once loved Wikipedia are now embarrassed and ashamed of how it is being abused to promote prejudices and political extremism. Certainly the page that has been recreated in my name is unbalanced, destructive and, to say the least, misleading. I have screen shots of the worst libels.

Larry Sanger was co-founder of Wikipedia and he certainly doesn't think much of what it has become in the hands of these people.

In his excellent recent book, *Essays on Free Knowledge* Sanger writes about the CIA and other government agencies editing pages, he excoriates Google which, he says, helped establish Wikipedia's undeserved popular perception of credibility and states baldly that 'Wikipedia has abandoned neutrality and is used as a tool for social manipulation'. Anyone who edits or uses Wikipedia should read his book to understand what has happened. Wikipedia is the modern version of the Witchfinder General.

An online encyclopaedia written largely by unskilled amateurs may have been a good idea when it began. But it's time Wikipedia was closed down. It's an insult to journalism, history, science, medicine and the essence of the encyclopaedia. It is, without doubt, now doing far more harm than good. There are honest editors who are interested in maintaining Wikipedia as a resource but they have allowed abuse on the site to be so widespread that an increasing number of people regard it as a joke. Some original thinkers now regard a defamatory Wikipedia page as a sign that they are doing something right but it is sad that the site's management appear to tolerate the bias and prejudices of some of the editors. I wonder how many innocent victims have committed suicide as a result of these character assassinations.

Most worrying of all, is the news that early modelling which helped guide the British government's approach in 2020, used Wikipedia – the disreputable site which is edited by all sorts of weirdos and freaks as well as by people with very particular political agendas to pursue.

I once heard two boys arguing in a shop.

'I read it on Wikipedia,' said one.

'Then it's probably wrong,' replied his pal.

And that says it all.

Wikipedia has been killed off by people with prejudices, and many sad and toxic editors are the online soldiers for the forces of fascism and disorder.

Like others who have been demonised, and had their professional lives ruined, I feel a sense of quiet despair but since my reputation has now been unfairly trashed I am now more determined than ever to continue to expose the truth.

Wilding

Wilding is the name given to the idea that if large areas of countryside are left unattended they will magically and mysteriously turn into flower meadows and pleasant bluebell filled woods. The trees will be filled with birds singing their hearts out, and below them acceptable mammals will roam what is left of the fields and pastures.

Sadly, none of this will happen.

In the UK, if land is allowed to go wild it will be overgrown with brambles, Japanese knotweed, giant hogweed and fast breeding animals such as rats. I imagine much the same sort of thing will happen in other countries – but with local variations.

But none of this troubles the wilding enthusiasts.

The original, official name for this nonsense was The Wildlands Project and the idea was to give back to nature huge areas of land with corridors of land connecting them all up. There are even plans to destroy dams (even those which generate electricity) so that huge amounts of land can be turned into lakes.

Moreover, the plan was, and is, to release all sorts of wild animals onto the land. In the United States, for example, wolves and bears are being released.

In the UK, bison are being released and two rangers are being recruited to look after them. It is, apparently, hoped that the animals (the largest land based mammals in Europe) will disrupt the ecosystem in woodlands. I bet they will. Heaven knows what this will do to the existing wildlife. There have been no bison (or relatives of bison) in the UK since the last Ice Age.

What's it all about?

Well, it isn't about letting huge areas of countryside turn into a conservation area for Japanese knotweed and huge rats.

And although, wilding or re-wilding appears to be the suburban woke version of good husbandry and preservation of the countryside, it certainly has nothing to do with conservation or respect for either humans or wildlife.

The aim of wilding (which is not at all understood by country folk and those who oppose it) is simply to force people to move into large cities where they can be more easily managed and controlled.

Wind farms

Wind farms are much favoured by the cultists who believe in global warming. If your aim is to kill a good many birds then look no further than a wind turbine. They are excellent if this is what you want. They are not, however, terribly good at generating electricity. There are several problems.

First, building a wind turbine (and digging out all the essential materials) uses up more energy than the windmill will produce in its lifetime.

Second, maintaining a wind turbine requires a good deal of electricity. When there is no wind (something which happens more often than you might think) the blades have to be turned round artificially in order to stop them seizing up. And guess what is used to keep the blades turning – electricity.

Third, when there is no wind then the turbine doesn't make electricity, and the people relying on it for heat, light, cooking and so on will freeze or starve to death. So, wind farms are really best for killing birds though it would be more profitable to hire a bunch of hedge fund managers and get them to pay £5,000 a day to shoot the birds.

World government

Every major dictator in history has dreamt of a world government – with themselves in charge. Alexander the Great wanted a world government and so did Julius Caesar. Charlemagne and Napoleon wanted to control the world. And so, of course, did Hitler.

Now, a world government is the target of people like Tony Blair – long discredited and widely regarded as a disreputable war criminal.

Zinc

Zinc is essential for a healthy immune system and it can help shorten the duration of a cold and make symptoms less severe. Zinc helps your body fight infections by boosting the production of antibodies. The WHO has reported that zinc deficiency may be responsible for 13% of diseases such as pneumonia and flu in children under the age of five. And zinc deficiency is common among the elderly – and a major reason why they are susceptible to infection. The easiest solution is regular supplements.

Part Three
Rescuing Our Future from the Past

If things go as Prince Charles, Boris Johnson, Klaus Schwab, Tony Blair, Bill Gates and others seem to hope, then the only future we will have is the future they will let us have.

So, what do we do about it? How do we change our governments in order to protect ourselves? Repelling the outrageous plans of the globalists will merely provide us with a temporary respite. We have to get rid of them permanently if we are to be free of their evil plans. And that means re-designing the world so we retain dignity and respect and repel the billionaires and control freaks who have designs on the world and on humanity itself.

The proponents of the global government condemn all opposition. If you don't approve of the Great Reset you must be a racist or something equally horrendous. The monstering, the demonising is done relentlessly and the collaborators are constantly recruited as foot soldiers in the war. Politicians and police officers constantly encourage collaborators to shame those with hidden disabilities and health problems, as well as those with free spirits and free minds.

Their aim is plainly visible; it is to dehumanise humans, to allow robots to take over the world, to deprive us all of our hearts and souls and of our freedom and democracy. The aim of the fourth industrial revolution is to control who we are as well as what we do and what we think. This is what they mean by the Great Reset. All babies will be programmed. Robots will take over virtually all jobs. The world population will be reduced by 95%. The UN's stated aim is for the industrialised nations to collapse. 'No one,' says the UN, 'will enter the New Age unless he will take a Luciferian initiation.'

They want to scare us, divide us and take away all our power.

They want to destroy small businesses and the middle classes and all ambition and all aspirations. They want to confiscate all private property and cause economic chaos so that they can reset the world. They want to install unelected regional governors – just as the EU planned to do – and to ban all manifestations of nationalism. So, for example, nation flags will be outlawed.

They have got us concentrating on the means not the end, the medium not the message. The purpose is lost in the undergrowth because they have got us studying the leaves, not the trees and certainly not the woods.

Afterword

Even when we have won this war, we will have to continue fighting to protect our society and our individuality. The threat to our freedom and democracy will never disappear because the people who planned Agenda 21, and the global warming fraud upon which Agenda 21 rests, will never go away and will remain determined to end democracy and all forms of freedom and to form a world government under their control. We and all future generations will have to remain eternally vigilant. It would help in the short term if all those identified as taking part in, and supporting and promoting, the plans for a new world order were imprisoned for life. Since they are responsible for millions of deaths, it will not be difficult to charge them under existing legislation.

The evil proponents of Agenda 21 may lose this battle but they will keep trying with a new law here, a new recommendation there and an endless series of guilt producing films and reports. They will never give up and we will have to remain on guard for eternity.

If we lose this war it will be because not enough people care enough to do something. And if we do lose then we will be nothing more than slaves in a totalitarian society that will make the USSR and China look like a benevolently run holiday camp.

Dear Reader

If you found this book useful, I would be enormously grateful if you would post a review on your preferred online site. It would help a great deal more than I can tell.

Thank you

Vernon Coleman

Essential Reading: Book List (In absolutely no particular order)

I used thousands of books, articles and scientific papers in the preparation of this book. To show off, and impress readers, I could have filled a hundred pages with the full list of all the scientific papers I consulted.

Showing off in this way seems common these days, and it is not uncommon to find a book of which a third or more consists of nothing but a huge list of references which no one will ever use and which the original author probably copied out of a reference book. (Anyone over the age of 70 who hasn't acquired a little scepticism, not to mention cynicism, has probably not been paying attention.)

However, listing all the sources I have used would have doubled the price of the book, and I have always preferred to make my books available as cheaply as possible. I would rather sell 100 copies of a book, and make 1 cent on each one, than sell 1 copy of a book and make a dollar.

But here is a list of some recommended books – most of which I have read several times and referred to while writing this book. The books are listed in no particular order. I didn't put them in alphabetical order because I couldn't decide whether to do so by author or by title. But I've kept the list as short as I could.

Fog Facts: Searching for Truth in the Land of Spin – Larry Beinhart
Wag the Dog – Larry Beinhart (a novel)
Civil Disobedience – Henry David Thoreau
The Social Contract – Rousseau
The Road to Serfdom – F.A.Hayek
Our Own Worst Enemy – Norman F Dixon
The Republic – Plato
The History of the Peloponnesian War – Thucydides
Without Conscience: The Disturbing World of the Psychopaths Among Us – Robert D.Hare PhD
Power Shift – Alvin Toffler

The Hidden Persuaders – Vance Packard
Snakes in Suits: When Psychopaths go to Work – Paul Babiak PhD and Robert D Hare PhD
Hidden Dangers: How governments, telecom and electric power utilities suppress the truth about the known hazards of electro-magnetic field (EMF) radiation – Captain Jerry G. Flynn
Technocracy – The Hard Road to World Order – Patrick M Wood
Climategate – The Dot Connector Library
The Invisible Rainbow: A History of Electricity and Life – Arthur Firstenberg
Understanding Media: The Extensions of Man – Marshall McLuhan
Griftopia – Matt Taibbi
Presstitutes: Embedded in the Pay of the CIA – Udo Ulfkotte
The Revolution: A Manifesto – Ron Paul
Behind the Green Mask: U.N. Agenda 21 – Rosa Koire
Illuminati: Agenda 21 – Dean and Jill Henderson
Shaping the Future of the Fourth Industrial Revolution: A Guide to Building a Better World – Klaus Schwab
Agenda 21 – Ron Taylor
The Creature from Jekyll Island: A Second Look at the Federal Reserve – G.Edward Griffin
Essays on Free Knowledge – Larry Sanger
On Liberty – John Stuart Mill
Brave New World – Aldous Huxley
Animal Farm – George Orwell
1984 – George Orwell
The Bible
Greta's Homework – Zina Cohen
Extraordinary Popular Delusions and the Madness of Crowds – Charles Mackay
Rural Rides – William Cobbett
The Road to Serfdom – F.A.Hayek
The Republic – Plato
Thomas Paine
Benjamin Franklin
The Greatest Minds and Ideas of All Time – Will Durant
The Prince – Machiavelli
Greek Lives – Plutarch
Tao Te Ching - Lao Tzu

The Art of War – Sun Tzu
The Lessons of History – Will and Ariel Durant
The Fifteen Decisive Battles of the World – Sir Edward Creasy MA
The Outsider – Colin Wilson
Greta's Homework – Zina Cohen
Roche versus Adams – Stanley Adams

Relevant Books by Vernon Coleman
How to Protect and Preserve Your Freedom Identity and Privacy
Coleman's Laws
Coming Apocalypse
How to Stop Your Doctor Killing You
Why and How Doctors Kill More People than Cancer
The Medicine Men (out of print)
Paper Doctors (out of print)
Health Scandal (out of print)
Betrayal of Trust (out of print)
What happens next?
Living in a fascist country
Why everything is going to get worse
Superbody
Meat Causes Cancer and More Food for Thought
Coming Apocalypse
OFPIS
Bloodless Revolution
The Shocking History of the EU
Anyone Who Tells You Vaccines are Safe and Effective is Lying
Moneypower
The Benzos Story
Bodypower
Mindpower
Spiritpower
Toxic Stress

The Author
Biography and reference articles

I have included this short biography (and reference articles) as a modest counter to the lies currently being told about me in most branches of the media.

Vernon Coleman was educated at Queen Mary's Grammar School in Walsall, Staffs. He then spent a year as a Community Service Volunteer in Liverpool where he was the first of Alec Dickson's 'catalysts'. (Ref 1 below). He studied medicine at Birmingham Medical School and qualified as a doctor in 1970. He has worked both in hospitals and as a GP. He resigned from the health service on a matter of principle. (Ref 2 below).

Vernon Coleman has organised many campaigns concerning iatrogenesis, drug addiction and the abuse of animals, and has given evidence to committees at the House of Commons and the House of Lords. For example, he gave evidence to the House of Lords Select Committee on Animals in Scientific Procedures (2001-2) on Tuesday 12.2.02

Dr Coleman's campaigns have often proved successful. For example, after a 15 year campaign (which started in 1973) he eventually persuaded the British Government to introduce stricter controls governing the prescribing of benzodiazepine tranquillisers. ('Dr Vernon Coleman's articles, to which I refer with approval, raised concern about these important matters,' said the Parliamentary Secretary for Health in the House of Commons in 1988.) (Ref 3 below).

Dr Coleman has worked as a columnist for numerous national newspapers including *The Sun*, *The Daily Star*, *The Sunday Express*, *Sunday Correspondent* and *The People*. He once wrote three columns at the same time for national papers (he wrote them under three different names, Dr Duncan Scott in *The Sunday People*, Dr James in *The Sun* and Dr Vernon Coleman in the *Daily Star*). At the same time he was also writing weekly columns for the *Evening*

Times in Glasgow and for the *Sunday Scot*. His syndicated columns have appeared in over 50 regional newspapers in the United Kingdom, and his columns and articles have appeared in newspapers and magazines around the world. Dr Coleman resigned from *The People* in 2003 when the editor refused to print a column criticising the Government's decision to start the Iraq War. (Ref 6 below)

He has contributed articles and stories to hundreds of other publications including *The Sunday Times, Observer, Guardian, Daily Telegraph, Sunday Telegraph, Daily Express, Daily Mail, Mail on Sunday, Daily Mirror, Sunday Mirror, Punch, Woman, Woman's Own, The Lady, Spectator* and the *British Medical Journal*. He was the founding editor of the *British Clinical Journal*. For many years he wrote a monthly newsletter called *Dr Vernon Coleman's Health Letter*. He has worked with the Open University in the UK and has lectured doctors and nurses on a variety of medical matters.

Vernon Coleman has presented numerous programmes on television and radio and was the original breakfast television doctor on TV AM. He was television's first agony uncle (on BBC1's The Afternoon Show) and presented three TV series based on his bestselling book *Bodypower*. In the 1980s, he helped write the algorithms for the first computerised health programmes – which sold around the world to those far-sighted individuals who had bought the world's first home computers. (Ref 4 below). His books have been published in the UK by Arrow, Pan, Penguin, Corgi, Mandarin, Star, Piatkus, RKP, Thames and Hudson, Sidgwick and Jackson, Macmillan and many other leading publishing houses and translated into 25 languages. English language versions sell in the USA, Australia, Canada and South Africa as well as the UK. Several of his books have appeared on both the *Sunday Times* and *Bookseller* bestseller lists.

Altogether, he has written over 100 books which have, together, sold over two million copies in the UK alone. His self-published novel, *Mrs Caldicot's Cabbage War* has been turned into an award winning film (starring Pauline Collins, John Alderton and Peter Capaldi) and the book is, like many of his other novels, available in an audio version.

Vernon Coleman has co-written five books with his wife, Donna Antoinette Coleman and has, in addition, written numerous articles (and books) under a vast variety of pennames (many of which he has now forgotten). Donna Antoinette Coleman is a talented oil painter who specialises in landscapes. Her books include, My Quirky Cotswold Garden. She is a Fellow of the Royal Society of Arts. Vernon and Antoinette Coleman have been married for more than 20 years.

Vernon Coleman has received numerous awards and was for some time a Professor of Holistic Medical Sciences at the Open International University based in Sri Lanka.

Reference Articles referring to Vernon Coleman
Ref 1
'Volunteer for Kirkby' – The Guardian, 14.5.1965
(Article re VC's work in Kirkby, Liverpool as a Community Service Volunteer in 1964-5)
Ref 2
'Bumbledom forced me to leave the NHS' – Pulse, 28.11.1981
(Vernon Coleman resigns as a GP after refusing to disclose confidential information on sick note forms)
Ref 3
'I'm Addicted To The Star' – The Star, 10.3.1988
Ref 4
'Medicine Becomes Computerised: Plug In Your Doctor.' – The Times, 29.3.1983
Ref 5
'Computer aided decision making in medicine' – British Medical Journal, 8.9.1984 and 27.10.1984
Ref 6
'Conscientious Objectors' – Financial Times magazine, 9.8.2003

Major interviews with Vernon Coleman include
'Doctor with the Common Touch' – Birmingham Post, 9.10.1984
'Sacred Cows Beware: Vernon Coleman publishing again.' – The Scotsman, 6.12.1984
'Our Doctor Coleman Is Mustard' – The Sun, 29.6.1988
'Reading the mind between the lines' – BMA News Review, November 1991
Doctors' Firsts – BMA News Review, 21.2.1996
'The big league of self-publishing' – Daily Telegraph, 17.8.1996

'Doctoring the books' – Independent, 16.3.1999
'Sick Practices' – Ode Magazine, July/August 2003
'You have been warned, Mr Blair' – Spectator, 6.3.2004 and 20.3.2004
'Food for thought with a real live Maverick' – Western Daily Press, 5.9.2006
'The doctor will see you now' – Independent, 14.5.2008

There is a more comprehensive list of reference articles on www.vernoncoleman.com

Printed in Great Britain
by Amazon

68981181R00159